# The Crucifixion and the Qur'an

# The Crucifixion and the Qur'an

## *A Study in the History of Muslim Thought*

TODD LAWSON

ONEWORLD
OXFORD

A Oneworld Book

Published by Oneworld Publications 2009


A CIP record for this title is available
from the British Library

ISBN 978–1–85168–636–0 (Hbk)
ISBN 978–1–85168–635–3 (Pbk)

Typeset by Jayvee, Trivandrum, India
Cover design by eDigital Design
Printed and bound in the UK
by Bell & Bain, Glasgow

Oneworld Publications
185 Banbury Road
Oxford OX2 7AR
England
www.oneworld-publications.com

Cover image: T414 f.102v, *The Ascension of Christ: Astonished Jews in a Grassy Landscape Watch Christ Ascend into Heaven with Two Angels*, from Zubdat al Tavarikh, completed after 1583 (vellum) by Lugman-i 'Ashur (late 16th century) ©The Trustees of the Chester Beatty Library, Dublin/The Bridgeman Art Library

# CONTENTS

# ACKNOWLEDGEMENTS

I would like to thank a number of people whose generosity and acumen have contributed to the final form of this book. Professor Sebastian Günther, colleague at the Near and Middle Eastern Civilizations Department, University of Toronto, and now Chair of Arabic and Islamic Studies at the University of Göttingen, offered numerous insightful suggestions on an earlier version of the manuscript. Professor Emeritus Michael E. Marmura, University of Toronto, also suggested improvements to the text. Dr Andrew Lane, University of Toronto, read an earlier draft and offered expert guidance in the reading of Zamakhsharī. Professor Walid Saleh, University of Toronto, made available to me a manuscript of the Tha'labī *tafsīr* and I am also very grateful to Professor Karin Ruehrdanz, Curator of Islamic Art, Royal Ontario Museum and the University of Toronto, for introducing me to the beautiful miniature that serves as the basis for the cover illustration. Professor Emeritus Michael G. Carter, Centre for Medieval Studies, Sydney University, read the manuscript and made several valuable suggestions for which I am most grateful. I would also like to thank Dr Stephen Lambden of Ohio University, who made numerous valuable suggestions as well. Three graduate students at the Department of Near and Middle Eastern Civilizations, University of Toronto, were also very helpful: Anne Clement offered excellent and very helpful advice in the reading of certain French texts, and Mina Yazdani supplied me with an unpublished typescript of her lucid study of the crucifixion in Bahā'ī thought. Mr Omid Ghaemmaghami was of great help at every stage, especially with research into some of the Shi'i literature. He also standardized the transliteration, footnote and bibliographic entries. I am especially grateful to him for all the time and care he has put into the final form of the book. I alone am responsible for any deficiencies, lapses and errors that remain. An earlier version of this study, published in 1991, benefited from the knowledge and expertise of Professors Wadi' Z. Haddad and Mahmoud Ayoub. I would also like to add here a word of special thanks to Mr Novin Doostdar of Oneworld for his interest in the subject and warm encouragement, Mr Mike Harpley and Dr Kate Smith of Oneworld for their expert advice and patience.

It is a particular pleasure to be able to express my gratitude to Professor Sidney H. Griffith of the Catholic University of America for kindly agreeing to write the foreword for the book. His words provide an uncommonly astute opening for the questions and problems raised and addressed in the following pages.

Finally, my wife Barbara Lawson has been involved in every aspect of the research, writing, organizing and publication of this book. Her judgement, diligence, patience, taste and generosity are impossible to acknowledge properly. This book is lovingly dedicated to her.

Todd Lawson
*Montreal*

# FOREWORD

The eminent French Islamicist Louis Massignon (1883–1962) once said of the Qur'an that in his estimation one could rightfully think of the Islamic scripture as 'a truncated, Arabic edition of the Bible'. He went on to say that in his view 'The Qur'an would be to the Bible what Ishmael was to Isaac.'[1] In fact, even a cursory reading of the Qur'an reveals its presumption that its audience is familiar with the scriptures of the Jews and the Christians, the Torah, the Prophets, the Psalms and the Gospels. What is more, the text discloses a familiarity with a wide range of Jewish and Christian lore, faith and practice. The Qur'an summons Jews, Christians and others to right faith in the one God, the God of Abraham, Isaac, Jacob, the prophets, and Jesus, the Messiah, the 'son of Mary'; it critiques what it takes to be excesses in the faith and practice of the 'People of the Book', 'Scripture People' (*Sūrat al-Nisā/The Women* 171).

There has been much scholarly discussion over the years about the identities of the Jewish and Christian groups whose doctrines and practices the Qur'an criticizes, or otherwise refers to. On the basis of their analyses of individual passages, some scholars have postulated the presence of one or another Jewish Christian community (Ebionites, Elchasaites or Nazoreans) in the milieu of the Qur'an, whose distinctive doctrines they think are discernible in particular passages of the Islamic scripture. Other scholars have proposed that the Qur'an's interactions with Christians were with the mostly Syriac-speaking, mainline communities of the early seventh century (Melkites, Jacobites, Nestorians) and they search for clues to which group's distinctive doctrines or

[1] Louis Massignon, *Les trois prières d'Abraham* (Paris: Éditions du Seuil, 1999), p. 6.

practices may still be disclosed from behind the text's highly allusive language. So far few scholars have considered these matters from the Qur'an's own point of view. Rather, they have brought their presuppositions about the text's indebtedness to pre-existent narratives to their readings of selected passages, seemingly without suspecting that the Qur'an may not intend so much to report or transmit earlier discourses as to comment on and critique the views of the 'People of the Book' or others in its own rhetorical style and within the horizons of its own concerns.

Perhaps no passage in the Qur'an has received more attention from scholars looking for the Islamic scripture's putative sources than *Sūrat al-Nisā* 157–8. On the face of it, the text says of the 'People of the Book', in this instance the Jews, that, in spite of their allegation to the contrary, 'they neither killed nor crucified' the Messiah, Jesus, son of Mary, and the Messenger of God. Rather, says the Qur'an, in a still puzzling Arabic phrase that has continued to draw the attention of commentators, *shubbiha lahum*; and the text goes on to say they did not kill him, 'God raised him up.' The puzzling phrase has been variously taken to mean something like 'it seemed so to them', or that 'a likeness was produced for them', readings that, while they are dictated by the root sense of the words, nevertheless leave the meaning as elusive as ever. Muslim scholars have had much to say about the appropriate way to interpret this passage; many have taken it to mean that Jesus Christ in fact did not die on the cross. Some Muslim and many non-Muslim scholars have busied themselves in searching for pre-Islamic, Christian sources that they think might lurk behind the difficult Arabic phrase just quoted, in which they have hoped to discern the influence of some group of Christian Docetists on the phrasing of *shubbiha lahum*, whose supposed presence in the Arabic-speaking milieu of the Qur'an might explain the sense of the puzzling language, suggesting that it means that Jesus Christ was only apparently crucified and that the Qur'an reflects these Docetists' understanding of the matter. From another point of view, one that presumes that the Qur'an refers to the pre-existing scriptures of the 'People of the Book', one enterprising commentator, whose suggestion has seldom been noticed, proposed that the obscure phrase includes 'an unconscious memory' on the Qur'an's part of a verse in St Paul's

Epistle to the Philippians, where the apostle speaks of Jesus and says of him that, 'being in the form of God', he was nevertheless 'made *in the likeness* of men' (Philippians 2:7).[2]

The problem with most of the suggestions about how to read and understand puzzling phrases in the Qur'an like the one in the passage under discussion here is that the interpretive focus has often been too narrow, confining attention to the immediate context of the troubling words and phrases and imagining a solution, either grammatical, lexical or historical, without taking a wider Qur'anic context into account, or a wider historical frame of reference, for that matter, or failing to find comparable phraseology in some alleged, non-Islamic source.

Finally, in this very welcome study, Todd Lawson brings the matter of the Qur'an's references to what the 'People of the Book' say about the crucifixion, death and resurrection of Jesus Christ into the wider framework of the testimony of the whole Qur'an about Jesus the son of Mary. What is more, Lawson pays close attention to the full range of understandings about the 'taking up' of Jesus, be it during his life or after his death, to be found in the works of the Muslim commentators on the Qur'an over the centuries. In this way he makes it clear that what is at stake in the discussion of the issue of the Qur'an's view of the crucifixion and/or the death of Jesus the Messiah is not just a matter of the right understanding of a particular Qur'anic phrase and its presumed historical background. Rather, one must consider the topic against the background of the entire Christology of the Qur'an, and indeed in view of the multiple Christologies of Islamic tradition. For the fact of the matter is that there is no simple solution to the famous *crux interpretum* of the *shubbiha lahum*. But there is a wide and wonderful range of theological thinking about Jesus, his life, his mission and his eschatological role in Islamic thinking. And it is into this whole narrative that Todd Lawson's work brings the discussion about the crucifixion of Jesus.

Sidney H. Griffith
*Institute of Christian Oriental Research*

[2] See R.C. Zaehner, *At Sundry Times: An Essay in the Comparison of Religions* (London: Faber & Faber, 1958), p. 211.

# INTRODUCTION

THEY DID NOT KILL HIM AND THEY DID NOT CRUCIFY HIM, RATHER, IT ONLY APPEARED SO TO THEM. (Qur'an 4:157)

وَمَا قَتَلُوهُ وَمَا صَلَبُوهُ وَلَكِنْ شُبِّهَ لَهُمْ

*wa-mā qatalūhu wa-mā ṣalabūhu wa-lākin shubbiha lahum*

This is the only verse in the Qur'an that mentions the crucifixion of Jesus. It has largely been understood both by Muslims and, in some ways more interestingly, by Christians as a denial of the historical and, to many, irrefutable 'fact' of the crucifixion of Jesus. Obviously, such a doctrinal position serves as a great obstacle separating Muslims and Christians on the grounds of belief. But, more importantly, such belief frankly serves to diminish Islam in the eyes of Christians and so-called 'Westerners' whose cultural identity is bound up, whether they are believers or not, with the axiomatic and unquestionable 'myth' of the death and resurrection of Jesus.

This book demonstrates that Muslim teaching, just like Christian teaching, on the life and ministry of Jesus is by no means consistent or monolithic. When it comes to the topic at hand, the understanding of the Qur'anic verse that mentions the crucifixion, it will be demonstrated that there are numerous forces at work at various levels of the Islamic learned tradition that impinge upon the hermeneutic culture out of which doctrine may be thought to have arisen and endured.

The uninitiated scholar or interested reader is likely to regard this standard Muslim teaching about Jesus with some surprise and bemusement. By far the vast majority of the followers of Islam hold that Jesus in fact was not crucified, but remains alive 'with God' in a spiritual realm from where he will descend at the end of time in an Islamic version of the Second Coming.

But, as will be seen in the following pages, any number of readers – Muslim or not – could read and have read the same verse without coming to this conclusion. If, for example, the reader were a follower of one of earliest Christian heresies, Docetism, they would in fact be able to agree completely with this statement.[1] 'Docetism' is a word that comes from the Greek verb *dokeō* ('to seem') or noun *dokesis* ('appearance'). It refers to a Christological tendency evident in emergent Christianity from the late first/early second century CE. For example, a form of Docetism is combated in the Johannine literature of the New Testament (e.g. John 1:14, 1 John 4:2–3 and 2 John 7). The term is used in a variety of ways from apostolic times and later by the Fathers of the Church. One of its usages is to describe a view that held that Jesus did not suffer on the cross, but only appeared to do so. An apocryphal gospel, *The Acts of John*, offers the following Docetic account of the crucifixion:

> After the Lord had so danced with us, my beloved, he went out. And we were like men amazed or fast asleep, and we fled this way and that. And so I saw him suffer, and did not wait by his suffering, but fled to the Mount of Olives and wept at what had come to pass. And when he was hung (upon the Cross) on Friday, at the sixth hour of the day there came a darkness over the whole earth. And my Lord stood in the middle of the cave and gave light to it and said, 'John, for the people below in Jerusalem I

[1] See the recent excellent discussion by Ronnie Goldstein and Guy G. Stroumsa, who draw attention to the likely origins of this 'heresy' in Jewish and Hellenic sources. In the course of this article the authors draw attention to the methodolological hazards of conflating Docetism with the rather elusive category of gnosticism: 'The Greek and Jewish Origins of Docetism: A New Proposal', *Zeitschrift für Antikes Christentum*, 10(3), 2007, pp. 423–41. My thanks to Dr Stephen Lambden of the University of Ohio for drawing my attention to this article.

> am being crucified and pierced with lances and reeds and given vinegar and gall to drink. But to you I am speaking, and listen to what I speak.'[2]

Docetism was a feature of a welter of Christologies current in the first several centuries of the Common Era that influenced the form of the Christianity which would eventually emerge as orthodoxy. A complex phenomenon, Docetism might be considered to have been a reaction to the notion of patripassianism, that God himself could suffer death through crucifixion. As such, it was connected to the great Christological debates that discussed the nature of Jesus: Was he fully human? Was he fully God? Was he half human? Was he half God? The defining consensus emerged at the famous Council of Nicea in 325 CE with the dogma: Fully God and Fully Human (incidentally, a classic, textbook example of the kind of *coincidentia oppositorum* that energizes much of religious thought). In any case, the Docetic view has a long history in Christianity and it holds that what was seen crucified on the cross was just an image: a phantom, not the real Jesus or perhaps even a substitute. In the following pages we will be using the term 'Docetic' in two distinct ways. The first may be called 'literal Docetism'. This refers to the belief found in some Christian heresies and the earliest Qur'anic exegesis that while there was indeed a crucifixion, the one who was crucified was only understood (wrongly) to be Jesus. In reality it was another person altogether, one upon whom the image of Jesus had been miraculously cast or one who was mistakenly thought to be Jesus. An early example of this type is found in the apocryphal *Apocalypse of Peter*, as noted by one of the foremost scholars of the Islamic Jesus writing today. Robinson offers the opinion that, based on this early Christian text, it may be possible to conclude that the Muslim exegetes who interpreted the verse as indicating there was an actual substitute for Jesus may have indeed interpreted the

[2] *The Acts of John* 97 in Edgar Hennecke, *New Testament Apocrypha*, ed. W. Schneemelcher, trans. A.J.B. Higgins et al., ed. R.McL. Wilson, 2 vols (Philadelphia: Westminster Press), vol. 2, pp. 232–3. See Henry Corbin's discussion of this passage in connection with a reading of Q. 4:157 in *Cyclical Time and Ismaili Gnosis*, trans. Ralph Manheim (London: Kegan Paul International in Association with Islamic Publications), pp. 71–4, 105–7.

verse 'correctly'.[3] The second way in which the term 'Docetic' may be used is as 'figurative Docetism'. Here the 'appearance' refers to the body of Jesus, which was certainly crucified, as distinct from his spiritual and eternal reality that, by its very nature, is invulnerable to suffering and death. It is this figurative Docetism that is evident in the story of the mystic/martyr hero Manṣūr ibn al-Ḥallāj (d. 309/922). According to none other than Abū Ḥāmid al-Ghazālī (d. 505/1111), al-Ḥallāj, as he was being crucified in Baghdad for his various sins, uttered our problematic verse from the gibbet: 'They did not kill him and they did not crucify him, it only appeared so to them.'[4] We are to understand from this account that al-Ḥallāj understood the verse to mean, in the case of both Jesus and himself, that it was only the human element and not the divine that was crucified.[5]

As Henry Corbin repeatedly pointed out many years ago, we can see how the above Qur'an verse (4:157) may be read perfectly in line with this early and apparently widespread Christian perspective.[6]

> Finally, the Qur'an (4:157) is resolutely 'docetist': Christ did not die on the cross; God raised him up unto Himself, for men did not have the power to kill the Word of God (*Kalām Allāh*), the Spirit of God (*Rūh Allāh*). But men had the illusion that they killed him.[7]

[3] Neal Robinson, 'Crucifixion', in *Encyclopaedia of the Qur'an*, ed. J.D. McAuliffe, vol. 1 (Leiden: E.J. Brill, 2001), pp. 487–9. See also Heribert Busse, *Islam, Judaism, and Christianity: Theological and Historical Affiliations*, trans. Allison Brown (Princeton, NJ: Markus Wiener, 1998), p. 136.

[4] Abū Ḥāmid al-Ghazālī, *al-Mustaẓhirī*, in Ignaz Goldziher, *Streitschrift des Ġazālī gegen die Bāṭinijja-Sekte* (Leiden: E.J. Brill, 1916), p. 30, l.8 ff. Indeed, as will be seen in Chapter Three, al-Ghazālī himself seems to have adopted this understanding of 4:157.

[5] Louis Massignon, 'Le Christ dans les évangiles selon Ghazali', *Revue des études Islamiques*, 6, 1932, p. 532, also draws attention to the alternative interpretation of *shubbiha lahum* (however grammatically problematic) found in Abū Ḥayyān's *tafsīr* which reads this as an allusion to the metamorphosis of the impious Jews into apes (cf. Q. 3:30).

[6] Henry Corbin, 'L'Ismaélisme et le symbole de la Croix', *La Table Ronde*, 120, 1957, pp. 122–34.

[7] Henry Corbin, 'Comparative Spiritual Hermeneutics', in *Swedenborg and Esoteric Islam*, trans. Leonard Fox (West Chester, PA: Swedenborg Foundation, 1999); first published as 'Herméneutique spirituelle comparée', in *Face de Dieu, face de l'homme* (Paris: Flammarion, 1984), p. 130.

Indeed, the following quotation from the celebrated *Lives of the Prophets* by the Sunni exegete al-Tha'labī (d. 427/1035) would appear to be a striking example:

> When he who was like Jesus was crucified, there came Mary, the mother of Jesus, and a woman for whom he had prayed and whom he had cured of devils, weeping over the crucified one. But Jesus came to them and said, 'For whom are you weeping?' 'For you,' they answered. 'But God has raised me up and nothing but good has befallen me. This person was but a likeness for them.'[8]

But even if our reader were not an actual, out and out Docete (if such an identity may be conceptualized), and was merely a believing Christian, it is not likely that reading the above verse – isolated from the early, formative Muslim exegesis – would necessarily cause much alarm. Apart from the Johannine texts referred to above, there are many other passages in the New Testament that are susceptible of such a reading. One that comes very close to paralleling the Qur'anic language in 4:157–8 is found in the hymn embedded in Philippians 2:5–11, cited by Gardner as an example of the traces of the dispute with Docetism remaining in the Bible:

> Have this mind among yourselves, which is yours in Christ Jesus, who, though he was in the form of God, did not count equality with God a thing to be grasped, but emptied himself, taking the form of a servant, being born in the likeness of men. And being found in human form he humbled himself and became obedient unto death, even death on a cross. Therefore God has highly exalted him and bestowed on him the name that is above every other name.[9]

[8] William Brinner (trans.), *'Arā'is al-Majālis ... al-Tha'labī* (Leiden, E.J. Brill, 2002), p. 671. See also Heribert Busse, 'Jesu Errettung vom Kreuz in der Islamischen Koranexegese von Sure 4:157', *Oriens*, 36, 2001, pp. 160–95, esp. pp. 186–9.

[9] Philippians 2:5–9 (*The New Oxford Annotated Bible*); cf. Iain Gardner, 'Docetism', in *Encyclopedia of Religion*, 2nd edn, ed. Lindsay Jones (Detroit: Macmillan, 2005), vol. 4, p. 2381. Cf. also the reference to Zaehner's citation of Philippians 2:7 as a parallel to Q. 4:157 in Sidney Griffith's preface to the present work.

As we will see below in Chapter Three, the Isma'ili scholars of the tenth and eleventh centuries saw perfect harmony between this Qur'anic verse and the Gospels, as for example when Jesus instructed his followers to fear not the one who can kill the body but fear the one who can kill both the body and the soul. Thus it is equally possible to state that these Muslim exegetes may also have been 'correct'. Such a Docetic reading may, in fact, be behind the following brief Nuṣayrī catechism:

> Question 75: Was Christ crucified and killed as the Christians say in their account of him?
>
> Answer: Know that there is no truth in that, for the Jews (Q. 4:157–8) 'did not slay him, neither crucified him, only a likeness of that was shown to them … But God raised him up to Him' as God says (Q. 3:169) 'Count not those who were slain in God's way as dead, but rather living with the Lord, by him provided.'[10]

As we will see, the Nuṣayrīs are not the only Muslim readers of the Qur'an to read Q. 4:157–8 in the light of Q. 3:169. Ultimately, in the Qur'an what the 'uninitiated' call death is quite illusory. And this would appear to be the chief message of this verse. That such a message is capable of being conveyed in a variety of forms is one of the factors at work in the vast array of exegetical and other literature on this problem. It may even be read in the recent observation by the contemporary Muslim scholar Farid Esack, who offers a distinctive translation of Q. 4:157 in observing that 'Muslims in general deny the crucifixion *although* the Qur'an merely states: THEY DID NOT SLAY HIM, NEITHER DID THEY CRUCIFY HIM, BUT IT ONLY SEEMED TO THEM AS IF IT HAD BEEN SO.'[11]

This book is the first extended study of the problem in which such an understanding of the verse by Muslims is taken seriously. Undoubtedly, one of the reasons such material has been ignored in the context of this problem has to do with what we now know

[10] Meir M. Bar-Asher & Aryeh Kofsky, *The Nuṣayrī-'Alawī Religion: An Enquiry into Its Theology and Liturgy* (Leiden/Boston: E.J. Brill, 2002), p. 191.

[11] Farid Esack, *The Qur'an: A User's Guide* (Oxford: Oneworld, 2005), p. 155 (emphasis added).

are unsuitable categories – especially in the case of Islam – of 'orthodoxy' and 'heterodoxy' as methodological guides in religious studies. In the past, in many scholarly circles, it was felt that 'real (cf. *orthodox*) Islam', which was naturally the most populous Islam, is what we should be studying. Whatever the 'real Islam' might be, we now know that the majoritarian version of Islam, that is to say Sunni Islam, represents a consolidation of doctrines and positions that were worked out over time and in discussion, sometimes heated, sometimes not, with alternative views of what 'real Islam' was. However much it is obviously true that the authors of the Shi'i material studied here represented either marginal groups or a group that would, through historical and political developments, be reduced to marginality, it is nonetheless the case that their voices were very much part of the debate which issued in what we now distinguish as 'Sunni Islam'. What they have to say gives us an insight into not only the formation of doctrine but the nature of the greater community of Muslims, the umma, at a specific time in its development. It shows us how things can and do change.

A factor that is frequently overlooked in discussions of the crucifixion is the history of the 'negative interpretation' – that is to say, the interpretation that holds that the Qur'an in 4:157 actually denies the historicity of the crucifixion of Jesus. It is important to recognize that the earliest textual evidence for such an interpretation is not Muslim at all; rather it is from the pen of none other than the last great Church Father, John of Damascus (d. 749).[12] This fact has also not been sufficiently noticed in previous studies.[13] It is not entirely clear that John 'knew that

[12] For the argument that Christians knew that Muslims themselves were interpreting the Qur'an as denying the crucifixion already early in the eighth century, see Mark N. Swanson, 'Folly to the *Ḥunafā'*: The Crucifixion in Early Christian–Muslim Controversy', in *The Encounter of Eastern Christianity with Early Islam*, ed. E. Grypeou, M. Swanson and D. Thomas (Leiden: E.J. Brill, 2006), pp. 237–56.

[13] Neal Robinson, *Christ in Islam and Christianity* (Albany: State University of New York Press, 1991), pp. 106–7. Here the author refers to the interpretation of John of Damascus as 'one of the earliest extant Christian writings to contain a reference to … the crucifixion'. But not only is it the earliest Christian writing, it is the earliest written interpretation of the verse by anyone, regardless of religious confession.

Muslims denied that Jesus had been crucified'.[14] Indeed, it is equally possible that John was offering his own original exegesis of the verse in order to present Islam to his audience as yet another heresy that in this instance offered yet another variation on what is probably the oldest heretical Christian doctrine, Docetism. Robinson observes in a very important rhetorical question, 'How accurately this reflects Qur'anic interpretation in John's day is impossible to tell.'[15] But at the same time, he seems not to notice the contradiction between this and his assertion, immediately following, that John 'knew' that Muslims denied the crucifixion. We know that John presented the Qur'an to his flock in a language Muslims did not understand – Greek – and could afford to say what he thought would best protect his community from this new, powerful and perhaps otherwise persuasive religion. The possible influence of John's interpretation on later Muslim exegesis is an extremely interesting question, but one that cannot be pursued here.

To return to our theoretical reader, they could hold a view that, whoever the THEY might be, it is clear that it is God himself who determines such important matters as the fate of his Son. Thus, even if to all outward appearances THEY did actually KILL AND CRUCIFY Jesus, it was only through the mysterious working out of the will of God, what Muslims might refer to as divine permission (*idhn*). THEY ultimately had no agency in the matter: 'it only appeared so to them'.

Now who are these THEY in the above Qur'anic citation? They are a group designated throughout the Qur'an by the Arabic word *yahūd*. This word is universally translated as 'JEWS'. So, do we see here an interesting case of the Qur'an absolving the Jews of a crime long charged against them by Christians: to have killed one whom they should have recognized as Messiah? Such a reading would in fact anticipate the recent study of Crossan, who reminds us that in fact the Jews did not kill Jesus, it was the Romans, despite the fact that the Gospels have been widely read as an anti-Jewish polemic.[16] Perhaps this is one of the intentions of the Qur'anic

[14] Ibid., p. 7. [15] Ibid.

[16] John Dominic Crossan, *Who Killed Jesus?* (San Francisco: Harper, 1995).

phrase. But in order to explore more thoroughly this greatest of stumbling blocks in Christian–Muslim dialogue, and one that has implications far beyond the somewhat parochial confines of theological debate, let us look briefly here, by way of introduction, at the entire verse in question in its Qur'anic context.

The theme being pursued in this section of the Qur'an (and we will return to this below) is not, it should be stressed and even repeated, not the life, suffering and death of Jesus. Rather the main topic here is 'faithlessness' in Arabic *kufr*, a subject much more native to the Qur'anic worldview. Those people who are burdened with this spiritual disability are referred to throughout the Qur'an as *kāfirūn* and they come from a variety of social, religious and ethnic backgrounds. The Qur'an contrasts this spiritual disease with *īmān* ('faithfulness, fidelity') and *islām* ('commitment and submission to the divine law'). As in the case of *kufr*, those who are blessed with faith also come from a variety of social, linguistic and religious backgrounds. It is a universal problem. The Qur'an is interested in describing traits and proclivities that are universally human, and not interested in the slightest in demonizing this or that group.[17]

The Qur'an, in the verses leading up to the 'crucifixion verse', says that an example of faithlessness may be found in the history of the Jews when they (1) 'killed their prophets without justification', (2) slandered Mary, the mother of Jesus, defaming her virtue, and (3) boasted that they had killed the Messiah. Note that their deeds are being singled out here as examples of *kufr* – for boasting that they could controvert the Will of God. They are not being castigated for having killed him. The verses run as follows, in the translation of Muḥammad Asad:[18]

> AND SO, [WE PUNISHED THEM] FOR THE BREAKING OF THEIR PLEDGE, AND THEIR REFUSAL TO ACKNOWLEDGE GOD'S MESSAGES, AND THEIR SLAYING OF PROPHETS AGAINST ALL RIGHT, AND THEIR BOAST, 'OUR HEARTS ARE ALREADY FULL OF KNOWLEDGE' – NAY, BUT GOD HAS SEALED THEIR HEARTS IN RESULT OF THEIR DENIAL

[17] W. Björkman, 'Kāfir', *EI*², vol. 4, p. 407.

[18] *The Message of the Qur'ān Translated and Explained by Muḥammad Asad* (Gibraltar: Dar al-Andalus, 1980).

> OF THE TRUTH, AND [NOW] THEY BELIEVE IN BUT FEW THINGS –; AND FOR THEIR REFUSAL TO ACKNOWLEDGE THE TRUTH, AND THE AWESOME CALUMNY WHICH THEY UTTER AGAINST MARY, AND THEIR BOAST, 'BEHOLD, WE HAVE SLAIN THE CHRIST JESUS, SON OF MARY, [WHO CLAIMED TO BE] AN APOSTLE OF GOD!' HOWEVER, THEY DID NOT SLAY HIM, AND NEITHER DID THEY CRUCIFY HIM, BUT IT ONLY SEEMED TO THEM [AS IF IT HAD BEEN] SO; AND, VERILY, THOSE WHO HOLD CONFLICTING VIEWS THEREON ARE INDEED CONFUSED, HAVING NO [REAL] KNOWLEDGE THEREOF, AND FOLLOWING MERE CONJECTURE. FOR, OF A CERTAINTY, THEY DID NOT SLAY HIM: NAY, GOD EXALTED HIM UNTO HIMSELF – AND GOD IS INDEED ALMIGHTY, WISE. (Q. 4:155–8)

Thus the Qur'an speaks of the crucifixion one time, and even in this single instance it is in the nature of parenthesis. It is not a topic central to the Qur'an. It is, however, a topic central to Muslim–Christian relations over the centuries. And over these centuries, since this verse was revealed in Medina, sometime between 622 and 632 CE, it has been interpreted by many Muslims and Christians as denying the crucifixion of Jesus. Islam and the Qur'an have thus come to be recognized and identified as denying the reality of arguably the most important doctrinal and historical values held by Christians. And, since an entire culture has been profoundly shaped and formed by Christian belief, and it could be argued 'Western' culture in particular, then all 'Westerners' (a very unsatisfactory designation) also have a stake in the truth of the crucifixion. When Hans Küng seems to suggest in his recent magisterial study of Islam that the denial of the crucifixion has a certain Islamic logic (while at the same time he acknowledges the ambiguity of the actual verse) it is as much a stated cultural position as an analysis of Qur'anic teaching.[19] In short, it would not only be a believing Christian who would say, 'How can the Qur'an be a divine book when it so obviously has it wrong about the crucifixion of Jesus?' And, if the Qur'an is not a divine book, then Islam is not a 'true religion'. Thus does this matter overflow the banks of mere theological debate.

[19] Hans Küng, *Islam: Past, Present and Future*, trans. John Bowden (Oxford: Oneworld, 2007), pp. 498–9. This work first appeared in German as *Der Islam: Geschichte, Gegenwart, Zukunft* (Munich: Piper Verlag, 2004).

The purpose of this book is not to try to demonstrate that Islam is a 'true religion'. Such a task is far beyond the ability of anyone. Such evidence as is needed will be found amply demonstrated in the lives, achievements and precious legacy of what Hodgson called 'The Venture of Islam' over time.[20] 'Venture' in this title refers as much, if not more, to a collective spiritual and moral epic as it does to a social and political history. It is one from which we all have a great deal to learn.

This book *is* an attempt to contextualize both a key element of the Qur'anic teaching about Jesus and to trace and analyse the all-important exegetical history of this verse. This latter task is divided into three major periods. The first is the pre-Ṭabarī period, which spans the time from the beginning of Islam to the death in 923 CE of the first major, encyclopedic exegete of the Islamic tradition, Muḥammad ibn Jarīr at-Ṭabarī (d. 310/923). The second part of the book deals with the history of the exegesis of this verse from the early tenth century to the dawn of the modern period, the time of the French Revolution in the West and the waning of the great Islamicate 'proto nation states' in the East: the Ottoman, the Safavid and the Mughal. The final section deals with the exegesis of this verse from that time until the present. This survey will show that while one particular exegetical stance has held sway over the centuries, Muslim scholars themselves – some of whom are among the most influential in Islamic intellectual history, were certainly divided as to the meaning and significance of these most important of Qur'anic words. The richness of this debate will enable the reader to acquire a deeper appreciation for the diligent and devout intellectual effort put forth in the pursuit of truth by the greater Muslim tradition. It may also enable us to read the Qur'an for ourselves and come to our own conclusions about what precisely it may mean: They did not kill him and they did not crucify him, rather it appeared so to them. Pound – aiming to express perhaps the same truth we read in the Qur'an, but in the key of English poetry – put it slightly differently:

[20] Marshall G.S. Hodgson, *The Venture of Islam: Conscience and History in a World Civilization*, 3 vols (Chicago: University of Chicago Press, 1975).

> If they think they ha' slain our Goodly Fere
> They are fools eternally.[21]

As we shall see below, John of Damascus's interpretation of the Qur'anic account is, in fact, unjustifiable. The Qur'an itself only asserts that the Jews did not crucify Jesus. This is obviously different from saying that Jesus was not crucified. The point is that both John of Damascus and many Qur'an exegetes (Arabic *mufassirūn*), though not the Qur'an, deny the crucifixion. The Qur'anic exegesis of verse 4:157 is by no means uniform; the interpretations range from an outright denial of the crucifixion of Jesus to a simple affirmation of the historicity of the event. The first and by far the most frequent interpretation is that God rescued Jesus from the crucifixion in a miraculous manner and that someone else was substituted for Jesus on the cross – literal Docetism. This explanation is based on various traditions that are sometimes demonized – e.g. by Ibn Kathīr – as intrusive to the Islamic tradition and are generally considered to fall into the category of *Isrā'īliyyāt*.[22] This book will show that at a relatively late date a trend developed in *tafsīr* that sought to free the verse from such perceived extra-Islamic influences. However, this tendency was abruptly abandoned shortly after it had begun, and from the fourteenth to the twentieth centuries the exegesis of this verse has generally reflected a need to deny the crucifixion of Jesus.

The primary concern here is not Muslim–Christian dialogue, but the Qur'an and its interpretation by Muslims. Thus in the following pages we will first approach verses 4:157–8 from a semantic perspective, then examine the history of their interpretation through comparative analysis of selected *tafsīr* works dating from the earliest Islamic times to the present.

It is interesting to speculate whether or not it would have been necessary for Muslims to deny the crucifixion of Jesus if that event

[21] Ezra Pound, 'The Goodly Fere', *Selected Poems of Ezra Pound* (New York: New Directions, 1957), p. 11. This poem, first published in 1909, explores the poetic or metaphorical – as distinct from the theological – structure of precisely the same kind of self-deception and arrogance, contrasted with moral and spiritual sovereignty, that is the subject of Q. 4:157. See Appendix.

[22] See G. Vajda, 'Isrā'īliyyāt', *EI*[2], vol. 4, pp. 211–12, and the commentary by Rashīd Riḍā below, Chapter Four.

were a doctrinally neutral issue. In other words, it would seem that a simple crucifixion, which did not carry with it such un-Islamic concepts as vicarious atonement, could easily be accepted. In light of the almost universal acceptance that 'someone' was crucified, it appears that the problem faced by the exegetes is not so much Jesus' death on the cross, but their inability to accept this and at the same time maintain their Islamic understanding of prophecy. This fits with Gibb's incisive comment of many years ago that Islam 'is distinguished from Christianity, not so much (in spite of all outward appearances) by its repudiation of the trinitarian concept of the unity of God, as by its rejection of the soteriology of the Christian doctrine and the relics of the old nature cults which survived in the rites and practices of the Christian church'.[23]

The twentieth-century preacher and prolific writer Sayyid Abū al-A'lā Mawdūdī (d. 1979) posed a question we will encounter below in Chapter 4: 'how could Jesus return in the last days if he were not living somewhere in the universe?' Such a question, it seems, could be answered by reference to the verses that discuss those who have died in the path of God: THINK NOT OF THOSE WHO ARE SLAIN IN GOD'S WAY AS DEAD. NAY, THEY LIVE, FINDING THEIR SUSTENANCE IN THE PRESENCE OF THEIR LORD (Q. 3:169). Indeed, this verse plays an important role in the Isma'ili understanding of the verse, as we will see in Chapter Three.

The Qur'anic notion of death, particularly for the righteous (among whom the Qur'anic Jesus holds an indisputable rank), is a paradox. That these verses are rarely, at least in the material surveyed for this study, cited in connection with 4:157–8 is symptomatic of what al-Fārūqī identified as a major shortcoming of modern exegesis. As such it lends itself to discussion under the principles enunciated in an article published by him almost thirty years ago. Although his major concern in this article is the derivation of a Qur'anic ethical code that has meaning for modern Islam, al-Fārūqī's thesis is applicable to the Book as a whole. Inasmuch as this notion of death represents an apparent contradiction in the Qur'an, the following quotation is especially pertinent.

[23] See the full quotation and reference below.

> In the methodology we are suggesting, we may surmount the limitations under which Suyuti, al-Razi and Shah Waliy Allah have laboured. Every contradiction or variance in either the Holy Qur'an or the Sunnah is apparent, including the cases of *naskh* which to their minds have seemed obdurate. The differentiation of the levels of meaning, the distinction of categorical real-existents from ideally-existent values and of higher and lower orders of rank among the latter makes possible the removal of all ambiguities, equivocations, variations, and contradictions without repudiating a single letter of the Holy Writ … What is, therefore, paramountly imperative upon all Muslims at this stage of their history … is a systematic restatement of the Holy Qur'an's valuational content.[24]

Al-Fārūqī called this process an 'axiological systemization' of values. Admittedly, his main concern was with the ethical content of the book; but the re-examination of scripture that he calls for is bound to have implications for questions of theology and metaphysics.

Depending on which translation of the Qur'an an interested Westerner reads, they will come away with an understanding (if there be any clear understanding at all) of the Islamic teaching on the death of Jesus which may or may not be justifiable. The primary reason for this is undoubtedly ascribable to the conspicuous paucity of Qur'anic data on this very specific subject. While Jesus himself is mentioned or referred to in almost a hundred separate verses, his crucifixion is treated in only one: an overall ratio of verses of less than one to six thousand. This alone should be enough to indicate to the intelligent observer that while the Qur'an does indeed concern itself with Jesus, it may emphasize aspects of his ministry that may or may not be of immediate relevance to traditional Christianity. It is obvious that the Book de-emphasizes what is generally considered to be – together with the resurrection – the single most important event in Christian salvation history. However, as we shall see, the Qur'anic de-emphasis need not be interpreted as a denial of the historicity of the crucifixion.

For a non-Muslim, an understanding of the Qur'anic view of

[24] Isma'il R. al-Fārūqī. 'Towards a New Methodology for Qur'anic Exegesis', *Islamic Studies*, 1(1), 1962, pp. 35–52.

the crucifixion event depends largely on which translation of the Qur'an they read. The difficult Arabic of verse 4:157 has led to a number of divergent translations. For convenience, the familiar and controversial 'crucifixion verse' (4:157) is reproduced, transliterated and translated here together with the short verse (4:158) that immediately follows it:

وَقَوْلِهِمْ إِنَّا قَتَلْنَا الْمَسِيحَ عِيسَى ابْنَ مَرْيَمَ رَسُولَ اللَّهِ وَمَا
قَتَلُوهُ وَمَا صَلَبُوهُ وَلَكِنْ شُبِّهَ لَهُمْ وَإِنَّ الَّذِينَ اخْتَلَفُوا فِيهِ لَفِي
يَقِينًا قَتَلُوهُ وَمَا الظَّنِّ اتِّبَاعَ إِلاَّ عِلْمٍ مِنْ بِهِ لَهُم مَا مِنْهُ شَكٍّ
بَلْ رَفَعَهُ اللَّهُ إِلَيْهِ وَكَانَ اللَّهُ عَزِيزًا حَكِيماً

> *wa-qawlihim innā qatalnā al-masīḥa 'Īsā ibna maryama rasūla Allāhi wa-mā qatalūhu wa-mā ṣalabūhu wa-lākin* shubbiha lahum *wa-inna al-ladhīna ikhtalafū fīhi lafī shakkin minhu mā lahum bihi min 'ilmin illā ittibā'a al-ẓanni wa-mā qatalūhu yaqīnan* [4:157] *bal rafa'ahu Allāhu ilayhi wa-kāna Allāhu 'azīzan ḥakīman* [4:158]

> AND FOR THEIR BOAST, 'BEHOLD, WE HAVE SLAIN THE CHRIST JESUS, SON OF MARY, [WHO CLAIMED TO BE] AN APOSTLE OF GOD!' HOWEVER, THEY DID NOT SLAY HIM, AND NEITHER DID THEY CRUCIFY HIM, *BUT IT ONLY SEEMED TO THEM [AS IF IT HAD BEEN] SO*; AND, VERILY, THOSE WHO HOLD CONFLICTING VIEWS THEREON ARE INDEED CONFUSED, HAVING NO [REAL] KNOWLEDGE THEREOF, AND FOLLOWING MERE CONJECTURE. FOR, OF A CERTAINTY, THEY DID NOT SLAY HIM. RATHER, GOD RAISED HIM TO HIMSELF. AND GOD IS MIGHTY, WISE. (Muḥammad Asad translation, slightly adapted)

The emphasized words isolate what is considered to be the most elusive phrase in this verse. *Shubbiha lahum* is a textbook example of a multivocal phrase. Chapter One will deal with the semantics involved here, as well as with the possible meanings of the other related Qur'anic material. But a few examples of the English rendering of this key verbal 'problem' are now offered in order to draw attention to the general puzzlement surrounding this verse. While it may not be strictly methodologically defensible (not to mention politically correct) the following examples are divided into two groups, those from the pens of Muslim scholars and those from others. This is to help illustrate one of the findings of this research, namely that modern Muslims have been less eager to read the Qur'anic text as denying the historicity of the crucifixion than other readers. A few Muslim translations are:

Maulvi Muhammad 'Ali (d. 1951): BUT [THE MATTER] WAS MADE DUBIOUS TO THEM
Yusuf 'Ali (d. 1953): BUT SO IT WAS MADE TO APPEAR TO THEM
Pickthall (d. 1936): BUT IT APPEARED SO UNTO THEM
Abdel Haleem (pub. 2004): THOUGH IT WAS MADE TO APPEAR LIKE THAT TO THEM
Bakhtiar (pub. 2006): BUT A LIKENESS WAS SHOWN TO THEM

A few Western or Christian translations are:

Sale (d. 1736): BUT HE WAS REPRESENTED *BY ONE* IN HIS LIKENESS
Bell (d. 1952): BUT HE WAS COUNTERFEITED FOR THEM
Arberry (d. 1969): ONLY A LIKENESS OF THAT WAS SHOWN TO THEM
Jones (pub. 2007): BUT IT WAS MADE TO SEEM SO TO THEM

Jones is here seen to be closer to Muslim translations than his Western fellows and it is a translation that may be considered to reflect accurately the Arabic. In contrast, the translations of Sale and Bell – along with others that are met with in Chapter One – will be seen to reflect certain themes of the formative exegesis of the verse, rather than the verse itself. It is significant that those who would be expected to be most familiar with and/or most bound by that exegesis, i.e. Muslims, appear here to have made a conscious effort to put the exegesis aside in their translations. The Ahmadiya translation of Maulvi Muhammad 'Ali does, of course, offer a further explanation – as does the translation of Yusuf 'Ali – but these explanations are consigned to footnotes, perhaps in order to preserve one of the more noteworthy and 'modern' aspects of the mood of classical *tafsīr* exemplified by the ubiquitous phrase *wa-Allāhu a'lam* ('but, really, God knows best', i.e. what the true interpretation of this verse should be). Their translations thus allow the Qur'an to speak for itself. However, Sale and Bell and those contemporary Muslim authors concerned with accentuating the distinctness (and perhaps superiority) of Islam in an atmosphere of heightened mistrust and phobia may have allowed the scriptures to become conditioned by extraneous ideas.

The problem in understanding the verse is that the reader who is unaware of its varied exegesis will not readily appreciate the wide range of interpretations that have been assigned to it. Nor will they appreciate to what extent some of these translations have been conditioned by only one of the several existing and influential types of exegesis. Therefore, when turning to modern studies of the Qur'anic Jesus, this same reader is apt to accept at face value a considerable body of scholarly opinion that asserts that the Qur'an categorically denies the crucifixion of Jesus. To be sure, the allegation varies from author to author, in both force and degree. The major purpose of this book is to claim that such assertions, no matter how they are presented, are not necessarily founded on evidence of the Qur'anic *ipsissima verba* alone. The evidence for such a reading is found principally in exegesis, and the bulk of this study is a comparative analysis of selected works of *tafsīr* – the technical Arabic term for exegesis – dating from the earliest Islamic times to the present.

This analysis will bring to light two important facts that have either been completely neglected or minimized in previous studies. The first is that exegesis itself is by no means unanimous on any given interpretation of the verse, and that these interpretations range from an outright denial of the crucifixion of Jesus to a simple affirmation of the historicity of the event. The first type is by far the most frequent, and this explains why it has had such influence. This interpretation maintains that someone else was substituted for Jesus, while God rescued Jesus from his fate in a miraculous manner. It is an explanation based on various traditions that, as a genre, have sometimes been considered intrusive to the Islamic tradition and are considered to fall under the category of *Isrā'īliyyāt*. It will be seen in Chapter Three that, at a relatively late date, a trend developed in *tafsīr* seeking to free the verse from such extra-Islamic influences. This tendency was abruptly abandoned shortly after it had begun, and from the fourteenth to the twentieth century the exegesis of this verse has generally reflected a need to deny the crucifixion of Jesus.

The second fact that will emerge is that most studies of the crucifixion event 'according to Islam' have ignored the Muslim exegetical tradition while being – perhaps unconsciously – influenced by it. In some cases where Western scholars have claimed to have studied the *tafsīr* of the verse, they have done so only partially. The effect of this incomplete treatment has been to misrepresent those Qur'an commentators (and therefore the Islamic tradition as a whole) who are seen to have thought far more creatively and extensively about the problem than one would have otherwise been led to believe. Thus misrepresentation occurs through marginalization and silencing by *not* allowing authentic Muslim voices to speak explicitly to the question.

It would be unfair to say that all scholars have made much of the so-called Qur'anic denial of Jesus' crucifixion. Nonetheless, they have done little to advance the study of the Qur'an on this very specific point beyond the position held by John of Damascus (676–749 CE). For these authors, the denial has become a fact of the Muslim–Christian encounter. Others have devoted a great deal of attention to the problem and have made valuable contributions to our understanding of the Qur'an. This book is indebted to the works of Elder, Parrinder, Michaud and Watt, all of whom have gone to some length in defusing the controversy. The attitude of Seale, that the Qur'an simply does not say enough on the subject to either confirm or deny the event, is the one that comes closest to the position presented in this study.[25] But no single writer has succeeded in emphasizing sufficiently the neutrality of the Qur'an on the subject of the crucifixion of Jesus and the great variety of Muslim understandings of the verse in question. For example, the third edition of Anderson's book, *The World Religions*, teaches us that, in the Qur'an, Muḥammad taught that Jesus was not crucified but someone else took his place on the cross.[26] The important distinction between scripture and the interpretation of scripture is blurred, and the result is nonsense because these two separate sources have been unwittingly mixed. The point is that

[25] Morris Seale, *Qur'an and Bible: Studies in Interpretation and Dialogue* (London: Croom Helm, 1978).

[26] J.N.D. Anderson, *The World's Religions*, 4th edn (Grand Rapids: W.M.B. Eerdmans, 1976), p. 62.

much *tafsīr*, not the Qur'an, denies the crucifixion. The Qur'an's assertion that the Jews did not crucify Jesus – *wa-mā ṣalabūhu* – is obviously different from saying that Jesus was not crucified – *wa-mā ṣuliba*. The first phrase is Qur'anic; the latter is found nowhere in the Book.

Modern and contemporary studies of John of Damascus (676–749 CE) confirm a need to revisit this question.[27] John of Damascus, the eighth-century Father of the Syrian Church, was the earliest author, Muslim or otherwise, to have charged the Qur'an with a denial of the crucifixion. Commenting on the latter's assertion that the Qur'an denies the crucifixion of Jesus, Sahas states,

> This passage is one of the most convincing evidences of the accuracy of John of Damascus' knowledge of the teaching and the wording of the Qur'an! The references to the Qur'an which we have given show that each of these points which John mentions has a Qur'anic origin and that he transmits to the Christians a most accurate account of the Muslim point of view with regard, especially, to the most delicate topic in a Muslim/Christian dialogue.[28]

What I wish to make crystal clear in the following pages is that although it is certainly true that 'each of these points … has a Qur'anic origin' such an origin is in the manner of a hermeneutic site that has been transformed in the process of exegesis carried out during a time when serious and incessant socio-religious pressures exerted themselves in formative ways on the reading of the Qur'an. These pressures were just as influential in the case of John of Damascus as they were in the case of the Muslim scholars who came after him. For John, much was at stake in explaining 'correctly' the formidable success and perhaps appeal of the claims and *da'wa* of the community of the Arabian Prophet. It may have been necessary for this last great Church Father to point out the similarities between the creed of the 'Hagarenes' and that

[27] Daniel J. Sahas, *John of Damascus on Islam: The 'Heresy of the Ishmaelites'* (Leiden: E.J. Brill, 1972).
[28] Ibid., p. 79.

of one of the oldest and in some ways most pernicious heresies of the Church, namely Docetism. As for those Muslim scholars who came after him, whether they were directly influenced by him or not – we know to what a high degree the Muslim 'men of the pen' venerated knowledge and scholarship, whether it came from beyond the borders of Islam or not – their task was quite different. Rather than demonstrate similarities with previous religions, in many instances it became a communal desideratum to show just how distinctive, in a sectarian milieu, this new religion was. This, together with quite unique orientations towards such eschatological problems as 'salvation', and, further, the multivocal or at least ambiguous wording of the Qur'an on the crucifixion, suggested to them that here might be an opportunity for asserting the true identity of Islam over against which the error of post-Jesus Christianity and therefore the truth of Islam as corrective, might be demonstrated.

On the achievement of the Church Father, Sahas adds, 'He presents the facts about Islam in an orderly and systematic way, although not at all complimentary; *he demonstrates an accurate knowledge of the religion, perhaps higher than the one an average Muslim could possess*' (emphasis added).[29] This remarkable statement preserves a kernel of truth in the sense that, at least according to the hypothesis advanced here, John's knowledge was superior precisely because he chose to tease out of the Qur'an teachings something that may have been of little interest or doctrinal importance for Islam. While salvation is mentioned throughout the Holy Qur'an, certainly it is a salvation intimately tied to deeds and behaviour. The redemptive value of the death of Jesus on the cross represents an alternative view that may have had little audience among the early followers of the Prophet Muḥammad. In short, if they adopted the interpretation of their sacred scripture put forth by one of the great, if not the greatest, religious scholars of their time and place, Muslims had nothing to lose with regard to the general ethos of their religion. After all, such religious scholars had already been quite instrumental in the growth and elaboration of the sacred history of Islam

[29] Ibid., p. 95.

(Waraqa b. Nawfal, Baḥīrā). So, there is a well-attested tradition of accepting the teaching of wise, venerated and especially highly placed Christian scholars. John was, after all, a key official in the bureaucracy of the Umayyads. And, as it happens, his interpretation of Q. 4:157–8 is the oldest extant written exegesis, Christian, Muslim or otherwise, asserting that the verses deny the crucifixion.

In the following study, John of Damascus's view will be analysed, and Sahas's claim will be shown to be extravagant and insupportable. This correction of Sahas's claim could be considered a contribution to the important but, in terms of this book, incidental concerns of Muslim–Christian dialogue. The primary concern here is not dialogue, but the Qur'an and its interpretation by Muslims. The majority of previous studies have approached the question from other angles and with other motives. One motive has been described by Welch as the interpretation of the Qur'an or the Bible 'for the purpose of establishing harmony between the two Scriptures'. Laudable as this purpose is, Welch's further observation that such harmonization of the two scriptures has often been attempted 'at points where none exists' is one fact behind the perpetuation of the mutual misunderstanding between Muslims and Christians.[30]

Attempts to study the Qur'anic crucifixion have often been conditioned by religious dispute, proselytization or apologetics. These attempts fall into two major categories. One may be described as an effort to define the type of Christianity that is reflected in the text. The purpose of such efforts is usually to present Muḥammad as well-meaning but ill-informed. The other strives to determine the actual circumstances in which the utterance was first heard. Often, the purpose here is to describe the Prophet's 'politics' by identifying the audience that Muḥammad, in a given instance, was trying to 'appease'. The first method has been the most popular, and the two sometimes overlap. This study should not be classified as either.

The reader will notice a lack of reference to works on the chronology of the Qur'an. Aside from the fact that our verse is never mentioned in the 'occasions of revelation' (*asbāb al-nuzūl*)

[30] Alford T. Welch, 'The Pneumatology of the Qur'an: Study in Phenomenology', PhD thesis, Edinburgh University, 1970, p. 19.

works, this writer believes that the question of chronology, while interesting to a point, has been addressed by Western scholars to a degree that inhibits or deflects an interest in the discrete text. Such discussions often replace interest in the text altogether, and what is actually said in the Qur'an is as a consequence simply ignored. The question of chronology is not basic to the subject at hand. This is a study of the ideas found first in the Qur'an, then elaborated and frequently transformed in *tafsīr*. A semantic approach to the former is offered in Chapter One, while an extensive review of the latter comprises the next three chapters.

The bulk of this study is concerned with the history of Muslim interpretation of Q. 4:157–8. The form of this study is adapted from Jane Smith's classic study of the term 'Islām'.[31] Like that work, it is repetitious, almost to the point of tedium. But *tafsīr* has been sadly neglected by Western students until recently, and the tedium that accompanies such a study is the price we pay for this neglect. Unlike Smith's work, which perceived a 'great unity' in the Muslim understanding of 'Islām', the following discussion will reveal a great divergence regarding the understanding by Muslims of the crucifixion in the Qur'an. A certain unity is nonetheless perceived, but the perception is by inference only. The unity perceived is the fundamental unity of Islam that was so appositely described by Gibb over sixty years ago:

> So far from professing to bring a new revelation Mohammed insisted that the Scripture given him was but a restatement of the faith delivered to the Prophets confirming their scriptures and itself confirmed by them. Yet the originality of Islam is nonetheless real, in that it represents a further step in the logical (if not philosophical) evolution of the monotheistic religion. Its monotheism, like that of the Hebrew Prophets, is absolute and unconditioned, but with this it combines the universalism of Christianity. On the one hand, it rejects the nationalist taint from which Judaism as a religion did not succeed in freeing itself; for Islam never identified itself with the Arabs, although at times Arabs have identified themselves with it. On the other hand, it is distinguished from Christianity, not so much (in spite of all

[31] Jane I. Smith, *An Historical and Semantic Study of the Term 'Islam' as Seen in a Sequence of Qur'an Commentaries* (Missoula, MT: Scholars Press, 1975).

> outward appearances) by its repudiation of the trinitarian concept of the unity of God, as by *its rejection of the soteriology of the Christian doctrine* and the relics of the old nature cults which survived in the rites and practices of the Christian Church.[32]

The results of the following four chapters will be restated in the conclusion, where many of the problems usually associated with an interpretation of 4:157–8 are seen to be the result of an Islamic rejection of Christian soteriology – the theory or doctrine of salvation. In the conclusion, there will also appear some tentative remarks on the question of the genesis of the notorious substitution legends that are the source of the denial of the crucifixion in *tafsīr*.

The variety of interpretation, whether by Muslim scholars or scholars from outside the Islamic religious tradition, encountered in the following pages may be arranged under three categories:

1. No one was crucified.
2. Jesus was crucified, but this happened only because God decided so; it was not a result of the plotting of the Jews.
3. A person other than Jesus was crucified. This is the view most widely held in the contemporary Muslim world.

In the main, the position put forth here agrees in part with the recent authoritative discussion found in the *Encyclopaedia of the Qur'án:*

> [T]he Qur'anic teaching about Jesus' death is not entirely clear-cut. Three things, however, may be said with certainty. First, the Qur'an attaches no salvific importance to his death. Second, it does not mention his resurrection on the third day and has no need of it as proof of God's power to raise the dead. Third, although the

[32] H.A.R. Gibb, *Islam: A Historical Survey*, 2nd edn (Oxford: Oxford University Press, 1989), p. 59; first published by Oxford in 1949 as *Mohammedanism: An Historical Survey*. Note the lucid discussion of this issue by Charles J. Adams, 'Islam and Christianity: The Opposition of Similarities', in *Logos Islamikos: Studia Islamica in Honorem Georgii Michaelis Wickens*, ed. Roger M. Savory and Dionisius A. Agius (Toronto: Pontifical Institute of Mediaeval Studies, 1984), pp. 287–306. There is, as a matter of interest, no article on 'Salvation' in *The Oxford Encyclopedia of the Modern Islamic World* (1995).

> Jews thought that they had killed Jesus, from God's viewpoint they did not kill or crucify him. Beyond this is the realm of speculation. The classical commentators generally began with the questionable premise that Q 4:157–9 contains an unambiguous denial of Jesus' death by crucifixion. They found confirmation of this in the existence of traditional reports about a look-alike substitute and hadiths about Jesus' future descent. Then they interpreted the other Qur'anic references to Jesus' death in the light of their understanding of this one passage. If, however, the other passages are examined without presupposition and Q 4:157–9 is then interpreted in the light of them, it can be read as a denial of the ultimate reality of Jesus' death rather than a categorical denial that he died. The traditional reports about the crucifixion of a look-alike substitute probably originated in circles in contact with Gnostic Christians. They may also owe something to early Shi'i speculation about the fate of the Imams.[33]

Robinson's summary is excellent. Another very useful and thorough study of the problem gathers and analyses a wide range of Qur'an commentary.[34] However, again, there is no attempt to treat divergent readings of the material as constituting part of the history of Muslim thinking about the problem. Of course, there is truth in the conclusion offered by Busse, that nothing can shake the Muslim belief that Jesus did not die on the cross.[35] I wish to offer here what might be considered a deeper reading of this statement. As indicated above, certain passages in the Johannine literature and Philippians can also be understood in the same way. Much of the material in this book was gathered and analysed nearly twenty years ago. This earlier study was published as a two-part article in 1991.[36] Thus

[33] Neal Robinson, 'Jesus', in *The Encyclopaedia of the Qur'ān,* ed. J.D. McAuliffe (Leiden: E.J. Brill, 2005), vol. 3, pp. 7–21. This represents an advance in the thinking of the author beyond the analysis he offered in his important *Christ in Islam and Christianity* (Albany: State University of New York Press, 1991).

[34] Heribert Busse, 'Jesu Errettung vom Kreuz in der islamischen Koranexegese von Sure 4:157', *Oriens*, 36, 2001, pp. 160–95.

[35] 'Nichts hat die Muslime in der Überzeugung erschüttern können, daß Jeus nicht am Kreuz gestorben ist.' Ibid., p. 191.

[36] Benjamin T. Lawson, 'The Crucifixion of Jesus in the Qur'an and Qur'anic Commentary: A Historical Survey (Part I)', *Bulletin of Henry Martyn Institute of Islamic Studies*, 10(2), 1991, pp. 34–62; idem, 'The Crucifixion of Jesus in the Qur'an and Qur'anic Commentary: A Historical Survey (Part II)', *Bulletin of Henry Martyn Institute of Islamic Studies*, 10(3), 1991, pp. 6–40.

many of the findings here overlap or dovetail with those published the same year in Robinson's fine book and later by Busse. But what is unique here is that the actual commentary is translated and presented to the reader in chronological order. More importantly, the writings of the Isma'ili authors, referred to above, are presented here for the first time in a general study of the problem of the crucifixion in the Qur'an, its exegesis or Islam as such. The result is that this book emphasizes and highlights the great variety of Muslim thought on this problem to a degree not previously encountered.

# 1

# THE QUR'ANIC CONTEXT

That the Qur'an itself is the first source of *tafsīr* needs no argument. It is an axiom held by the greater Muslim exegetical tradition and it is one subscribed to here. It also happens to concur with a first principle in literary theory, namely that a text is a discrete entity and provides its own context for understanding its contents. Our enquiry is restricted, however, by the fact that the crucifixion of Jesus is mentioned only once in the Qur'an and may be said to occupy no more than two verses: one directly (4:157) and the other by inference (4:158). It is of the first importance to determine the context of these otherwise isolated statements.

This small portion of the Qur'an falls into the major category of non-legal or non-prescriptive material, which, in this instance, has as its main objective the general edification of its audience on matters pertaining to the nature of *kufr*.[1] In this case, the Jews are being singled out as an example and condemned for various transgressions: idol worship (4:153); breaking their covenant, disbelieving revelation, slaying prophets, for saying OUR HEARTS ARE HARDENED (4:155); general disbelief/*kufr* and defaming or insulting Mary (4:156); FOR THEIR SAYING, WE KILLED THE MESSIAH, JESUS, SON OF MARY, THE MESSENGER OF GOD (4:157); general wrongdoing/*ẓulm*, hindering others from GOD'S WAY [*sabīl Allāh*]

[1] Toshihiko Izutsu, *Ethico-religious Concepts in the Qur'an*, ed. Charles J. Adams and John A. Williams (Montreal: McGill University Press, 1966), pp. 105–77. Here the author emphasizes the root meaning of *kufr* as 'ingratitude'.

(4:160); taking usury, and DEVOURING PEOPLE'S WEALTH [*aklihim amwāl al-nās*] BY FALSE PRETENSES (4:161). Immediately following this list of transgressions comes the promise of an IMMENSE REWARD to those who avoid such behaviour (4:162).

Thus it is clear that the 'crucifixion verse' is located in a context that does not have any aspect of Christian belief or doctrine as its theme or purpose. The information about the event itself, THEY DID NOT KILL HIM AND THEY DID NOT CRUCIFY HIM, BUT IT APPEARED SO UNTO THEM, must be seen as parenthetic in support of the condemnation of *kufr*, which in this case is located in a few especially reprehensible actions of a group who esteemed themselves JEWS. In this context it is no more than an apostrophe meant to underscore the vanity and futility of *kufr.* As we shall see, this is the way the Muslim specialists, the *mufassirūn*, read it; and it is also the way it is understood by a few Western scholars of the Qur'an.[2] This, of course, raises the question: If the Qur'an insists that the Jews did not really kill or crucify Jesus, then what is it about their actions, depicted in 4:157, that is being condemned? On this point there is near unanimity: they are being condemned for their boast that they were able to contravene the will of God by killing his prophet and messenger, Jesus the son of Mary. Thus the concerns of this verse come more sharply into focus. It is not really a discussion about the historicity of the crucifixion of Jesus.

The context of 4:157–8 thus fixed, we are in a position to examine these verses in more detail. They are seen to contain a few words or phrases that form the nuclei of much of the ensuing

[2] For example, 'Seine [Muḥammad's] Aussagen über die Kreuzigen zeigen demnach einen stark polemischen, antijüdischen Akzent', in Claus Schedl, *Muḥammad und Jesus: Die christologisch relevanten Texte des Korans, Neu übersetz und erklärt* (Vienna: Herder, 1978), p. 470. But if by 'polemical' the author intends an actual dispute as the *Sitz im Leben* of this verse, I would strongly disagree. That the Jews are referred to throughout this series of verses indicates that they merely represent a 'historical' example of that class of people known in the Qur'an as *kāfirūn*. See also Giulio Basetti-Sani, *The Koran in the Light of Christ: A Christian Interpretation of the Sacred Book of Islam* (Chicago: Franciscan Herald Press, 1977), p. 163. But the 'first intention' of the context is to preach against *kufr*, not to 'deprive the Jews of the victory they claimed was theirs in Jesus' death'. This latter function must be considered of secondary importance, similarly to the statement in 4:159 that ultimately the People of the Book will come to recognize the station of Jesus. See also Geoffrey Parrinder, *Jesus in the Qur'an* (London: Faber & Faber, 1965), pp. 108–9.

exegesis. Foremost among these is undoubtedly *shubbiha lahum*: BUT IT/HE ONLY APPEARED SO TO THEM. But there are others of equal or at least determinate value. I am not aware of any serious argument against the *'Īsā* of the Qur'an being synonymous with the Jesus of the Gospels.[3] This, then, is the only lexical item in the passage that has escaped controversy. Because of their tangential pertinence to the subject, the words *masīḥ* (MESSIAH) and *rasūl* (MESSENGER) will not be dealt with here. All of the other major words will be treated in the following pages in the light of their general Qur'anic usage.

The first major idea in the two verses is introduced by the verb *q-t-l* ('to kill'). Thus our first task is to determine what is meant in the Qur'an by 'death'. As O'Shaughnessy discovered, this is not a simple matter. In his effort to prove that Muḥammad's ministry was 'not an unexpected explosion but an office assumed after careful preparation and much reflection with the close collaboration of his best friends',[4] he discovered that the concept is a rich one which defies any attempt at categorization. Nevertheless, one of his chapters is of special importance in a discussion of the death of Jesus.

It should be pointed out first that the death of Jesus is directly mentioned in three other verses (19:33; 3:55; 5:117), and indirectly in one (5:17). Qur'an 4:159 is also read to indicate the death of Jesus, but this verse is further embroiled in exegetical debate, the details of which are too involved to discuss here.[5] The usual Qur'anic word for death is *mawt* and it occurs in 19:33: PEACE WAS ON ME THE DAY I WAS BORN, AND THE DAY I DIE, AND THE DAY I SHALL BE RAISED ALIVE! Here, Jesus is miraculously speaking from the 'cradle', as it were. Apart from the resonances such a scene has with the Infancy Gospel, a number of other salient features require analysis. The exegetes have usually seen this verse as referring to Jesus' death in the Last Days when he will have returned to earth, killed the Antichrist, lived for a while and then

[3] The statement of al-Ṭabāṭabā'ī (see Chapter Four) may be considered an exception.

[4] Thomas O'Shaughnessy, *Muḥammad's Thoughts on Death: A Thematic Study of the Qur'anic Data* (Leiden: E.J. Brill, 1969).

[5] The exegesis of the verse is complicated by the existence of a variant reading (*qirā'a*).

died a natural death. Then he will be buried next to Muḥammad, with whom he shall rise on the Day of Resurrection.[6] In verses 3:55 and 5:117, another word is used, which in other contexts is generally construed as physical death. This is a derivation of the root *w-f-y*. In the former verse, it appears as the active participle of the Vth form with the possessive second-person pronominal suffix: *mutawaffīka*. In the latter, it appears as the second-person perfect verb of the same form with the objective first-person ligature: *tawaffaytanī*. In both cases, the originator of the action is God.

> [AND REMEMBER] WHEN GOD SAID: O JESUS! LO! I AM GATHERING THEE AND CAUSING THEE TO ASCEND UNTO ME, AND AM CLEANSING THEE OF THOSE WHO DISBELIEVE UNTIL THE DAY OF RESURRECTION. THEN UNTO ME YE [ALL] RETURN, AND I SHALL JUDGE BETWEEN YOU AS TO THAT WHEREIN YE USED TO DIFFER. (3:55)

> I SPAKE UNTO THEM ONLY THAT WHICH THOU COMMANDEDST ME, [SAYING]: WORSHIP GOD, MY LORD AND YOUR LORD. I WAS A WITNESS OF THEM WHILE I DWELT AMONG THEM, AND WHEN THOU TOOKEST ME THOU WAS THE WATCHER OVER THEM. THOU ART WITNESS OVER ALL THINGS. (5:117)

Each of these verses has its respective problems of interpretation, but they are both important because of the occurrence of *w-f-y*. Of the sixty-six times this root appears in the Qur'an, twenty-five are in the Vth form (4:97; 6:61; 47:27; 5:17; 16:28; 16:32; 10:46; 13:40; 40:77; 8:50; 39:42; 6:60; 10:104; 16:70; 32:11; 4:15; 7:37; 3:193; 7:126; 12:101; 22:5; 40:67; 2:234; 2:240; 3:55). Of these, the majority unequivocally convey the idea of physical death,

[6] 'Abd al-Raḥmān Sā'ātī, *Minḥat al-ma'būd fī tartīb musnad al-Ṭayālisī Abī Dā'ūd*, vol. 1 (Cairo: Maṭba'at al-Munīrīya, 1372/1952) 335 (*ḥadīth* no. 2575). According to Arent Jan Wensinck, *A Handbook of Early Muḥammadan Tradition* (Leiden: E.J. Brill, 1927), and his later *Concordance et Indices de la Tradition Musulmane*, 5 vols (Leiden: E.J. Brill, 1936), this *ḥadīth* transmitted from Muḥammad on the authority of Abū Hurayrah (d. 59/678–9) is the only one available from any source which mentions the death of Jesus in any context. The eschatological import of this isolated instance tends to support the theory that the subject of the crucifixion was not one that occupied the early community. That it was of interest to al-Ṭayālisī (d. 203/818) is a possibility that has implications for a study of the history of Islamic eschatology. An extensive discussion of Jesus in *ḥadīth* literature can be found in William Paul McLean, 'Jesus in the Qur'an and the Ḥadīth Literature', MA thesis, McGill University, 1970.

including one instance where the death of Muḥammad is the issue (40:77). Those verses which are not quite so direct appear also to connote death, e.g. 47:27: THEN HOW (WILL IT BE WITH THEM) WHEN THE ANGELS GATHER THEM, SMITING THEIR FACES AND THEIR BACKS!

The lexical meaning of this form is 'to take' or 'to redeem'. In the verses listed above, it offers a parallel to the English 'to get what is coming to one' or perhaps the less formal 'to be called home'. As mentioned above, the two verses in this group that mention Jesus are fraught with their own exegetical problems. Many of these are a result of – or at least related to – the questions surrounding the 'Qur'anic crucifixion' in 4:157–8. Thus we are in the midst of an exegetical ellipse. Many of these questions will be satisfactorily, if indirectly, addressed in the following pages. The main point here is to emphasize that, according to Qur'anic usage, it is quite permissible to understand these two verses as indicating the death of Jesus:[7] Jesus, according to the Qur'an, can die a normal 'biological' death.

The other direct reference is the negative one in 4:157, but the indirect statement of Jesus' death in 5:17 bears examination here:

> THEY INDEED HAVE DISBELIEVED WHO SAY: LO! GOD IS THE MESSIAH, SON OF MARY. SAY: WHO THEN CAN DO AUGHT AGAINST GOD, IF HE HAD WILLED TO *DESTROY* THE MESSIAH, SON OF MARY, AND HIS MOTHER AND EVERYONE ON EARTH? GOD'S IS THE SOVEREIGNTY OF THE HEAVENS AND THE EARTH AND ALL THAT IS BETWEEN THEM. HE CREATETH WHAT HE WILL. AND GOD IS ABLE TO DO ALL THINGS.

[7] Verse 3:55 has special significance for this subject. *Muṭahhiruka*, translated as CLEANSING YOU, is based on the root *ṭ-h-r*. This root is found in the form *ṭahhirnī* in a tradition that recounts the story of a repentant adulterer who uttered it ('purify me') to Muḥammad with the result that he was stoned to death. See Ignaz Goldziher, 'Das Strafrecht im Islam', *Zum ältesten Strafrecht der Kulturvölker: Fragen zur Rechtsvergleichung gestellt von Th. Mommsen, beantwortet, von H. Brunner, u.a.* (Leipzig, 1905), cited by Th.W. Juynboll, 'Crimes and Punishments (Muḥammadan)', in *Encyclopedia of Religion and Ethics*, ed. James Hastings (Edinburgh: T. & T. Clark, 1908–26), vol. 4, p. 290. The author uses this as an example of the ancient Arabian belief that crime was regarded as impurity and punishment as purification. This need not imply that the Qur'an considers Jesus to have been guilty of some crime. On the contrary, the verse is specific: God is CLEANSING Jesus OF THOSE WHO DISBELIEVE. Cf. Izutsu, op. cit. 241; and further contrast with the findings of Jacob Neusner, 'History and Purity in First-Century Judaism', *History of Religions*, 18(1), 1978, pp. 1–17.

The italics mark the translation of *yuhlika*, which is derived from the frequent (sixty-eight instances) Qur'anic root *h-l-k.* The IVth form here has the straightforward meaning 'to ruin, destroy', while the first form means 'to perish, die, be annihilated'. The first is by far the most frequent form of the verb in the Qur'an. Obviously, the meaning of the above verse is conditional and cannot be construed as indicating the fact of Jesus' destruction or death. Rather, the purpose is to assert the humanity of Jesus, in opposition to the belief in his divinity. But the Book here is categorical: Jesus is, like other men, susceptible of physical death.

The next major root in the passage under discussion is *ṣ-l-b* ('to crucify'). Because the verb is 'denominative', i.e. derived from a noun rather than being a 'natural' Arabic verb form, Jeffery asserts its non-Arabic origin, claiming that its source is Iranian.[8] It occurs in the Qur'an eight times (4:157; 12:41; 7:124; 20:71; 26:49; 5:33; 86:7; 4:23). Six of these are as a verb with the accepted meaning of 'to crucify'. The others are as a noun meaning 'back' or 'loins' (86:7; 4:23). Aside from its use in 4:157, the five remaining positive uses refer to (respectively): the fate of one of Joseph's fellow prisoners (12:41); Pharoah's threat to his magicians (7:124; 20:71; 26:49); and a prescription of punishment for those who fight against God and his messenger (5:33). There is no reason to doubt that the verb indicates the punishment of crucifixion, as it is usually understood.[9]

[8] Arthur Jeffery, *The Foreign Vocabulary of the Qur'an* (Baroda: Oriental Institute, 1938), p. 197.

[9] A cursory look at the history of crucifixion shows that the procedure was adopted for two distinct, if sometimes combined, reasons: (1) as a means of execution; (2) to provide a forceful deterrent to future crime. In the second case, the criminal was killed by separate means before their corpse was publicly displayed on a pike or cross. These grisly details are in line with the Shāfi'ī ruling for one convicted of highway robbery and murder, in which this second procedure was to be followed. The sequence of events – execution then crucifixion – may be reflected in the unchanging order of the two distinct ideas of 'killing' and 'crucifixion' in every *tafsīr* consulted for this study. It is also possible that this reflects nothing more than the Qur'anic word order, in which case hyperbaton (*taqdīm*) could be expected to have been invoked by Muslim rhetoricians; but which fact alone might lead the student of the history of religion to investigate seventh-century Arab methods of punishment. See the brief study by O. Spies, 'Über die Kreuzigung im Islam', in *Religion und Religionen* ... (Bonn: Rohrscheid), pp. 143–56. For the image of crucifixion in Arabic poetry see M. Ullman, *Das Motiv der Kreuzingung* ... (Wiesbaden: Harrasowitz).

*Shubbiha lahum* is by far the most difficult idea presented in verse 4:157, and thus merits careful consideration. Some form of the root *sh-b-h* appears twelve times in the Qur'an in eight separate verses (4:157; 2:70; 3:7 [twice]; 13:16; 2:118; 6:99 [twice]; 2:25; 39:23). The meaning of the root varies, of course, according to the six different forms it assumes in these contexts. The most frequent meaning is a function of the IIIrd-form verbal usage, *to be similar or nearly identical to the point of confusion of true identity*:

> LO! COWS ARE *MUCH ALIKE* TO US (2:70)
>
> THEIR HEARTS ARE ALL *ALIKE* (2:118)
>
> OR ASSIGN THEY UNTO GOD PARTNERS WHO CREATED THE LIKE OF HIS CREATION (WHICH THEY MADE AND HIS CREATION) *SEEMED ALIKE* TO THEM (13:16)
>
> BUT THOSE IN WHOSE HEARTS IS DOUBT, PURSUE, FORSOOTH, THAT WHICH *IS UNCLEAR* (3:7)

The root also appears as an adverbial VIth-form active participle:

> AND IT IS GIVEN TO THEM *IN RESEMBLANCE* (2:25)
>
> HE IT IS WHO PRODUCETH GARDENS TRELLISED AND UNTRELLISED, AND THE DATE-PALM, AND CROPS OF DIVERSE FLAVOUR, AND THE OLIVE AND THE POMEGRANATE, *LIKE AND UNLIKE* (6:141)
>
> GOD HATH [NOW] REVEALED THE FAIREST OF STATEMENTS, A SCRIPTURE CONSISTENT, [WHEREIN PROMISES OF REWARD ARE] *PAIRED* [WITH THREATS OF PUNISHMENT] (39:23)

The active participle is used again, but this time in a negative grammatical construction (*iḍāfa*): WE BRING FORTH ... GARDENS OF GRAPES, AND THE OLIVE, AND THE POMEGRANATE, *ALIKE* AND *UNLIKE* (6:99).

The VIIIth-form active participle is also used in this verse and is translated above as ALIKE. This brings us to the last usage which itself is of primary importance here: BUT *IT APPEARED SO* UNTO THEM (4:157).[10]

This phrase represents the single Qur'anic usage of this form of the root. As an example of *hapax legomenon*, it is among some of the most controversial locutions in exegesis.[11] This distinction should not be forgotten in the following chapters, where lexical equivalents are rarely offered for *shubbiha*. All definitions of the verb have been obtained by deducing a general meaning of 'substitution' from the legends, to be explored in detail below. An exception is the gloss *ḥuyyila* offered by al-Zamakhsharī and later commentators. This hesitancy to define, by lexical means, words of single instance in the Qur'an[12] appears to be an old and accepted tradition. Thus, Ibn 'Abbās is reported to have refused to offer a meaning for *anfāl* – which occurs only once in *sūra*

[10] The following few examples indicate the difficulties facing the translator of this phrase. A more extensive study of the way this verse has been translated would include works listed in the preface to Muhammad Hamidullah's *Le Saint Coran*, preface by Louis Massignon (Paris: Club Français du Livre, 1959), pp. xliii–lxvii.

i. Arberry: ONLY A LIKENESS OF THAT WAS SHOWN TO THEM.
ii. Bell: BUT HE WAS COUNTERFEITED FOR THEM.
iii. Sale: BUT HE WAS REPRESENTED *BY ONE* IN HIS LIKENESS.
iv. Blachère: MAIS QUE SON SOSIE A ÉTÉ SUBSTITUÉ À LEURS YEUX.
v. Hamidullah: MAIS ON LEUR A APPORTÉ QUELQUE CHOSE DE RESSEMBLANT!
vi. Kasimirsky: UN HOMME QUI LUI RESSEMBLAIT FUT MIS À SA PLACE.
vii. Savary: UN CORPS FANTASTIQUE A TROMPÉ LEUR BARBARIE.
viii. Paret: VIELMEHR ERSCHIEN IHREN (EIN ANDERER) ÄHNLICH (SO DASS SIE IHN MIT JESUS VERWECHSELTEN UND TÖTETEN).
ix. Schedl: VIELMEHR WAR ER IHNEN (NUR) ÄHNLICH GEWORDEN.
x. Bausani: BENSI QUALCUNO FU RESO AI LORO OCCHO SIMILE A LUI.
xi. 'Abd al-Haleem: THEY DID NOT KILL HIM, NOR DID THEY CRUCIFY HIM, THOUGH IT WAS MADE TO APPEAR LIKE THAT TO THEM. THOSE WHO DISAGREED ABOUT HIM ARE FULL OF DOUBT, WITH NO KNOWLEDGE TO FOLLOW, ONLY SUPPOSITION: THEY CERTAINLY DID NOT KILL HIM, GOD RAISED HIM UP TO HIMSELF. GOD IS ALMIGHTY AND WISE.

[11] See John Wansbrough, *Quranic Studies: Sources and Methods of Scriptural Interpretation* (Oxford: Oxford University Press, 1977), pp. 117–18.

[12] For example: *tafsīr*, *ilhām*, *khatām* – to name only three of the 450-plus words of single occurrence in the Qur'an. It would be interesting to know what percentage of these *hapax legomena* have become centres of controversy, not forgetting that scripture in general classically endures thorough word-by-word dissection at the hands of its votaries. A study of the exegesis of these words might disclose a general tendency, signalled by the following refusal of Ibn 'Abbās to discuss *anfāl*, cited by Wansbrough, op. cit., p. 172.

eight. This undoubtedly reflects a sincere impulse, as illustrated by the famous statement of the second caliph, to avoid ascribing to the Book of God something that it does not convey, and underscores the basic scripturalist hermeneutic principle upon which I have undertaken this chapter, a principle that was given systematic doctrinal status in the fourteenth century by Ibn Taymiyya (d. 728/1328).[13]

The fact that 4:157–8 is not treated in the *mutashābihāt* works may indicate that the Qur'anic usage of *shubbiha* was quite idiomatic. This, combined with the elaborate legends that embellished Qur'anic usage, may have neutralized incipient controversy over a verse that did not, in any case, pertain directly to questions of jurisprudence – questions that, in the early days, tended to be the prime locus of *ikhtilāf.* The phrase *shubbiha lahum*, as we have seen above, may be translated in a variety of ways. In exegetical literature, it is almost always explained elliptically; that is, by some form of the root *sh-b-h-* it is obvious that such a method does not enrich one's understanding of semantics. The following is a brief summary of Lane's lexical analysis:

> Active: *Shabbahahu bihi* = He made it to be like it or resemble it. He assimilated it to it (syn. of *mathalahu*). *Shabbahtu al-shay' bi al-shay'* = I put the thing in the place of or in the predicament of the other thing, *by reason of an attribute* connecting them or common to them; which attribute may be real or ideal … *Shabbaha* [apparently for *shabbaha shay'an bi-shay'in*] = He made a thing equal to a thing, or like a thing. [Hence] *shabbaha 'alayhi* = He rendered it confused to him [by making it to appear like some other thing]. *He rendered it ambiguous, dubious or obscure, to him.*[14]

Lane tells us that the passive verb of this form is synonymous with the VIIth and the Vth, giving the following examples: '*shubbiha 'alayhi al-amr* = The thing or affair was rendered confused or dubious to him. *Tashabbaha lahu annahu kadhā* = It became to

[13] Taqī al-Dīn Aḥmad ibn Taymiyya, *al-Muqaddima fi uṣūl al-tafsīr* (Beirut: Dār al-Qur'ān al-Karīm, 1399/1979), pp. 93–105.

[14] Abridgement of 'Shabaha', in Edward William Lane, *An Arabic–English Lexicon*, Bk I, pt 4. (London: Williams & Norgate, 1872), pp. 1499–1501.

him [in the mind, i.e. it seemed to him] that it was so. Synonymous with *ḥuyyila* and *shubbiha*.'[15]

This rather dreary inventory of definitions was thought to be justified for obvious reasons. Although such an idea as 'substitution' could possibly be implicated in the second definition of the active voice, this would seem to be quite a reach in the context of the dictionary meaning of the verb. Of course, the Qur'an existed before dictionaries and lexicons were compiled. It is, therefore, interesting to note that this active voice does appear in a Qur'anic variant (*qirā'a*) of 4:157.[16] As in the case of the exegetes, the only synonym offered that is not derived from the same root *is ḥuyyila.* However if, as Lane suggests, the passive voice is synonymous with certain uses of the Vth and VIIIth forms, then some indication of its semantic range may be obtained by reference to extra-Qur'anic usage. The terms *tashbīh, mutashābihāt* and *mushtabih* are frequent technical terms in exegesis and other religious discussions. The first can mean: comparison, allegory, simile, metaphor, parable or anthropomorphization. The remaining words can mean: obscure, suspicious or doubtful. These latter are generally used when speaking of unclear Qur'anic passages that are sometimes interpreted allegorically or metaphorically, or are explained by reference to heretofore unsignalled or extra-Qur'anic events.[17]

[15] Ibid., p. 1500.

[16] See Arthur Jeffery, *Materials for the History of the Text of the Qur'an: The Old Codices, etc.* (Leiden: E.J. Brill, 1937), pp. 38, 127. The first variant is simply *shabbaha* as opposed to *shubbiha*; the second is more elaborate: *shubbiha lahum wa-ma qatalahu al-ladhīna ittahamū bihi*. In the first variant we face the problem of subject: is it God or Jesus? The second is sufficiently vague, adding little to our knowledge of the identity of the victim. The whole problem of variants is notoriously vexed, and while it may not be possible to prove they represent anything more than *tafsīr* (Jeffery, *Materials*, p. 10) the hypothesis in John Burton, *The Collection of the Qur'an* (Cambridge, England: Cambridge University Press, 1977) certainly could be used to support such a claim. It may not be out of place to draw attention to the variant for 4:159 (Jeffery, *Materials*, p. 127): *layu'minanna*, trans. = 'will believe' (third-person sing.) as opposed to *layu'minunna* (pl.). Likewise, it is only the number that varies in the other variant word of this verse: *mawtihi* changes to *mawtihim*. Thus, this variant cannot be speaking of the death of Jesus, which death, in any case, is interpreted eschatologically.

[17] Wansbrough, op. cit., pp. 212–16 and index: *mushtabih/mutashābih*. An example of this type of exegesis is that of Muqātil, *Mutashābih fī al-Qur'ān*, portions of which are reproduced in Abū al-Ḥusayn Muḥammad b. Aḥmad al-Malaṭī, *al-Tanbīh wa-al-radd* (Cairo: Maktab Nashr al-Thaqāfat al-Islāmiyya, 1363/1949), pp. 44–63.

By this, I am not proposing a semantic leap. It would be difficult, if not impossible, to argue from these facts that the phrase *shubbiha lahum* should be translated as 'it was allegorized to them'. But the fact is that quite early in the history of the exegesis of this phrase the meaning of the verbal phrase was enhanced with a new layer of drama by way of the substitution legends. The main point here is to highlight the fact that the Qur'an neither supports nor rejects the substitution of another human being for Jesus in this context, being serenely indifferent to the entire question.

Turning to the next major word in verse 4:157, we encounter the root *ẓ-n-n* ('conjecture, fancy'). This root occurs a total of sixty-nine times in the Qur'an. However, the main concern here is with the noun *ẓann*, which occurs fifteen times and which Pickthall has translated variously as: 'thought' (3:15; 10:60; 48:6; 48:12); 'conjecture' (4:157; 10:36; 10:66); 'opinion' (6:116; 6:148; 38:27); 'suspicion' (49:12, twice); and 'guess' (53:23; 53:28, twice). In six of these instances, including the verse under discussion, *ẓann* is that which is followed (*tubi'a*) by representatives of that class of Qur'anic dramatis personae known as *kāfirūn*. Thus we are presented with the normative Qur'anic usage, a situation much preferable to the controversial locutions surrounding *shubbiha lahum*.

Still, the interpretation of *ẓann* is by no means clear-cut. Izutsu classes *ẓann* as one of the 'value words' in the Qur'an, and notes that it is best understood in contrast to *'ilm*, another value word. The overshadowing importance of this latter term – translated as 'knowing, knowledge' – as constitutive of Islamic theodicy is too involved to treat here. Suffice it to say that it represents a kind of knowledge which is certain and unchallengeable, denotative in its way of a kind of immutability usually ascribed to natural laws (and may itself represent the only immutable reality), and transcendent in that its source is divine.[18] *Ẓann*, therefore, in a general way, represents everything antithetical to this knowledge. It implies that which is at odds with revelation. While it may indeed mean 'conjecture' in verse 4:157, it also connotes a blindness to true

[18] Toshihiko Izutsu, *God and Man In the Qur'an: Semantics of the Koranic Weltanschauung* (Tokyo: Keio Institute of Cultural and Linguistic Studies, 1964), pp. 59–62.

religion on all levels, whether ethical, moral, spiritual or communal. So in our context it is those who disagree about the crucifixion, either among themselves, or with the Qur'an, who are at the mercy of religiously dysfunctional forces, which in the context described above are summarized as *kufr.* Thus, *ẓann* represents far more than simple opinion, thought or guess. Its complex and sinister reverberations well up from a source much deeper than the intellect.

Brief notice should be taken here of *y-q-n*, which is another familiar (twenty-eight occurrences) Qur'anic root. The noun form with which we are concerned is another antonym of *ẓann*.[19] Usually translated as 'certainty', it is used in the Qur'an to describe matters of Revelation, Faith, Prophets, God and the Hereafter. It is also used to describe the less lofty, or at least more contingent ideas of Knowledge, Truth, Vision, Tidings and general certainty about 'what is right'. In addition, it is used in its negative sense on four occasions: in speaking of general awareness, Faith, The Hour, and the death of Jesus. Qur'an 15:19 and 74:47 are particularly interesting in that while the application concerns the certainty of the Judgement Day, it seems also to imply a primary correspondence to 'death'. Indeed, one of the dictionary meanings of *yaqīn* (in Persian) is 'death'.[20] The root as it appears in 4:157 is in a unique form, and although discussion of it in *tafsīr* is always restricted to the question of what exactly was uncertain,[21] further enquiry into its semantic value could reveal a larger field than that proscribed by the word 'certainty', particularly in light of its relation to *ẓann*.[22]

The last root to be dealt with is *r-f-'*. In the Qur'an, it appears twenty-two times as a verb and six times as a noun. The verbal

[19] See the discussion of litotes in Wansbrough, op. cit., p. 230.

[20] See 'Yaqīn' in F. Steingass, *Persian–English Dictionary* (New Delhi: Oriental Books Reprint Corporation, 1973).

[21] But cf. the opinion of Abū Ḥātim al-Rāzī cited by Massignon, op. cit., p. 534 (discussed below).

[22] See Rosalind Ward Gwynne, *Logic, Rhetoric, and Legal Reasoning in the Quran: God's Arguments* (London/New York: RoutledgeCurzon, 2004), p. 138 for a discussion of the important Qur'anic technical terms '*ilm, shakk, ẓann* and *yaqīn*. The importance of Q. 4:157 is underlined, as it is the only place in the Qur'an where all these terms occur together.

uses are evenly divided into two general meaning-groups. The first carries the idea of raising as in the lifting of an object from a surface (12:100; 13:2; 88:18; 79:28; 2:63; 2:93; 4:154; 55:7; 49:2; 2:127). The second means, or can mean, the exaltation of a thing or person in rank or value (2:253; 6:175; 43:32; 94:4; 7:176; 19:57; 4:158; 6:83; 12:76; 58:11; 35:10; 24:36). In addition, there are various noun forms that occur with a similar distribution of meaning (56:3; 3:55; 40:15; 52:5; 56:34; 80:14). Among the verses in which *r-f-'* occurs, we find verse 3:55, a verse we analysed earlier in a discussion of *w-f-y*. This intimate lexical relationship between 3:55 and 4:157–8 no doubt explains the exegetes' frequent reference to the former verse in their discussion of the crucifixion. What is not clear, however, is why this reference is made to the exclusion of almost all other verses that have been seen to have a semantic relationship to the subject.[23] It is also worth mentioning that included in this group is verse 19:57, which mentions the raising of Idrīs (Enoch), one of the four prophets who, according to tradition, were physically raised to heaven. It is also significant that Pickthall translates this verse as AND WE RAISED HIM TO A HIGH STATION rather than the more literal alternative.

Here any idea of physical raising is left purely to the imagination. And such an imagination, in light of the English translation chosen by Pickthall, would need to be particularly inventive in order to arrive at such a conclusion. Although the prepositional phrase used with this verb in 4:158 does indicate a spatial dimension, it should be remembered that God, as the object of this preposition, is placeless.[24] That early exegetes persisted in interpreting the verse 'anthropomorphically' makes sense in the context of the well-known connections between and among exegesis, storytelling and preaching.[25] It solved textual problems in an instructive, edifying and, dare we say, entertaining fashion. Nevertheless, it

[23] The most common Qur'anic clarification cited for 4:157 is 26:27 (or similar verses) in order to confirm that the Jews, not God, spoke these words in ridicule. A notable exception is Rashīd Riḍā (see Chapter Four).

[24] See the presentation of the exegesis of Fakhr al-Dīn al-Rāzī (d.1209) in Chapter Three.

[25] J. Pedersen, 'The Islamic Preacher: Wa'iz, Mudhakkir, Qass', in *Goldziher Memorial Volume*, vol. 1, ed. Samuel Lowinger and Joseph Desomogyi (Budapest: Globus Nyomdai Munitezet, 1948).

required centuries of theological and terminological refinement before such interpretations were challenged in *tafsīr*, as will be seen below. This says as much about the genre of *tafsīr* as it does about anything else.

Undoubtedly, a major influence on the early interpretation of this verse, and probably 19:57 as well, was the legend of the ascension of the Prophet Muḥammad – the *mi'rāj* tradition as a whole, and the reality this tradition represented to Muslims.[26] Whatever the case may be, it is quite clear that the Qur'an does not favour one meaning over the other.

## THE QUR'ANIC CONCEPT OF DEATH

With the above observations on the semantics of verses 4:157–8 thus registered, we are free to pursue the Qur'anic concept of death. The death of those who are particularly favoured by God is the type that has the most significance for this study. O'Shaughnessy has singled out fourteen instances of such deaths, four of which are quoted here for reference:

> THOSE WHO FLED THEIR HOMES FOR THE CAUSE OF GOD AND THEN WERE SLAIN [*qutilū*] OR DIED [*mātū*], GOD WILL PROVIDE FOR THEM A GOOD PROVISION. (22:58)

> O YE WHO ARE JEWS! IF YE CLAIM THAT YE ARE FAVOURED OF GOD APART FROM [ALL] MANKIND, THEN LONG FOR DEATH [*al-mawt*] IF YE ARE TRUTHFUL. (62:6)

> [PHAROAH] SAID: [TO HIS MAGICIANS] … 'I WILL CUT OFF YOUR HANDS AND YOUR FEET ALTERNATELY, AND VERILY I WILL CRUCIFY YOU EVERY ONE.' THEY SAID: 'IT IS NO HURT, FOR LO! UNTO OUR LORD WE SHALL RETURN.' (26:49–50)

[26] Geo Widengren, *Muḥammad the Apostle of God, and His Ascension (King and Saviour V)* (Uppsala, Sweden: Almqvist & Wiksells, 1955), evaluates the importance of this tradition for Islam along with a study of its pre-Islamic history. For direct correspondence between this tradition and *tafsīr*, see Chapter Two and Chapter Four.

> AND CALL NOT THOSE WHO ARE SLAIN [*yuqtalu*] IN THE WAY OF GOD 'DEAD' [*amwāt*]. NAY THEY ARE LIVING, ONLY YE PERCEIVE NOT. (2:154, similar to 3:169)

The idea, reality and inevitability of death is an unbroken obbligato heard throughout and behind the shifting themes and movements of the Qur'an. That this does not impose an undifferentiated mood of melancholy, despair and impotence upon the reader is due in part to the many other contrasting themes that are also present. But perhaps the most important reason for this overall effect has to do with the basic Qur'anic teaching on death.[27] This idea is best understood by contrasting it with pre-Islamic notions. The Qur'an itself indicates as much:

> AND THEY [the Jāhilī Arabs] SAY: THERE IS NAUGHT BUT OUR LIFE IN THIS WORLD; WE DIE AND WE LIVE, AND NAUGHT DESTROYETH US SAVE TIME [*dahr*]; WHEN THEY HAVE NO KNOWLEDGE WHATSOEVER OF [ALL] THAT; THEY DO BUT GUESS [*yaẓunnūna*]. AND WHEN OUR CLEAR REVELATIONS ARE RECITED UNTO THEM THEIR ONLY ARGUMENT IS THAT THEY SAY: BRING [BACK] OUR FATHERS THEN, IF YE ARE TRUTHFUL. SAY [UNTO THEM, O MUḤAMMAD]: GOD GIVETH LIFE TO YOU, THEN CAUSETH YOU TO DIE, THEN GATHERETH YOU UNTO THE DAY OF RESURRECTION WHEREOF THERE IS NO DOUBT. BUT MOST OF MANKIND KNOW NOT [*lā ya'lamūna*]. (45:24–6)

According to Izutsu, the ideas present in the above passage are a clear reflection of the semantic tensions within the Qur'an, which derive from the tensions between two opposing worldviews. One, the pre-Islamic (*jāhilī*), which is strongly coloured by 'the problem of *khulūd*, "the eternal life," the absolute unattainableness of which they were so painfully aware … and which drove them to their characteristic philosophy of life, the pessimistic nihilism'.[28] The other, the Islamic, is discussed as follows:

> The inevitability of death in the form of *ajal*, however, does not lead, in the Islamic conception, as it used to do in Jahiliyyah, to a gloomy pessimistic view of human existence, because the *ajal*

[27] Izutsu, *God and Man*, pp. 123–30; idem, *Ethico*, pp. 47–54.
[28] Izutsu, *God and Man*, p. 123.

> in this sense is not, in the new *Weltanschauung*, the real terminal point of existence. It is, on the contrary, the very threshold of a new and entirely different kind of life – the eternal life (*khulūd*). In this system, the *ajal*, i.e. death, of each individual man is but a middle stage in the whole length of his life, a turning-point in his life history situated between the Dunya and the Hereafter. Unlike the Jāhilī view of life which would see nothing beyond the *ajal*, the Koranic view sees precisely beyond the *ajal* the real life, real because it is 'eternal' (*khālid*).[29]

Thus, even if our verse said that Jesus did not die, we would be compelled to ponder the more profound meaning such a statement demands. But it does not say this. The verse states that the Jews did not kill him. The semantic constitution of such a statement strongly points to a reading that would go well beyond the mundane realms of murder and physical death. By extension the same applies to the statement that they did not crucify him inasmuch as the 'him' can be understood, in light of the above quotation, as the eternal reality (*khālid/khuld*) of Jesus. This will be the thrust of certain 'dissident' Muslim interpretations of this verse by, for example, Abū Ḥātim al-Rāzī, al-Sijistānī and the *Ikhwān al-Ṣafā'*, below.

To the assertion that the denial of the crucifixion is in 'perfect agreement with the logic of the Kur'ān', it need hardly be pointed out that while it may indeed be '"God's practice" ... to make faith triumph finally over the forces of evil and adversity',[30] it is also obvious that this triumph may have a more mysterious character than Jesus' putative and chance escape – however exciting – from his misguided opponents. After all, Jesus the prophet, as demonstrated above, is among those in the Qur'an who are vulnerable to physical death, e.g. Muḥammad (7:28), Moses (7:155) and Yaḥyā (John the Baptist) (19:15). Moreover, a distinctive characteristic of Qur'anic prophethood is the unremitting opposition that greets those upon whom it is bestowed. That this opposition frequently ends in the murder of a prophet is well known (e.g. 2:61; 2:87;

[29] Ibid., p. 130.

[30] Georges C. Anawati, "Īsā', *Encyclopaedia of Islam*, 2nd edn (hereafter *EI* followed by a numerical superscript indicating the edition), vol. 4, p. 84, includes the preceding quotation.

2:91; 3:21; 3:183; 4:155[!]). Finally, it is quite clear that such a death, though seemingly the result of human perfidy, is really a work of less fallible design:

> No soul can ever die except by God's leave and at a term appointed. Whoso desireth the reward of the world, We bestow on him thereof; and whoso desireth the reward of the Hereafter, We bestow on him thereof. We shall reward the thankful. (3:145)

# 2

# PRE-ṬABARĪ *TAFSĪR*: EXEGETICAL TRADITIONS

Qur'anic exegesis is divided into two basic categories: (1) *tafsīr bi-al-ma'thūr*, founded on received traditions (*aḥādīth*), which are traced to the prophet Muḥammad, his companions (*aṣḥāb*) or recognized early authorities on scriptural exegesis (*mufassirūn*);[1] and (2) *tafsīr bi-al-ra'y*, which allows the exegete to offer opinions without being bound by the interpretations of the verse found in the traditions. This chapter is primarily concerned with the first type of commentary, which also represents the earliest stages of exegesis. The second type is a later development and will be treated in subsequent chapters.

[1] Rashid Ahmad Jullandri, 'Qur'anic Exegesis and Classical Tafsīr', *Islamic Quarterly*, 12(1), 1968, p. 81. In addition to this article, see the following on early *tafsīr* in general: Hartwig Hirschfeld, *New Researches into the Composition and Exegesis of the Qoran* (London: Royal Asiatic Society, 1902); Ignaz Goldziher, *Die Richtungen der Islamischen Koranauslegung*, 2nd edn (Leiden: E.J. Brill, 1952), pp. 1–98; Harris Birkeland, 'Old Muslim Opposition against Interpretation of the Koran', *Avhandlinger utgitt av del Norske Vldenskaps-Academic: Oslo, II, Hist.-Filos, Klasse., 1955, No. 1* (Uppsala, Sweden: Almqvist & Wiksells, 1956); Nabia Abbot, *Studies in Arabic Literary Papyri: II, Qur'anic Commentary and Tradition* (Chicago: University of Chicago Press, 1967); Jane I. Smith, op. cit., pp. 35–56; Helmut Gätje, *The Qur'anic and Its Exegesis: Selected Texts with Classical and Modern Muslim Interpretations*, trans. and ed. Alford T. Welch (London: Routledge & Kegan Paul, 1976); M.O.A. Abdul, 'The Historical Development of Tafsīr', *Islamic Culture*, 50, 1976, pp. 141–53; Wansbrough, op. cit.; Mujāhid Muḥammad al-Ṣawwāf, 'Early Tafsīr – A Survey of Qur'anic Commentary up to 150 A.H.', in *Islamic Perspectives: Studies In Honour of Mawlanā Sayyid Abū A'lā Mawdūdī*, ed. Khurshid Ahmad and Zafar Ishaq Ansari (London: Islamic Foundation, 1979), pp. 135–45.

Much of this early material is taken from al-Ṭabarī,[2] although some of it has been found in independent editions of the works of various authors. The following is a review in chronological order, based upon the death dates of the several commentators, of the thinking of the *mufassirūn* of the first three centuries of Islam on the problem of the crucifixion.

## 'ABD ALLĀH IBN 'ABBĀS (d. 68/687)

This quasi-legendary figure is esteemed, especially by the Sunni exegetical tradition, to be the 'father of Qur'an commentary' and is known by the honorifics '*The* doctor' (*al-ḥibr*) and 'the Ocean [of knowledge]' (*al-baḥr*). This excerpt from the *Encyclopaedia of Islam* captures the veneration the Islamic tradition holds for him:

> From his youth he showed a strong inclination towards accurate scholarly research, in so far as such a conception was possible at that time. We know indeed that the idea soon occurred to him to gather information concerning the Prophet by questioning his Companions. While still young, he became a master, around whom thronged people desirous to learn. Proud of his knowledge, which was not based only on memory, but also on a large collection of written notes, he gave public lectures, or rather classes, keeping to a sort of programme, according to the days of the week, on different subjects: interpretation of the Qur'an, judicial questions, Muḥammad's expeditions, pre-islamic history, ancient poetry. It is because of his habit of quoting lines in support of his explanations of phrases or words of the Qur'an that ancient Arabic poetry acquired, for Muslim scholars, its acknowledged importance. His competence having been recognized, he was asked for *fatwā*s (especially famous is his authorization of *mut'a* marriage, which he later had to vindicate). The

[2] Abū Ja'far Muḥammad b. Jarīr al-Ṭabarī, *Jāmi' al-bayān 'an ta'wīl āy al-Qur'ān*, ed. Maḥmūd Muḥammad Shākir and Aḥmad Muḥammad Shākir (Cairo: Dār al-Ma'ārif, 1374/1955). This is the edition used for this research. See also the more recent modern edition: *Jāmi' al-bayān 'an ta'wīl āy al-Qur'ān*, 30 vols (Cairo: Muṣṭafā al-Bābī al-Ḥalabī, 1986).

> Qur'an explanations of Ibn 'Abbās were soon brought together in special collections, of which the *isnād*s go back to one of his immediate pupils ... his *fatwā*s were also collected; today there exist numerous manuscripts and several editions of a *tafsīr* or *tafsīr*s which are attributed to him.[3]

Thousands of exegetical traditions are ascribed to him by both Sunni and Shi'i authors. The *Tanwīr al-miqbās* is a short *tafsīr* ascribed to Ibn 'Abbās, and, like works attributed to other early figures in Islamic history, carries many questions of authenticity. Indeed, the current debate on whether or not it is accurate to speak of *tafsīr* as an early activity casts a certain amount of perplexity over any discussion of the subject.[4] For several reasons, the traditions associated with Ibn 'Abbās are generally thought to be untrustworthy, at least as far as the ascription is concerned. As observed by Smith,

> One issue that must be dealt with by anyone undertaking a specific study of this question is why so little of the material concerning specific passages of the Qur'an attributed to this man by later writers of *tafsīr* is not to be found, or is found in different form, in his own [i.e. the work at hand] *tafsīr* ... one hopes that in the near future we may be able to discuss these questions armed with fewer opinions and more facts.[5]

Fortunately, one fact has recently come to light: the *Tanwīr al-miqbās* is an abridgement by al-Dīnawārī (d. 308/920) of perhaps a Muḥammad al-Kalbī (d. 146/763) *tafsīr*.[6] Hence, it is with a certain amount of abdication that the following discussion is related to Ibn 'Abbās; rather, we should associate it with al-Kalbī, who,

[3] Laura Veccia Vaglieri, "Abd Allāh ibn al-'Abbās', *EI*², vol. 1, pp. 40–1.

[4] That is, *tafsīr* as a discipline distinct from the general study of Qur'an and *ḥadīth*; see Jullandri, op. cit., p. 78; al-Ṣawwāf, op. cit. In addition, Abbot's discussion of the theories of Goldziher and Birkeland, op. cit., pp. 106–13, and Wansbrough's criticism of this, op. cit., pp. 157–8, are important.

[5] Smith, op. cit., p. 42.

[6] Andrew Rippin, 'The Exegetical Works Ascribed to Ibn 'Abbās: An Examination', in *The Qur'an and Its Interpretative Tradition* (Aldershot, England: Variorum, 2001).

nevertheless, cited much on the authority of Ibn 'Abbās.[7] Here is a translation of the relevant passage:

> BECAUSE OF THEIR SAYING: because of their statement WE KILLED THE MESSIAH, JESUS SON OF MARY, THE MESSENGER OF GOD, God destroyed one of their [the Jews'] friends, Naṭyānūs BUT THEY KILLED HIM NOT, NOR DID THEY CRUCIFY HIM, BUT SO IT WAS MADE TO APPEAR TO THEM, the likeness [*shibh/shabah*] of Jesus was cast upon Naṭyānūs, so they killed him instead of Jesus AND THOSE WHO DIFFER THEREIN about his killing ARE FULL OF DOUBTS about his killing THEY HAVE NOTHING CONCERNING IT concerning his killing OF KNOWLEDGE, ONLY CONJECTURE and not even conjecture AND THEY DID NOT KILL HIM IN CERTAINTY i.e. certainly they did not kill him RATHER, GOD RAISED HIM TO HIMSELF to heaven AND GOD IS EXALTED IN POWER in revenging His enemies WISE with support for His intimate friends [*awliyā'*] and His prophet, and He destroyed their friend Naṭyānūs.[8]

This example of the *tafsīr* of verses 4:157–8 gives us the essence of what may be termed, for the purposes of this study, the 'substitution legend'. Although this is by no means the only device employed to explain the two verses, it is by far the most frequently encountered. As such, it is undoubtedly responsible for the debate on the actuality of the crucifixion of Jesus. This legend will be met with many times and in many forms in the following pages. A brief enumeration of the points of 'future' exegetical dispute is therefore offered here for convenience:

1. The meaning of THEIR SAYING (*qawlihim*) – whether it denotes a simple statement or a boast.
2. The identity of the speaker of the words THE MESSENGER OF GOD (*rasūl Allāh*) – whether it is God or the Jews.
3. What is meant by BUT SO IT WAS MADE TO APPEAR TO THEM (*shubbiha lahum*). As we noted earlier, this phrase is at the heart of the controversy, and its explanation accounts for

[7] As is evidenced in the work at hand, Abū Ṭāhir Muḥammad ibn Ya'qūb al-Fīrūzābādī, *Tanwīr al-miqbās min tafsīr ibn 'Abbās*, 2nd edn (Cairo: al-Bābī al-Ṭabarī, 1370/1951).

[8] *Tanwīr al-miqbās*, p. 68. Qur'anic quotations provided in small caps.

many of the variant interpretations of the verse, especially the substitution legends.

4. Whether the antecedent of the third-person object pronoun HE/IT (*hu*) in the phrase THEY DID NOT KILL HIM/IT IN CERTAINTY (*ma qatalūhu yaqīnan*) is HIM or IT (i.e. Jesus or DOUBT about the event of the crucifixion); and the meaning of IN CERTAINTY (*yaqīnan*).
5. The meaning of [GOD] RAISED (*rafa'a*), the antecedent of the pronoun (*hu*), and the meaning of TO HIMSELF (*ilayhi*) in the phrase, RATHER, GOD RAISED HIM TO HIMSELF (*bal rafa'ahu Allāh ilayhi*).
6. In addition, and with special reference to the various substitution legends, the most changeable element is the identity of the victim of the crucifixion. Another is the number of disciples (*ḥawārīyūn/aṣḥāb*) with Jesus during the events recounted in these legends. Other minor variations will also be noticed.

The above excerpt from the *Tanwīr al-miqbās* ascribed to Ibn 'Abbās also displays a concern for many of the usual exegetical questions. To point out the obvious, the *tafsīr* acknowledges that a crucifixion took place. Thus, the question presents itself: 'Why was it so important to grant this, but at the same time deny that Jesus was crucified?' Whatever the answer may be, it is obvious that the later exegetes went to great lengths to uphold the historicity of *a* crucifixion. The most important issue here is the identity of the victim. In this rather short commentary, the name Naṭyānūs is mentioned three times. Contemporaries of al-Kalbī suggested a different identity. For example, Muqātil, to be dealt with at greater length below, claimed that the victim was Yāhūdhā, a Jew. It could thus be argued that even at this early date the Muslim community was in agreement on the event of the crucifixion, but not on who was crucified, except that it was not Jesus. Why it could not have been Jesus is a problem to be dealt with in the conclusion. We now turn to an examination of other early traditions.

As mentioned above, traditions are of various kinds depending on the ultimate authority to which they are attributed. Research has been unable to produce any *aḥādīth* on the crucifixion of Jesus that go back to the Prophet (*ḥādīth nabawī*), or of that category termed *ḥādīth qudsī*, i.e. *ḥādīth* that transmit the direct speech of God.[9] The oldest authority for any tradition on the subject is Ibn 'Abbās. Aside from the *tafsīr* attributed to him, later exegetes cite him as an authority for traditions about this verse. None of these agrees with the *Tanwīr al-miqbās*.[10] This would seem to support, at least partially, Rippin's analysis referred to above.

## MUJĀHID B. JABR AL-MAKKĪ (d. 104/722)

Mujāhid, an exponent of the Meccan school of *tafsīr*[11] – which considered Ibn 'Abbās its master – is the accepted authority for countless exegetical traditions. A volume of these, which have been collected and edited from various sources,[12] has been used in this study. The commentary on 4:157–8 is quite brief:

> BUT SO IT WAS MADE TO APPEAR TO THEM they crucified a man other than Jesus while they reckoned that he was Jesus because this other man 'was made to look like [Jesus] to them' (*shubbiha lahum*).[13]

[9] On the subject of *ḥadīth qudsī* see William A. Graham, *Divine Word and Prophetic Word in Early Islam: A Reconsideration of the Sources with Special Reference to the Divine Saying or ḥadīth Qudsī* (The Hague: Mouton, 1977). The standard analysis of the general question of *ḥadīth* is, of course, Ignaz Goldziher, *Muslim Studies*, vol. 2, trans. C.R. Barber and S.M. Stern, ed. S.M. Stern (London: George Allen & Unwin, 1971), pp. 17–251. A response to non-Muslim scholarship on the subject is: Mohammad Mustafa Azmi, *Studies in Early ḥadīth Literature: With a Critical Edition of Some Early Texts* (Beirut: al-Maktab al-Islāmī, 1968). See also Leonard T. Librande, 'Three Western Scholars and Islamic Tradition: Opinions on Its Early Development', MA thesis, McGill University, 1972. For the specific topic of Jesus in *ḥadīth*, see McLean, op. cit., and Arent Jan Wensinck, *A Handbook of Early Muḥammadan Tradition: Alphabetically Arranged* (Leiden: E.J. Brill, 1960).

[10] For example, see the discussion of al-Māturidī and al-Suyūṭī ((in Chapter Three).

[11] Al-Sawwāf, op. cit., p. 141. The other schools were: (1) the 'Irāqī school, headed by Ibn Mas'ūd; and (2) the Medinan school whose most prominent leader was 'Ubayy b. Ka'b.

[12] Mujāhid b. Jabr, *Tafsīr Mujāhid*, ed. 'Abd al-Raḥmān al-Ṭāhir b. Muḥammad al-Surtī (Qatar: Maṭābi' al-Duḥā al-*Ḥadītha*, 1395/1976).

[13] Ibid., p. 180. The *isnād* is: 'Abd al-Raḥmān; Ibrāhīm; Ādam; Waraqā'; Ibn Abī Najīḥ, Mujāhid. The *matn* here is similar to that connected with al-Ṭabarī's variant *isnād*, no. 10787, vol. 9, p. 373.

No further explanation is offered here – no attempt to identify the victim of the crucifixion. Likewise, there is no discussion of the other key terms of the sequence (e.g. *yaqīnan, rafa'a*). A note to the text gives another example from Mujāhid's *tafsīr*:

> They crucified a man whom they saw as [*shabbaha*] Jesus, and God raised Jesus to Himself, living.[14]

Here the pivotal verb *shubbiha* is used in the active voice in order to specify more clearly that what was doubtful to the observers was the identity of the one crucified; also, *rafa'a* is here given a meaning: that Jesus was raised to God. But the same root is used in the commentary, along with the adverb 'living' (*ḥayyan*), neither of which is specified further. As was the case in the preceding example, the point to be made is that someone else died.

## WAHB IBN MUNABBIH (d. 114/732)

By far the most popular versions of the substitution legend are related on the authority of Wahb. He is the Yemeni scholar of earliest times who is best known for his knowledge of Judaism and Christianity. Ground-breaking scholarship on him and his literary legacy was published by Professor Khoury of Heidelberg.[15] Wahb, highly regarded in many traditional learned circles, is the source of many traditions dealing with other biblical subjects and, in modern times especially (but not exclusively), much of his exegetical and biblical tradition has been anathematized as

[14] Ibid., p. 180 (no. 2), where the other two traditions of Mujāhid used by al-Ṭabarī are mentioned (i.e. nos 10788 and 10789). Neither of these agrees with the *isnād* here. See Heribert Horst, 'Zur Uberlieferung im Koran-kommentor at-Ṭabaris', *Zeitschrift der Deutschen Morganländischen Gessellschafl*, 103, 1953, pp. 290–307, for an analysis of the *asānīd* in al-Ṭabarī. Of special relevance here are pp. 295 and 296.

[15] Raif Georges Khoury, *Wahb b. Munnabih Pt. I: Leben und Werk des Dichters* (Wiesbaden: Otto Harrassowitz, 1972). See the same author's excellent article 'Wahb b. Munnabih', *EI*[2], vol. 11, p. 34.

*Isrā'īliyyāt.*[16] In light of this, it is somewhat ironic that the most influential traditions denying that Jesus was crucified are traced to his authority. As the author of several books on various subjects, Wahb acquired a reputation that varied from trustworthy to 'audacious liar'.[17] The earliest known form of the substitution legend ascribed to this author comes in two versions from al-Ṭabarī [18] and can be summarized as follows:

1. It happened that Jesus was in a house with seven disciples when the Jews surrounded them. When the Jews entered the house God changed all of the disciples to look like Jesus. The Jews, claiming they had been bewitched, demanded that Jesus be pointed out to them, otherwise they would kill all of them. Jesus then said to his disciples, 'Who would purchase for himself paradise today?' One of them volunteered, announced to the Jews that he was Jesus, and was killed and crucified by them.

   THUS IT APPEARED TO THEM; and they thought that they had killed Jesus, and the Christians likewise thought that he was Jesus, and God raised Jesus from that day [to this] (*wa-rafa'a Allāhu 'Īsā min yawmihi dhālika*).[19]
2. When God revealed to him that he would soon leave the world, Jesus became troubled. He gathered his disciples for a meal. Jesus served them, washing their hands and drying[20] them with his garment. The disciples recoiled at this, thinking it to be beneath Jesus. Jesus chided them for their reaction, telling them that they should follow his example, that none should vaunt

[16] For the argument that condemnation of Isrā'īliyyāt began quite early in the Islamic learned tradition and *is not* a modern or contemporary development, see G. Vajda, 'Isrā'īliyyāt', op. cit.

[17] Aḥmad b. Muḥammad ibn Khallikān, *Wafayāt al-a'yān wa-anbā' abnā' al-zamān*, trans. William M. DeSlane, 4 vols (Paris: Oriental Translation Fund of Great Britain and Ireland, 1257–87/1842–71), vol. 3, p. 673, cited by Earl E. Elder, 'The Crucifixion in the Koran', *Muslim World*, 13, 1923, pp. 242–58, at p. 246.

[18] Al-Ṭabarī, vol. 9, pp. 368–70.

[19] This translation differs slightly from Elder, op. cit., pp. 246–7.

[20] *Masaḥa*; *masīḥ* 'MESSIAH', in 4:157, is derived from this verb. Its literal meaning is 'to rub' as in 'rub oil in or on', thus its equivalence with *Christos* ('annointed'). See Lane, *Lexicon*, q.v. M-S-Ḥ. The use of this verb here is an excellent example of the subtle and skilful manner in which the exegetes built their arguments.

himself over another; they should sacrifice their selves for each other as Jesus has sacrificed his self (*nafs*) for them. Then he said: 'Pray fervently to God that my death be postponed.'

They began to pray but were unable to fend off sleep, it being late. Jesus aroused them, scolding them for sleeping. Then he said: 'When the shepherd disappears, the flock scatters … The truth is, one of you will deny me before the cock crows three times. And one of you will sell me for a paltry price …' The disciples then dispersed.

The Jews were looking for Jesus and encountered Sham'ūn (Simon Peter). They accused him of being a disciple, which he denied; they met another disciple and the same thing happened. The cock crew, reminding him of Jesus' warning and he was saddened. Then one of the disciples came to the Jews and offered to lead them to Jesus for a price. At some point previous, this disciple was changed into the likeness of Jesus [*wa-kāna shubbiha 'alayhim qabla dhālika*], so the Jews took him, sure that he was Jesus. They bound him and led him around, saying: 'You have raised the dead, driven away devils, and cured the insane; why not therefore free yourself from this rope?' The Jews spat upon him and placed thorns upon his head. When they came to the post upon which they intended to crucify him, God raised him [the antecedent of 'him' is unclear; according to the text it should be the disciple, but what follows indicates that it is Jesus], and they crucified what APPEARED TO THEM. And he remained crucified seven hours.

Then Jesus' mother, and the woman he had treated and whom God had freed from madness, came weeping before the crucified one. Jesus appeared to them and asked them why they were weeping. They said, 'For you.' He said: 'Verily, God has raised me to himself, and nothing but good can befall me. This thing ONLY APPEARS SO TO THEM; so, send for the disciples that they may meet me at such-and-such a place.'

Eleven disciples met him at the designated place. Jesus discovered that the one who had betrayed him was missing; upon enquiry he was told that he had repented and hanged himself. Jesus said: 'If he repents may God forgive him.' Then Jesus enquired about a youth who was following them. His name

> was Yāhannā [sic] and Jesus appointed him a disciple and instructed them all to preach to the people in their language and summon them.[21]

These two accounts attributed to Wahb contain several significant elements that justify their inclusion here. Foremost is the fact that the first legend is the one chosen by al-Ṭabarī as the best explanation of 4:157.[22] Al-Ṭabarī's influence on later *mufassirūn* was enormous and requires no further comment.[23] This second legend, aside from being the lengthiest exegetical *ḥadīth* on the topic of Jesus' crucifixion, seems also to have been favoured by al-Ṭabarī, although it was not his first choice. It may be helpful, therefore, to try to discern just why these particular stories had such appeal.

Contrary to tradition, Wahb was more likely born a Muslim, not a Jew.[24] He was the author of several works, much of which deals with biblical tradition. Classed among the *tābi'ūn* of Persian origin, his knowledge of biblical tradition was said to come from his associations with Christians and Jews of his native Dhimār.[25] His *Kitāb al-mubtada'* is a source for later historians such as al-Mas'ūdī (d. 345/956) and al-Tha'labī. The *Kitāb al-Isra'īliyyāt* is not extant and probably never existed, although an attempt has been made to reconstruct it.[26] Early exegetes such as

[21] This is an abridged translation. For a complete translation, see Elder, op. cit. pp. 247–8. (Note error on p. 248: 'Fear you' should read 'For you'.) Cf. also Mahmoud Ayoub, 'Towards an Islamic Christology: II: The Death of Jesus. Reality or Delusion? (A Study of the Death of Jesus in *Tafsīr* Literature)', *Muslim World*, 70, 1980, pp. 91–121. For the relationship between this second account and Docetism, see Parrinder, op. cit., pp. 109–11. See also Robinson, 'Crucifixion'.

[22] Al-Ṭabarī, vol. 9, p. 374.

[23] The recent study by Walid Saleh, *The Formation of the Classical* Tafsīr *Tradition: The Qur'ān Commentary of al-Tha'labī (d. 427/1035)* (Leiden: E.J. Brill, 2004), offers a compelling revision of the classical history of *tafsīr*.

[24] Khoury, 'Wahb b. Munabbih', *EI*[2], pp. 34–6 (and see the earlier article by Josef Horovitz, 'Wahb b. Munabbih', *EI*[1], vol. 4, p. 1084). See also Raif Georges Khoury, *Wahb b. Munabbih, Codices Arabici Antiqui*, vol. 1, 2 pts (Weisbaden: Otto Harrassowitz, 1972), pt 1, p. 215.

[25] Horovitz, op. cit..

[26] 'A *K. al-Isrā'īliyyāt* … is attributed to Wahb, but this does not seem to have been known in the literature of the first century of Islam (Khoury, *Wahb Codices*, pp. 205, 247–57).' Khoury, 'Wahb b. Munnabih', p. 34. Cf. the reconstruction

al-Ṭabarī and Ibn Qutayba freely quoted him. However, much of this material is contradictory, as is the material used by Ibn Hishām (d. 213/828) in his *Kitāb al-tījān* when compared with Wahb's *Kitāb al-mubtada'*.[27] Although Wahb's work was used by Ibn Isḥāq (d. 150–1/767–8) for the latter's history of the beginnings of Christianity, he was completely avoided as a source for the Prophet's biography.[28] As with so many early traditionists, Wahb's reputation is uneven. It is possible his notoriety alone made his name an attractive one for exegetes dealing with biblical subjects.

The above extracts illustrate perfectly the utility of his traditions. In these two stories, no lexical item of 4:157–8 is left unexplained, except the question of the connotation of *qawlihim* and of the 'speaker' of *rasūl Allāh*. In addition, the stories explain the phrase in the verse that reads, AND THOSE WHO DIFFER THEREIN ARE FULL OF DOUBTS, WITH NO CERTAIN KNOWLEDGE, BUT ONLY CONJECTURE TO FOLLOW. This is explained in the first of Wahb's accounts, where the text reads, 'they thought that they had killed Jesus'. The Arabic here is *ẓannū* ('they thought/conjectured') and shares the same root with the Qur'anic noun translated as CONJECTURE above. Also contributing to the popularity of the two accounts is the fact that both are full of characters, helping to explain who 'those' who differed about the crucifixion were: the Jews, the disciples, 'his mother and the woman' and finally Yūḥannā. Thus, not only is the verse completely explained, the stories themselves are entertaining while remaining very close – but not identical – to 'orthodox' Christian teaching. Note, also, the near perfect correspondence between the longer version and the excerpt from the apocryphal *Acts of John* quoted in the Introduction above.

The vocabulary of the above 'explanations' is, for the most part, identical with the Qur'anic language of the immediate subject of exegesis. The roots *sh-b-h* and *ẓ-n-n* are repeatedly used in the stories without ever being more fully defined. Even the root *m-s-ḥ*

attempt by Vincent Charles Chauvin, *La récension egyptiénne des Mille et une nuits* (Brussels: Société belge de librairie, 1899), also discussed in Khoury, *Wahb Codices*, pp. 224–5. See also Horovitz, op. cit.

27 Ibid.

28 Horovitz, op. cit., p. 1085.

(which forms *masīḥ*), 'Messiah', is used to describe Jesus washing the disciples' hands. It is questionable, as Elder observed, whether this kind of elliptical commentary can actually be considered an explanation.[29] Nevertheless, the fact remains that it has been accepted by the Muslim community and so has exerted enormous influence in the formation of Islamic Christology. Before leaving this discussion of Wahb's accounts, it should be repeated that the second story summarized above is quite close to the Gospel accounts in many of its details. Aside from displaying external literary dependence, this also must have commended it to the exegetes who were eager to accept the scriptures of previous communities but were at the same time wary of their corruption (*taḥrīf*).[30]

## QATĀDA IBN DI'ĀMA (d. 117–8/735–6)

Al-Ṭabarī cites two traditions from this exegete who was renowned for his powerful memory and dislike of writing.[31] Both accounts are quite brief:

1. About God's statement: VERILY, WE KILLED THE MESSIAH, JESUS SON OF MARY, THE MESSENGER OF GOD; AND THEY DID NOT KILL HIM AND THEY DID NOT CRUCIFY HIM up to God's statement: AND GOD IS MIGHTY, WISE: The Jews were the enemies of God, and they had decided to kill Jesus son of Mary, the messenger of God, and they claimed to have killed him and crucified him. And it was related to us that the prophet of God, Jesus son of Mary, said to his disciples: 'Who of you will have my likeness [*shibh/shabah*] cast upon him and thereby be killed?' One of the disciples said 'I, O prophet of God!' Thus that man was killed and God protected [*mana'a*] His prophet as HE RAISED HIM TO HIMSELF.

[29] Elder, op. cit., p. 250.

[30] Hava Lazarus-Yafeh, 'Taḥrīf (a.)', *EI²*, vol. 11, p. 111.

[31] He was a student of Sa'īd ibn al-Musayyib (d. 94/712), who was disturbed by Qatāda's reluctance to write down dictation. See Abbot, op. cit., p. 198.

2. Concerning His statement: AND THEY DID NOT KILL HIM AND THEY DID NOT CRUCIFY HIM, BUT IT APPEARED SO TO THEM. Qatāda said: 'The likeness of Jesus was cast upon one of his disciples, and he was killed. Jesus had appeared before them and said: "Whoever of you will have my likeness cast upon him will have paradise." And one said: "Upon me!"'[32]

As was the case in the previous traditions, these two from Qatāda make no attempt to identify or name the substitute. They both agree with Wahb's second account in that they portray Jesus as actively seeking to avoid crucifixion. Why such a portrayal would have been so popular is somewhat puzzling. There is evidence to suggest that al-Ṭabarī himself thought such a thing unlikely, perhaps because it would have been beneath the dignity of a prophet to flee death.[33] Moreover, the many Qur'anic passages, already cited earlier, which laud death in the way of God (*fī sabīl Allāh*) would also seem to argue that such action was unbecoming a true Muslim; and Jesus, according to Islam, was a true Muslim.[34]

## AL-QĀSIM IBN ABĪ BAZZA (d. 124/742)

He is said to have been the only student of Mujāhid's who made a complete copy of his teacher's *tafsīr*.[35] The tradition in al-Ṭabarī is

[32] Al-Ṭabarī, vol. 9, p. 370. The *isnād* nos are 10781 and 10782. See Horst, op. cit., pp. 301 and 296, respectively.

[33] Al-Ṭabarī, vol. 9, p. 374. His choice of Wahb's first account might be thought to support this.

[34] See the Qur'anic citations in Thomas O'Shaughnessy, *Muḥammad's Thoughts on Death: A Thematic Study of the Qur'anic Data* (Leiden: E.J. Brill, 1969), pp. 61–6. For Jesus as a Muslim, see, for example, Claus Schedl, *Muḥammad und Jesus*, p. 33. On the whole question of death in Islam, see Jane Idleman Smith and Yvonne Yazbeck Haddad, *The Islamic Understanding of Death and Resurrection* (New York : Oxford University Press, 2002); originally published: Albany: State University of New York Press, 1981. For the related topic of martyrdom, see Todd Lawson, 'Martyrdom', in *The Oxford Encyclopaedia of the Modern Islamic World*, ed. J. Esposito (New York: Oxford University Press, 1995), vol. 3, pp. 54–9, and also David Cook, *Martyrdom in Islam* (Cambridge, England: Cambridge University Press, 2007).

[35] Abbot, op. cit., p. 98.

quite similar to Mujāhid's and those just examined from Qatāda. As it offers nothing new, it will not be examined in detail.[36]

## ISMĀ'ĪL IBN 'ABD AL-RAḤMĀN AL-SUDDĪ (d. 127/744)

This scholar is one of a handful of early exegetes credited with actually writing his own *tafsīr.* His authority is widely used by al-Ṭabarī, but other Muslim scholars have classed him among the least reliable of early commentators.[37] Al-Suddī's account is similar to the preceding, but a few points deserve special notice. The first is that he specifies the number of disciples as nineteen, though no names are mentioned. The second is that he makes an attempt to define *rafa'a*, the verb 'to raise'. Rather than merely repeat the verb, al-Suddī used the passive of *ṣa'ada* – which is, in effect, a synonym – to express God's raising Jesus to heaven.[38] In addition, the commentator uses the verb *shakka* to say that the Jews (*Banū Isrā'īl*) 'suspected' that the substitute was Jesus, which nicely echoes the Qur'anic expression TRULY FULL OF DOUBT ABOUT IT (*la-fī shakkin minhu*).

## JA'FAR IBN MUḤAMMAD AL-ṢĀDIQ (d. 148/765)

This exegete is not quoted by al-Ṭabarī. Much has been attributed to the sixth imam of the Shi'a, little of which can be authenticated according to the strict requirements of textual scholarship.[39] His reputation as a scholar, legist and mystic, and the influence of his position as a divinely commissioned spiritual leader combined

[36] Al-Ṭabarī, vol. 9, p. 371; Horst, op. cit., p. 298.

[37] Jullandari, op. cit., p. 80.

[38] A popular device in *tafsīr* discussed at length in Wansbrough, op. cit., pp. 130–1, 145.

[39] *Geschichte des Arabischen Schrifttums* (Sezgin), vol. 1, pp. 529–30. The *tafsīr* manuscripts listed are: (1) Bankipore XVIII, 2,143, no. 1460; (2) Buhar 13; (3) Nafiz 65; (4) Ch. Beatty 5253; (5) Aligarh 2976 111/28.

at an early stage to give his name special authority. Sunnis and Shi'is alike honour him for his learning. One of the chief justices of Baghdad, during the caliphate of Hārūn al-Rashīd (d. 193/809), considered Ja'far one of the most reliable sources for questions of jurisprudence.[40] Ja'far is said to have transmitted traditions from such divergent types as Abū Ḥanīfa (d. 150/767) and Mālik ibn Anas (d. 179/796); from Hijazi and Iraqi scholars, Sunni or Shi'i. He is also credited with compiling a book of traditions, which unfortunately is no longer extant.[41]

Among other works attributed to Ja'far is a *tafsīr*, a manuscript of which was consulted for this study. It contains a brief commentary on verse 4:157.[42] In 1968, Paul Nwyia published a critical edition of the *tafsīr* of Ja'far as it appears in Sulamī's *Ḥaqā'iq al-tafsīr*. Comparison of that work with the manuscript at hand shows the two have little in common on the treatment of our subject, reference to 4:157 being absent in the former.[43] The commentary itself is quite brief, but it is interesting in that it is also quite different from anything studied earlier in these pages. This might have been expected in light of what is known about the nature of Ja'far's mystical exegesis,[44] since the *tafsīr* is attributed to a contemporary of

[40] His name was Abū al-Bakhtarī Wahb ibn Wahb (d. 200/815–16). For a discussion of his use of tradition, see Abbot, op. cit., pp. 224, 229.

[41] Ibid., p. 229.

[42] Ch. Beatty 5253.

[43] See Paul Nwyia, 'Le tafsīr mystique atribué à Ga'far Ṣādiq', *Mélanges de l'Université Saint Joseph*, 43(4), 1968, pp. 182–230.

[44] Paul Nwyia, *Exégèse coranique et langage mystique: nouvel essai sur le lexique technique des mystiques musulmans* (Beirut: Dar el-Machreq, 1970), pp. 156–88. For a discussion of methodological differences between Ja'far and Muqātil, see esp. pp. 160–4. Nwyia points out Ja'far's use of four levels of interpretation: (1) *l'expression*; (2) *l'allusion*; (3) *les touches de la grace*; (4) *les realites* (p. 167). His method has also been seen as the utilization of two main approaches to the Qur'anic text, i.e. through (1) a combination of literal and allegorical (*'ibāra* and *ishāra*) exegesis, and (2) a concern for mystical subtleties and spiritual realities (*laṭā'if* and *ḥaqā'iq*). These two categories with their four components are seen to correspond to Ja'far's division of humanity into the common man, the mystic man, saints and prophets in Gerhard Bowering, *The Mystical Vision of Existence In Classical Islam: The Qur'anic Hermeneutics of the Ṣūfī Sahl at-Tustarī (d. 283/896)* (Berlin: Walter de Gruyter, 1980), p. 141. See also p. 142 for comments on the question of Dhū al-Nūn as the first editor of Ja'far's *tafsīr*, a question first opened by Louis Massignon, *Essai sur les origins du lexique technique de la mystique musulmane*, 2nd ed. (Paris: Vrin, 1954), pp. 201–6.

such exegetes as *Ibn Jurayj*, Muqātil and Ibn Isḥāq. Inasmuch as all these exegetes will be found below to have taught some version of the substitution explanation, this work deserves to be mentioned, if only as a deviation from the norm. At the very least, it shows that the greater Muslim tradition also values commentary on this troubling verse which does not attempt to address the somewhat polemical problem of the historicity of the crucifixion.

The most striking aspect of this *tafsīr* is that the author restricts his comment to only a small phrase in the verse: VERILY, WE KILLED THE MESSIAH. No attempt is made to identify the subject, or indeed anyone else usually associated with the verse. In fact, Jesus himself is not even mentioned by name and is only referred to by a pronoun identifying him as one of an anonymous group called here simply the 'prophets of God'. The main business of the *tafsīr* is to discuss the implications of the killing. Killing is described as being of three types: (1) 'killing of the world [*qatl al-dunyā*] by abandoning it to the enemies'; (2) 'killing of the sins of a lover'; and (3) 'killing of the passion of a knower [*'ārif*]'. The author then says that 'he' – Jesus? – gained a high rank (*rif'a*) by being killed, just as God raised his other prophets (*wa-lahu fī qatlihi rif'a kamā rafa'a Allāh anbiyā'ahu*). God seated 'him' – Jesus – on the throne of intimacy (*uns*) and reunion (*liqā'*).[45] The paradox – reading the *wa* in the previous phrase as 'while' rather than 'and' – of appearing to be nailed to a cross in humiliation but in reality being seated on a throne is thus indicated. And this paradox will be met with again in the following chapter and found to be made explicit.

An attempt to define the terms 'enemies', 'lover' and 'knower' would be beyond the scope of this study.[46] Their nature and order suggest a discourse usually found later in the history of Islam. It seems clear that the author's purpose here is to affirm that Jesus died and was spiritually exalted, although it is impossible to conclude that, because of this, Ja'far himself opposed the idea of substitution. This is partly due to the problem of authenticity mentioned above, and partly due to the problems inherent in what

[45] Ch. Beatty 5253, fol. 33b.

[46] An index of Ja'far's technical language is found in Nwyia, *Exégèse*, pp. 188–207.

might be called the 'logic of the crucifixion'. It is obvious that it was not an issue that here concerned him (or whoever the author was), since there is mention *and acceptance of the reality* of 'his killing', not of any crucifixion. It is also noteworthy, in light of the discussion in the next chapter, that there is no reference here to a human dimension (*nāsūt*) as distinct from a divine dimension or nature (*lāhūt*). We will see that one of the crucial hermeneutic presuppositions of the Isma'ili material presented below depends on this syzygy and then the division of these two natures so that Jesus' human nature may be crucified while his divine nature is preserved, in Qur'anic language RAISED, forever invulnerable to the machinations of the enemies of God.

It may also be that the substitution legend was thought to be so familiar, perhaps even axiomatic, that it did not require special mention; or, perhaps more likely, that it was simply irrelevant.[47] Nonetheless, it is significant that early exegetes, such as Ja'far, are seen to have read the verse in such a way. Furthermore, since this *tafsīr* must also be considered part of the vast textual heritage of Shi'ism, it will be interesting to remember its more salient features when we turn to the very interesting question of the preservation of a distinct debate on the crucifixion within the greater Shi'i tradition by representatives of, on the one hand, the Isma'ili branch, who argued for the historicity of the death and crucifixion of Jesus and, on the other, representatives of the Ja'farī or Ithnā 'asharī branch, who, like their Sunni counterparts, argue that it was not really Jesus who was killed and crucified.

## 'ABD AL-MALIK B. 'ABD AL-'AZĪZ, *IBN JURAYJ* (d. 149–50/766–7)

This transmitter of Mujāhid's *tafsīr* does not provide any information that has not been already presented in the latter's

[47] That Jesus was raised to heaven alive was considered a plausible event by later Ṣūfīs is affirmed by the reference to Ruzbihan Baqlī (d. 606/1209) in Annemarie Schimmel, *Mystical Dimensions of Islam* (Chapel Hill: University of North Carolina Press, 1978), p. 202. See below for Ruzbihān's *tafsīr* on this verse.

commentary. The *ḥadīth* is quite short and states simply that Jesus asked a disciple to take his likeness, which the disciple did before being killed. Jesus was raised to God.[48]

## MUQĀTIL B. SULAYMĀN AL-BALKHĪ (d. 150–1/767)

Scholars have recently studied the *tafsīr* of Muqātil, but it is still not possible to certify the provenance of works attributed to him.[49] A manuscript of such a *tafsīr* was consulted for this study and found to contain some interesting variations on the substitution legend.[50] In this account, the author deals with the usual exegetical points, starting with his insistence that the Jews did not say MESSENGER OF GOD, but rather it was God who spoke here. According to Muqātil, the eventual substitute for Jesus was the guard whom the Jews had placed over him. He was given the likeness of Jesus as punishment for assaulting him physically and accusing him of blasphemy by claiming to be a messenger of God. This guard's name here is Yāhūdhā, but it is clear that he is not the disciple Yāhūdhā (Judas), whom other exegetes[51] reported was substituted for Jesus.

Muqātil makes it quite definite that THOSE WHO DISAGREE about the crucifixion are the Christians: 'some of them say the Jews killed him, while some of them say he was not killed, but they are in doubt about his killing'.[52] Muqātil adds that the Jews were also unsure of the true identity of the one they were killing, and relates this nicely to the commentary on THEY DID NOT KILL HIM/IT[53] IN, CERTAINTY by saying that the Jews did not kill the

[48] Al-Ṭabarī, vol. 9, p. 373, *isnād* no. 10786; see Horst, op. cit., p. 295.

[49] Abbot, op. cit., pp. 92–113; Nwyia, *Exégèse*, pp. 25, 108; Wansbrough, op. cit., index.

[50] *Beyazit Umumi* 561.

[51] For example, Ibn Isḥāq; see below.

[52] This, of course, is historically correct, as was pointed out in the Introduction. The Christian traditon is far from unanimous on the problem of the crucifixion. We will return to this topic in our conclusion.

[53] *-hu* in *mā ṣalabūhu wa-mā qatalūhu* is the masculine Arabic pronominal objective suffix. It can mean either 'him' or 'it'. There are only two genders in Arabic grammar: masculine or feminine. There is no neuter.

victim in absolute certainty.[54] As we saw earlier, Ibn 'Abbās held that the Jews CERTAINLY did not kill Jesus.

The author adds that Jesus was raised alive to heaven, 'during the month of Ramaḍān, on the night of Power, and he was thirty-three years old when he was raised from the mount of Jerusalem'. The exegesis ends by saying that GOD IS MIGHTY, WISE, 'more MIGHTY in forbidding Jesus' killing, and WISE when he decreed raising him'. That Muqātil chose the most auspicious day in the Muslim calendar as the time for these events indicates that Jesus is to be regarded as the spiritual kin of Muḥammad. This date witnesses such significant events as the first revelation and the famous *mi'rāj* of Muḥammad. Whether Jesus' prophethood was doubted by Muqātil's Muslim contemporaries, it is impossible to say. Certainly, there is no ground for such doubts in the Qur'an. Why al-Ṭabarī ignored this version is also puzzling, inasmuch as it differs so little in intent from others cited by him. Perhaps the lack of gospel allusions in it was a factor or perhaps he was simply unaware of it. None of the later *mufassirūn* mentions this account.[55]

## MUḤAMMAD IBN ISḤĀQ (d. 150–1/767–8)

Ibn Isḥāq's lengthy *tafsīr*[56] of 4:157–8 is actually composed of three separate *aḥādīth* – the *sanadayn* of the first two are identical; Ibn Ḥumayd, Salama, Ibn Isḥāq. The third *isnād* differs only in that the final authority is an unnamed Christian convert to Islam. In the first tradition, Ibn Isḥāq says that none of the servants of God could have been responsible for issuing the order to kill Jesus. Rather, it was Dā'ūd, King of the *Banū Isrā'īl.* We are told that the action did not bother the King, nor did he pray to God to keep him from it. Ibn Isḥāq also notes that when the Jews

[54] A similar argument will be found in Chapter Three with the Mu'tazilite scholars al-Jubbā'ī, as quoted by al-Ṭūsī and 'Abd al-Jabbār.

[55] See *Beyazit Umumi 561*, fol. 88b–89a.

[56] From al-Ṭabarī, vol. 9, pp. 371–3, *isnād* no. 10785 subsumes all three *asānīd*. See Horst, op. cit., p. 303.

entered the house where Jesus and *thirteen* of his disciples were, they were SURE (*yaqīn*) that they had found Jesus.[57]

The second *ḥadīth* says that one of the thirteen disciples was a man named Serjes, whom the Christians do not recognize. It was Serjes who was substituted for Jesus. It goes on to say that 'they' (not specified) repudiated what the prophet Muḥammad said concerning this incident. This last item is quite interesting in that no *ḥadīth* about the crucifixion has been found to go all the way back to Muḥammad. It is possible that this simply refers to the Qur'anic verses. However, the utilization of the word *khabar* makes this seem unlikely, unless here it does not have its later technical meaning as a synonym for *ḥadīth* and indicates merely the 'information' that came from God through Muḥammad in the Qur'an.

The third *ḥadīth*, on the authority of a Christian, says that when God told Jesus he would raise him (3:55), Jesus appealed to his disciples to save him by accepting his likeness (*ṣūratī* – 'my image'). The same Serjes volunteered, took Jesus' seat and Jesus was RAISED up. When the Jews entered, they took Serjes and CRUCIFIED AND KILLED HIM. In all three *aḥādīth,* much is made of the number of the disciples. This is seen to be the point that corresponds to the Qur'anic AND THOSE WHO DIFFER HEREIN. So the text here says, 'And their number, when they entered with Jesus, was CERTAIN – they had seen them and counted them.' But when the Jews actually went in after Jesus, they discovered one of them missing (Jesus having already been raised up). Moreover, the Jews did not really know what Jesus looked like, so they offered Yūdas Zakariyyā Yūṭa' (i.e. Judas) thirty dirhāms to lead them to Jesus. Yūdas did so by kissing the one whom he thought was Jesus but in reality was Serjes. Then the latter was crucified. Yūdas then repented and hanged himself. We are told that the Christians cursed him, and that some of them even believe that it was Yūdas who was crucified. The commentary ends judiciously with, 'And God knows best how it really was.'[58]

[57] Explication of *yaqīna* in Ibn Isḥāq is centred on the question of the exact number of disciples with Jesus. This represents a variation in the exegesis of this word.

[58] Al-Ṭabarī, vol. 9, p. 373. This oft-repeated formula deserves more respect than scholars, particularly 'Western', have heretofore been willing to afford it. Assuming that its author here is sincere, and there is certainly no reason not to, it connotes, if not denotes, a certain critical attitude towards the accounts just cited.

It is curious that none of this appears in Ibn Isḥāq's *sīra* (biography of the Prophet).[59] In the passage that portrays Muḥammad as trying to resolve differences between Christians and Jews by pointing out their respective doctrinal errors and calling both communities to Islam, there is extensive *tafsīr* on much of *sūra* three. At 3:54–5 the following appears:

> Then God referred to His taking up of Jesus to Himself when the Jews decided to kill him, He said: AND THEY PLOTTED AND GOD PLOTTED, AND GOD IS THE BEST OF PLOTTERS. Then He told them – refuting what they assert of the Jews in regard to his [Jesus'?] crucifixion – how He took him up and purified him from them.[60]

One might have thought that this would have provided an excellent opportunity to present the account found in al-Ṭabarī, particularly since 4:157 is mentioned nowhere in the *sīra.* However, most of the exegetical passages in the *sīra* are themselves relatively short. Nevertheless, it is odd that on a subject of such doctrinal importance no mention of an actual substitute is made. It is clear that the purpose here is to 'refute' Christian notions about the Jews, just as the object throughout the context in which the above passage appears is to assert to the Jews the prophethood of Jesus, the Messiah.[61] In this passage of the *sīra*, Muḥammad is portrayed as a peacemaker and a uniter of divergent faiths, though this might be difficult to detect in the standard English translation where the verb 'to unite' (*jam'*) is translated as 'to combine'.

## YAḤYĀ IBN ZIYĀD AL-FARRĀ' (d. 207/822–3)

Yaḥyā ibn Ziyād al-Farrā' was the Kūfan author of one of the earliest extant works on Qur'anic sciences. His sobriquet is a pun.

[59] Muḥammad ibn Isḥāq, *al-Sīrat al-nabawīya li-ibn Hishām*, ed. Muṣṭafā al-Shaqqā, Ibrāhīm al-Ubyārī and 'Abd al-Ḥāfiẓ Shālabī, 3rd edn, 2 vols (Cairo: al-Bābī al-Ṭabarī, 1370/1955).

[60] Ibid., vol. 1, p. 582.

[61] Ibid., pp. 573–84. Cf. Alfred Guillaume, *The Life of Muḥammad: A Translation of Isḥāq's Sīrat Rasūl Allāh* (Karachi: Oxford University Press, 1974), pp. 270–7.

Thus he is remembered as one who 'skins' or rigorously analyses language, not a furrier.[62] His expertise and reputation are confirmed by the fact that he was appointed tutor to two sons of the Caliph al-Ma'mūn (d. 218/833). His *Ma'ānī al-Qur'ān* is mainly concerned with basic grammatical questions, much like the later work of the same title written a century later by al-Zajjāj, whom we will briefly notice in the next chapter.[63] Inclusion here, even if there is very little to report from his book, helps to close the nearly hundred-year gap separating Ibn Isḥāq from Ibn Qutayba. It also demonstrates an important fact, namely the incessant and continuous concern for proper understanding of the Qur'an on the part of Muslims. Here on Qur'an 4:157–8 the effort is sparsely in evidence.

At 4:157, al-Farrā' is concerned only to say that the pronominal suffix *hā'* ending the verbal cluster *mā qatalūhu* (the HIM of THEY DID NOT KILL HIM) refers to KNOWLEDGE rather than to Jesus 'as when one says: "I knew it perfectly (*qataltu 'ilman*)" and it means "I knew it certainly" instead of [mere] opinion, verbal report or conjecture'.[64] We shall see this grammatical explanation repeated or referred to several times in the following pages. The important thing here is that this influential scholar and exemplary Muslim did not find it necessary to include a statement either for or against the Christian belief in the historicity of the crucifixion. As such, his commentary is a good example of the proposition that one of the frequently unacknowledged factors at play in discussions of this issue is that it is simply not as relevant as one might otherwise think. That al-Farrā' also explicitly indicates that it is not Jesus whom the Qur'an is saying was not killed is also quite significant as a development in the history of the formal exegesis of the verse.

[62] R. Blachère, 'al-Farrā'', *EI²*, vol. 2, pp. 86–8.
[63] Abū Zakariyyā' Yaḥyā ibn Ziyād, *al-Farrā', Ma'ānī al-Qur'ān bi-taḥqīq Aḥmad Yūsuf Najātī & Muḥammad 'Alī al-Najjār*, 3 vols (Beirut: Dār al-Surūr, 1988). On al-Zajjāj, see Chapter Three.
[64] Al-Farrā', *Ma'anī al-Qur'ān*, vol. 1, p. 294.

## ABŪ MUḤAMMAD ʻABD ALLĀH B. MUSLIM B. QUTAYBA AL-DĪNAWARĪ (d. 276/889)[91]

To further close the more than hundred-year gap that separates Ibn Qutayba from Ibn Isḥāq, an attempt was made to gain material from exegetes such as Abū ʻUbayda (d. 209/824) and Sūfyān al-Thawrī (d. 161/778). Unfortunately, the works that were available contained nothing of direct pertinence.[65] It should also be mentioned that the *tafsīr* of Sahl al-Tustarī (d. 283/896) is equally silent on the verse in question.[66] Consequently, this author is the last to be studied at any length in this chapter.

As its name implies, Ibn Qutayba's *Kitāb tafsīr gharīb al-Qur'ān* deals with the difficult passages in the Qur'an.[67] Given the varied interpretations of 4:157 circulating during the time of this author, it comes as no surprise that the verse is treated in this work. What is surprising, however, is that the 'strange' word chosen for comment is not *shubbiha* or *rafaʻa*, but *yaqīnan.* The entire explication runs as follows:

> THEY DID NOT KILL HIM/IT CERTAINLY (*mā qatalūhu yaqīnan*) that is: the knowledge (*ʻilm*) that they 'killed the knowledge' of him (lit.). [This means that they did not have absolute, certain knowledge, certain in the way that death is certain. 'Death' in Arabic poetry is known by the euphemism *al-yaqīn* ('the [only thing which is] Certain').] The saying [*taqawwul*], 'I killed him certainly (*yaqīnan*) and I killed him in knowledge (*ʻilman*)' is a similar metaphor (*istiʻāra*) used in connection [with discussions] of opinion (*ra'y*), *ḥadīth*, and *kalām.* Thus God says: THEY DID NOT KILL HIM/IT CERTAINLY, that is, they were neither sure nor certain about it. The reason for that is that the killing of a thing

[65] See Abū ʻUbayda, *Majāz al-Qur'ān*, ed. Fuad Sezgin, 2 vols (Cairo: Muḥammad Sāmī Amīn al-Khanjī, 1374–81/1954–62); Sūfyān al-Thawrī, *Tafsīr al-Qur'ān al-Karīm* (Rampur, India: Hindūstān Brintik Wurks, 1385/1965).

[66] See Abū Muḥammad Sahl ibn ʻAbd Allāh al-Tustarī, *Tafsīr al-Qur'ān al-ʻAẓīm* (Cairo: al-Ḥalabī, 1329/1911).

[67] In *al-Qurtayn li-ibn Muṭarrif al-Kinānī aw kitāb mushkil al-Qur'ān wa-gharīb li-ibn Qutayba*, ed. ʻAbd al-ʻAzīz al-Khanābī, 2 pts in 1 vol. (Cairo: al-Khanābī, 1355/1936). See Gérard Lecomte, *Ibn Qutayba (mort en 276/889): l'homme, son oeuvre, ses idées* (Damascus: Institut Français de Damas, 1965), pp. 135, 141. On Ibn Qutayba's *tafsīr* method, see pp. 275–301.

> is by way of vanquishing (*qahr*), and superiority (*isti'lā'*), and total victory (*ghalaba*). Thus God is saying: 'They did not know about the killing of the Messiah with true knowledge, thoroughly comprehending the matter; rather it was CONJECTURE.'[68]

A thorough examination of Ibn Qutayba's work would undoubtedly shed more light on this verse.[69] This brief commentary makes it clear that the author considers it proper to understand that the Jews were not sure of what they had done. This is contrary to translations that read, 'They certainly did not kill him,' and should be considered an important development in the interpretation of the verse.

## AL-QUMMĪ (d. 309/921)

This contemporary of al-Ṭabarī was the author of the oldest unquestionably authentic work of Shi'i exegesis. Unfortunately, it offers no explanation for our troublesome verse. Al-Qummī does mention the phrase *wa-lākin shubbiha lahum*, but only in the context of his eschatological concerns expressed in connection with Q. 4:159. However, al-Qummī does offer some very interesting discussion on the Qur'anic charge of 'killing prophets'.[70]

## SUMMARY

Having thus closely examined the early traditions and pre-Ṭabarī exegesis of the crucifixion question, we can identify the following facts. All of the exegetes who broach the problem agree that someone was crucified, but few agree on the victim, except that it was not Jesus. In one instance, the commentary ascribed to Ja'far

[68] *Al-Qurtayn*, pt 1, 133.

[69] Lecomte suggests that the entire body of his work constitutes 'en quelque façon un vast commentaire du Coran' (op. cit., p. 275).

[70] Al-Qummi, *Tafsīr*, p. 165.

al-Ṣādiq, the death of Jesus would appear to be affirmed. The substitution legends can be divided into two major categories: (1) those favouring 'volunteer substitution' and (2) those claiming punishment substitution. The former appears to have been preferred. Those exegetes who did not employ traditions did not find it necessary to reject the crucifixion of Jesus. One of them, Ja'far, or perhaps better 'pseudo-Ja'far', commented only on the nature of 'killing', while Ibn Qutayba was concerned with the meaning of CERTAINTY (*yaqīnan*). None of the exegetes whose commentaries we examined displayed any concern for the grammatical problems surrounding *shubbiha lahum*. Rather, the ambiguity of the phrase (attested by later exegetes below) was explained by narrative embellishment.

# 3

## CLASSICAL AND MEDIEVAL *TAFSĪR* (923–1505)

With this chapter, we begin to explore the way in which Muslim exegetes, *mufassirūn*, applied and critiqued the traditional exegesis discussed in the previous chapter. Although the early traditions carried with them many difficult questions of authenticity and historicity, the authors and works treated here may be considered genuine. As we will see, many of them support – or, more accurately, are supported by – the substitution legends. However, there are exceptions, and it is the existence of these exceptions that warrants a careful examination of the *tafsīr* of the classical and medieval period. This chapter covers exegetical material composed or collected after the death of al-Ṭabarī in 923 and up until the late medieval period. Here we look at the standard and influential Sunni *tafsīr*s composed in this period by Tha'labī, Zamakhsharī, Bayḍāwī, Fakhr al-Dīn al-Rāzī and Ibn Kathīr. We will also study the Sufi *tafsīr* of Qushayrī.[1] And we return to the topic of Shi'i

[1] For a fuller discussion of specifically Sufi exegesis on this verse, see Robinson, *Christ*, pp. 178–90, where, in addition to Qushayrī, the work of 'Abd al-Razzāq al-Kāshānī (d. 1329), the famous exponent of the school of Ibn 'Arabī (d. 1240), is examined. Two useful adjuncts to a fuller treatment of this complex and fascinating subject would be the recent books by Keeler and Sands (see Bibliography). Such research ought to focus considerable attention on the still unpublished (in a satisfactory edition) *tafsīr* of Ruzbihān Baqlī (d. 1209), the great 'rehabilitator' of Ḥallāj. A prelimary examination of the *Arā'is al-bayān fī ḥaqā'iq al-Qur'ān* confirms the infiltration of such Isma'ili terminology as *nāsūt/lāhūt* in his treatment of the verse (see below). The margin of this publication carries text purporting to be yet another *tafsīr* by Ibn al-'Arabī. This one has been noticed: O. Yahya, *Histoire et*

*tafsīr* introduced above in examination of a *tafsīr* ascribed to the sixth Shi'i imam, Ja'far al-Ṣādiq (d. 148/765). Here, we will see how controversies between the two main divisions of Shi'ism, the Isma'ili and the Twelver or Imami, left their mark on the history of the 'Islamic understanding' of this verse. The earlier part of this period is designated by historians of Islam as 'the Shi'i Century' because of the political success of the Fatimids (910–1171) in the west and the Hamdanids and the Buyids in the central and more eastern Islamic lands. It is also one in which key and enduring religious identities were consolidated. After all, it is only in the context of a 'Sunni Islam' that something designated as 'Shi'ism' can make sense. The reverse, it seems, is also the case.

As for the problem of the historicity of the crucifixion of Jesus, it could be thought that this issue might possibly represent a distinguishing feature between and among the various schools and divisions of Islam. It is surmised, for example, in the *Encyclopaedia of Islam* article by Anawati on 'Īsā, that the denial of the death of Jesus on the cross is a perfectly unexceptionable and characteristic Sunni Islamic teaching that reflects a distinctively Sunni triumphalist ethos. True prophets are successful in the way that Sunni Islam asserted itself over not only other religious communities but also all other competing versions of Islam. Thus, it would make sense to expect to find in Shi'ism, the Islamic 'church' in which the mirror – that is to say, reversed – image of a triumphalist ethos occurs, an alternative exegesis of the famous verse. However, this does not occur, at least not in the form of a categorical disagreement with the Sunni exegetes in the classical exegetical works of Twelver Shi'ism, such as those composed by al-Ṭūsī (d. 460/1067) and al-Ṭabrisī (d. ca. 620/1223). Both classical Sunni and Shi'i exegetical traditions disagree and dispute the orthodox Christian teaching that Jesus Christ was crucified on Good Friday and his dead body placed in a tomb from which it was revivified and ultimately raised to heaven 'to sit at the right hand of God … there to judge between the quick and the dead'.

*classification de l'oeuvre d'Ibn 'Arabi, étude critique* (Damascus: Institut français de Damas, 1964), vol. 2, pp. 483–4. It is also mentioned in Brockelmann, *GAL*, 1, pp. 571–3, who identifies it as al-Kāshānī's.

## AL-ṬABARĪ (d. 310/923)

The periodization of the history of *tafsīr* is a problem confronting any student of the subject.[2] In al-Ṭabarī, however, we clearly encounter a new development in the historical life of this science. Al-Ṭabarī's enduring legacy of exegetical traditions has exerted inestimable influence on later *mufassirūn* down to the present day.

In light of the actual form and contents of the work, however, it might be most appropriate to classify al-Ṭabarī's efforts as 'supercommentary', since his method is to list the various traditions and choose the most acceptable, giving his own reasons for his choices. Thus, while on the surface the work appeals to the authority of the *ḥadīth* tradition, the reality is that al-Ṭabarī's authorial presence is everywhere to be encountered throughout this large work. And it is encountered in his commentary on Q. 4:157–8. Not only does al-Ṭabarī explicitly comment on the acceptability or appositeness of certain traditions, he also indicates a certain authorial intervention just in the way he orders them. While he does not give any indication or reason why certain *aḥādīth* are presented before others, the emerging sequence certainly describes a distinctive scriptural flow or narrative that is solely the product of our 'compiler'.[3] This is all the more true in light of the complete absence of grammatical analysis or reference to poetry in any of the traditions cited, or al-Ṭabarī's discussion of these.[4] In Chapter Two, a brief examination of his choice of Wahb's account was offered. We return to this issue now in the hope of gaining a more complete understanding of the reasoning behind his choice.

In 1923, a provocative article on the crucifixion of Jesus and its treatment in Islam was published by Elder.[5] This author's task was to probe the traditional literature on this issue with the hope

[2] See the reference to Saleh, above.

[3] The most thorough and illuminating examination of al-Ṭabarī's exegetical work is still the work of Claude Gilliot, *Exégèse, langue et théologie en Islam: l'éxègese coranique de* Ṭabari *(m. 311/923)* (Paris: J. Vrin, 1990).

[4] Although al-Ṭabarī does employ these methods elsewhere in his *tafsīr*, their absence, in this instance, contrasts with the methods of later exegetes, e.g. al-Bayḍāwī (on whom see below).

[5] Elder, op. cit., pp. 242–58.

of finding that which Christians could use to win Muslims 'to the gospel of Christ'.[6] Although Elder makes numerous references to other sources, the bulk of his article is concerned with al-Ṭabarī's *tafsīr*. It is pointed out that al-Ṭabarī treated this subject very fully, seeing as his main task the sorting through of a 'mass' of tradition and treating the attendant problems of accuracy and credibility.[7] In fact, al-Ṭabarī cites only eleven traditions on this subject before giving his appraisal. As we have seen, these eleven vary mainly in length, all of them upholding some form of substitution. It is therefore remarkable that even after this array of rather homogeneous commentary al-Ṭabarī's verdict is unclear.

Al-Ṭabarī first states that the most accurate of all reports is the one from Wahb in which the likeness of Jesus was cast upon all of the disciples. His possible reasons for this choice were given above, mainly because it most closely resembled the gospel account. However, al-Ṭabarī's final opinion is as follows:

> Or the affair was according to what 'Abd al-Ṣamad related (that is the second tradition) from Wahb ibn Munabbih, that is, that the people who were with 'Īsā in the house scattered from the house before the Jews came upon him. 'Īsā remained, and his LIKENESS was cast upon one of his companions, who still remained with him in the house. And 'Īsā was RAISED UP, and one who was changed into the LIKENESS of 'Īsā was killed. And his companions thought that the one CRUCIFIED was 'Īsā, because of what they saw happen to the one who was made to look like him. And the truth of the matter was hidden from them, because his being RAISED UP and the changing of the one who was killed into his LIKENESS happened after the SCATTERING of his friends. And [because] they [had] heard 'Īsā that night announce his death, and mourn because he thought that death was approaching him. And they related what happened as true, but the affair with God was really quite different from what they related. And those disciples who related this do not deserve to be called liars.[8]

Further evidence of al-Ṭabarī's preference for this second tradition may be seen by its inclusion in his history to the exclusion

6 Ibid., p. 242. 7 Ibid., p. 248.

8 Elder's translation, slightly adapted, ibid., pp. 249–50; cf. al-Ṭabarī, vol. 9, p. 374.

of all other traditions on the subject.[9] Be that as it may, all we can really be sure of is that the great exegete preferred Wahb's account to others. This is undoubtedly also a function of Wahb's reputation as an expert on Jewish and Christian learning. Hence, this second tradition is preferred perhaps because of its closer proximity to the gospel accounts.[10] However, the first tradition is also attractive in that it does not present Jesus as actively seeking to avoid death.

Elder questions whether such traditions may be considered proper explanations; yet, in light of what is known about early *tafsīr*, they are not only proper but extremely thorough. In the present context, that these explanations of Jesus' crucifixion are unsatisfactory for Christians is neither here nor there. In many cases, the object of the exegete was to link scripture to actual concrete, if not dramatic, events – not to define individual words.[11] A measure of al-Ṭabarī's greatness, however, is to be found in his attempt to absolve the Christians from the charge of propagating false beliefs. This may have been an answer to a specific debate, an attempt to promote a kind of 'Islamicate' tolerance, or simply a logical conclusion. Whatever the reason, this new development in the understanding of 4:157–8 is found first in al-Ṭabarī and as such should be noted as another stage in the understanding of our verse.

## AL-ZAJJĀJ (d. 310/923)

Abu Isḥāq Ibrāhīm ibn al-Sarī al-Zajjāj, a contemporary of al-Ṭabari, was a highly regarded grammarian, living and working for the most part in Baghdad. He was the author of several works

[9] Elder, op. cit., p. 250.

[10] Ibid. See also Chapter Two, note 9.

[11] John Wansbrough, *Qur'anic Studies: Sources and Methods of Scriptural Interpretation* (Oxford: Oxford University Press, 1977), pp. 119–48, esp. pp. 147–8. His lengthy analysis of Muqātil and Ibn Isḥāq characterizes much of the early exegetical traditions as 'public oratory' that was both 'didactic and entertaining' and in which 'anecdotal accreta appended to scriptural texts conformed admirably to the … concept of pious and edifying tradition symbolized in the formula *ḥadīthun ḍa'īfun walākin musta'nisu* (poorly accredited but of therapeutic [*sic*] value)'.

on lexicography.[12] In a work on the Qur'an he offers some interesting alternative and innovative approaches to the understanding of this verse, specifically a concern with grammar, something we have not seen previously.[13]

> It is related in *al-tafsīr* that when God wanted to raise Jesus to Himself and purify him from them, Jesus said to his companions: 'Who among you will accept to have my likeness cast upon them and thus be killed and crucified and enter the Garden?' One of the men answered: 'Me!' So his likeness was cast upon him and he was killed while God raised Jesus to Himself. And all of this is not impossible and I have no doubt that HE/IT APPEARED SO TO THEM.
>
> As for His utterance: AND VERILY THOSE WHO DISAGREE ARE IN GRAVE DOUBT ABOUT IT.
>
> This means that those who disagree about his killing are unsure (doubting) because some of them claimed that he was a god and was thus not killed and some of them said that he was killed. Because of this they are doubters (*shākkūn*).
>
> THEY HAVE NO KNOWLEDGE THEY FOLLOW ONLY CONJECTURE
>
> This is an accusative of exception ... The meaning (*al-ma'nā*) is they have no KNOWLEDGE, but they follow CONJECTURE.
>
> Some of them said: 'the *hā'* (i.e. the pronoun) refers to [their] knowledge. The meaning here is: "they did not kill their knowledge with certainty (*mā qatalū 'ilmahum yaqīnan*)" as one says: "I killed something with knowledge." The *ta'wīl* of this is: "I knew it with perfect knowledge (*'ilman tāmman*)."'
>
> And some say: AND THEY DID NOT KILL HIM. The *hā'* refers to 'Īsā, as [God] said: AND THEY DID NOT KILL HIM AND THEY DID NOT CRUCIFY HIM.
>
> And both of these readings are permitted.
>
> As for His utterance: NAY, RATHER GOD RAISED HIM TO HIMSELF
>
> Here the *lām* (of *bal*: NAY, RATHER) is assimilated to the *rā'* (of *rafa'a*: he raised). This is a 'reading' which has implications for the two above readings. It is also permitted not to [assimilate].[14]

[12] C.H.M. Versteegh, 'al-Zadjdjādj, Abū Isḥāḳ Ibrāhīm b. al- Sarī', *EI*$^2$, vol. 11, p. 377.
[13] Zajjāj Abu Isḥāq Ibrāhīm ibn al-Sarī, *Ma'ānī al-Qur'ān wa i'rābuh*, 5 vols (Beirut: 'Ālam al-Kutub, 1988).
[14] Ibid., 129–30.

## AL-MĀTURĪDĪ (d. 320/933)

In contrast to what may be considered al-Ṭabarī's irenic approach to the problem, his younger contemporary Abū Manṣūr al-Māturīdī is distinguished by both his method and his concerns. His *tafsīr*[15] of this verse includes no supporting *isnād* for the three varying traditions offered. The first of these appears to be a combination of the two reports from Wahb, but is not offered on anyone's authority. The second relates that it was a Jew who was crucified instead of Jesus. No name is offered, but the story is similar to Muqātil's (reproduced above): When Jesus took refuge in a house, knowing he was about to be killed, one of the Jews went in after him. It was this Jew who was made to look like Jesus. When he came out of the house, his companions thought he was Jesus and killed him. Al-Māturīdī does not mention Jesus' being raised by God.

Al-Māturīdī objects to this story because it has not been attested by a sufficient number of tradents or witnesses – it is *khabar wāḥid*, a single report as distinct from *khabar mutawātir*, a widely attested report transmitted by a variety of different chains of transmission. He further suggests that just because the report is considered *mutawātir*, one cannot discount that it might be a lie. He says that the confusion (*tashbīh*) in *wa-lākin shubbiha* refers to the reports about the event rather than to the event itself. That is to say, the Jews did not want to admit that they could not find Jesus, and thus they falsely claimed to have killed him.[16]

Obviously, we would want to stop at this point and ask the commentator if this reading of *wa-lākin shubbiha* (RATHER IT APPEARED SO TO THEM) could apply to all reports, *mutawātir* or otherwise, that claim to explain the verse. Although we cannot guess al-Māturīdī's answer, we know that he had serious questions about the relationship between *tafsīr* and *ḥadīth*. A further study of his exegesis could shed more light on this interesting and significant problem.[17]

[15] Abū Manṣūr al-Māturīdī, *Ta'wīlāt, Halet Effendi*, ms. #22.

[16] Ibid., fol. 179.

[17] Al-Māturīdī's role in establishing a distinction between *tafsīr* and *ta'wīl* is discussed in M. Gotz, 'Māturīdī und Sein Kitāb Ta'wīlāt al-Qur'ān', *Der Islam*, 91, 1965, pp. 27–70.

To return to the text, al-Māturīdī goes on to say that if the matter were as the other exegetes (*ahl al-ta'wīl*) said, i.e. that Jesus was raised up and someone else was crucified, then it must be accepted as one of God's miraculous signs (*āyāt*). In closing the exegesis, he is compelled to underline the errors of both Jews and Christians, saying that they (unspecified) were in doubt about the killing of Jesus, and in doubt they (presumably the Christians) said he was the son of God. Then al-Māturīdī gives a reading for *mā qatalāhu yaqīnan* (THEY DID NOT KILL HIM/IT CERTAINLY) reminiscent of Ibn Qutayba's (above), by adding that THEY (unspecified, presumably Jews and Christians) did not kill their doubts about the affair. He concludes by citing Ibn 'Abbās (his only mention of an outside authority in the whole commentary) for the exegesis of the final words MIGHTY, WISE of 4:158, saying, 'God is MIGHTY and WISE in protecting his messengers.'[18]

## THE SHI'I APPROACH

At the risk of violating the strict chronological order of our discussion so far, it may be helpful to anticipate the future here in order to contextualize more helpfully what follows. As seen above, early *tafsīr* works ascribed to Shi'i authors carry no discussion of the crucifixion question. Those ascribed to the fifth imam Muḥammad al-Bāqir (d. 127/745), the eleventh imam al-Ḥasan al-'Askarī (d. 260/874), Furāt ibn Ibrāhīm al-Kūfī (fl. ca. 236–87/850–900), 'Alī ibn Ibrāhīm al-Qummī (d. 309/921) and Muḥammad ibn Mas'ūd al-'Ayyāshī (d. ca. 320/932) all form a foundation for the later development of Imami or Twelver Shi'i exegesis. Of some interest also is the fact that there is not even any mention of the verse in the voluminous collection of Shi'i traditions, *Uṣūl al-kāfi*, compiled by the early Twelver scholar al-Kulaynī. Indeed, it is not until the first major *tafsīr* work of Twelver Shi'ism by Abū Ja'far al-Ṭūsī that the problem is broached at all

[18] *Halet Effendi*, ms. #22, fol. 179.

in works of Twelver exegesis. I am not including in this group the work ascribed to the sixth imam Ja'far al-Ṣādiq because it seems certain that it was fathered upon him by a much later author. In fact, it is preferable to refer to this work as 'pseudo-Ja'far'.

From 874 CE two historical developments within central Islamic lands began to unfold. One was the occultation of the Muḥammad ibn al-Ḥasan al-'Askarī who is more widely known as the Hidden or Twelfth Imam of the Ithnā 'asharī Shi'i community. The other development of interest here is the emergence of the Isma'ili Shi'i mission (*da'wa*).

> After a period of concealment, the Ismailis first appeared on the stage of world history around 874 AD, when their propagators and missionaries began to operate, and in less than a quarter of a century they had founded a network of communities extending from the Maghrib in the west to Sind (today's Pakistan) in the east, from the mountains of Daylam on the southern shore of the Caspian Sea to the highlands of the Yemen in the south. [19]

It is well known that the Isma'ili community did not produce a genre of literature known as *tafsīr.*[20] However, the religious and philosophical writings of the early Isma'ili intellectuals are full of exegesis of the Qur'an, commentary and explanation, which goes by the name of *ta'wīl*. This is not the place to enter into a discussion of the meaning of these terms. Suffice it to say that *ta'wīl* as the designation of scriptural hermeneutics eventually came to be demonized by a Sunni establishment that sought to differentiate its own exegetical activity as normative or 'orthodox'. Thus the *tafsīr* genre and the enormous prestige it enjoys in the hierarchy of Islamic religious sciences today. But before the term had become thus reified, it is important to know that even major Sunni exegetes referred to their own work as *ta'wīl* – or the search for the original meaning of a text. Thus the title of none other than the great al-Ṭabarī's work: *Jāmi' al-bayān 'an ta'wīlāy al-Qur'ān.*

[19] Heinz Halm, *The Fatimids and Their Traditions of Learning* (London/New York: I.B. Tauris in association with the Institute of Ismaili Studies, 1997), p. 1.

[20] Ismail K. Poonawala, 'Ismā'īlī *ta'wīl* of the Qur'ān', *Approaches to the History of the Interpretation of the Qur'an*, ed. A. Rippin (Oxford: Clarendon Press, 1988), pp. 199–222.

In what follows we will look at a few selected Isma'ili texts that offer an alternative understanding of Q. 4:157. Before proceeding directly to the Isma'ili authors, it is of interest to note that another representative of the Shi'i community, this time the Zaydīs, also appears to have taught a seriously divergent understanding of Q. 4:157. The influential scholar and jurist al-Qāsim ibn Ibrāhīm al-Rassī (d. 246/860), founder of the Yemeni Zaydī legal *madhhab*, upheld the historicity of the crucifixion of Jesus. The precise details of his teaching on this topic are as yet unclear. But there seems to be no compelling reason to doubt that he understood the Qur'an as *not* denying that the historical Jesus was actually put on the cross and crucified.[21] In one passage he explains and justifies the crucifixion of Jesus as a 'ransom to God'.[22] This indicates that a study of the image and discussion of Jesus in specifically Zaydi literature is likely to yield interesting results.

In an important article published in 1932, Louis Massignon brought attention to what might be thought a somewhat anomalous instance of the great 'renewer of religion' (*mujaddid*), Abū Ḥāmid al-Ghazālī, affirming the historicity of the crucifixion of Jesus.[23] The authorship of the particular work in which this affirmation occurs, *al-Radd al-Jamīl*, has long been disputed, some preferring to ascribe it to one of al-Ghazālī's students, and has recently become once again the topic of vigorous scholarly debate.[24] But there is still no completely compelling reason to fully doubt

[21] My thanks to Dr Tobias Mayer for this information. See Tobias Mayer, 'A Muslim speaks to Christians', *Priests and People: Pastoral Theology for the Modern World*, January 2003, p. 11. It has also been pointed out that his distinctive anti-anthropomorphism was in agreement with contemporary Christian doctrine. See Wilferd Madelung, 'Al-Rassī', *EI²*, vol. 8, pp. 453–4.

[22] A.J. Wensinck [D. Thomas], 'al-Ṣalīb', *EI²*, vol. 8, pp. 980–1.

[23] Massignon, 'Le Christ dans les évangiles selon Ghazali'. Many thanks to doctoral candidate Anne Clement for her help with this article.

[24] Thus Hava Lazarus-Yafeh, *Studies in al-Ghazzali* (Jerusalem: Magnes Press, Hebrew University, 1975), pp. 458–87, disagrees with Massignon's acceptance of its authenticity. The topic was recently broached in G.S. Reynolds, 'The Ends of *al-Radd al-Jamīl* and Its Portrayal of Christian Sects', *Islamochristiana*, 25, 1999, pp. 45–65, who rejects al-Ghazālī's authorship, and Maha El-Kaisy Friemuth, '*Al-Radd al-Jamīl:* al-Ghazālī's or Pseudo-Ghazālī's?', in *The Bible in Arab Christianity*, ed. David Thomas (Leiden: E.J. Brill, 2007), pp. 275–94, who is more optimistic.

al-Ghazālī's authorship.[25] Even if there were, the important point in this context is that such a work could have been read by generations of scholars as representing the views of al-Ghazālī. This has not been sufficiently appreciated in scholarship on the 'Muslim Jesus'. The question emerges: what occurred between the death of the great Sunni exegete al-Ṭabarī (923 CE) and the death of al-Ghazālī (1111 CE), the great Sunni theologian, to allow or cause such a startling reversal in understanding of our verse to occur?

Massignon's conclusion was that al-Ghazālī, in the process of studying the writings of one of his main theological opponents, namely the Isma'ili preachers and intellectuals from Abū Ḥātim al-Rāzī (d. 322/933–4) to Nāṣir-i Khusraw (d. ca. 471/1078), had become persuaded of the correctness of some of their beliefs. As Massignon points out, al-Ghazālī had been studying these works long before his sojourn in Jerusalem and Alexandria (ca. 1095–7) and it was already widely known by this time that the Isma'ili-inspired *Ikhwān al-Ṣafā'* (tenth century) taught that Jesus had really been crucified (see below). In addition to this text, Massignon knew of two others by Isma'ili philosophers. The first was the *A'lām al-nubuwwa* by Abū Ḥātim al-Rāzī, whose interpretation of the verse as affirming the historicity of the crucifixion of Jesus will be examined in detail below. The other work in which Massignon found a positive reading was the *Majālis* of Mu'ayyad fī al-Dīn Shīrāzī (d. 1077), where this scholar cites Q. 3:163, that martyrs do not really die but are alive with God, in order to refute the so-called *zindiq* Ibn al-Rāwandī (d. mid–late tenth century), who, in his *Kitāb al-zumurrudh*, questioned the veracity of the Qur'an precisely because it negated the crucifixion of Jesus. This, according to Mu'ayyad, was in clear opposition to an overwhelming agreement among 'concordant' (perhaps *mutawātir*?) testimonies coming from two major religious communities.[26] Thus, it was not only Ash'arism and Avicennan phi-

[25] Thus I differ with Robinson, *Christ*, p. 48, who categorically rejects the possibility. For a more measured approach to the problem see Gerhard Böwering, 'Ghazālī', *Encyclopaedia Iranica*, vol. 10, pp. 358–63 See also the positive view in Friemuth, op. cit.

[26] 520th *majlis*; see Massignon, op. cit., p. 534 and note to the Kraus edition. Massignon adds here that, following al-Ghazālī, his brother Aḥmad and his disciple 'Ayn al-Quḍāt al-Hamadānī referred to such exegesis, one that Fakhr al-Dīn Rāzī

losophy that formed al-Ghazālī's theological and philosophical thinking. The Isma'ili authors did not serve only as his adversaries. Massignon observed that the *Tahāfut* was more than likely immediately positively influenced by the writings of Isma'ili philosophers and thinkers such as Abū Ḥātim al-Rāzī, al-Muḥammad al-Nasafī (d. 331/943), Abū Ya'qūb al-Sijistānī (d. ca. 360/971), Ḥamīd al-Dīn al-Kirmānī (d. early eleventh century) and Nāṣir-i Khusraw. The works of these men show a 'sustained effort at religious apologetics reacting above all against the agnostic or atheistic consequences of Hellenistic philosophy, in other words a "first draft" of the *Tahāfut*'.[27] Completed in early 1095, the *Tahāfut* was obviously not the result of al-Ghazālī's much later 'conversion' to mysticism and can therefore not be ascribed to it. According to Massignon, what we see reflected in it is rather 'two centuries of passionate anti-Hellenism on the part of the Isma'ili philosophers ... The *tahāfut* would have been inspired to Ghazali by the reading of Abū Ḥātim Rāzī and Kirmānī; just as the Nizamiya university, where Ghazali taught in Baghdad, was founded on the Fatimid model of al-Azhar university in Cairo.'[28]

In this same article Massignon also offers the reasonable and, in the context of the foregoing, somewhat paradoxical hypothesis that the origins of the so-called Docetic[29] exegesis of Qur'an 4:157 are to be sought in the early history of the Shi'a, although it is obvious that it entered Sunni exegesis at a very early stage as well. Massignon explains that such an exegesis is in harmony with the explanation of the violent death suffered by the imams given by the 'extremist sects who deified them'. For example, it

(on whom see below) declared in his *al-Tafsīr al-Kabīr* to be that of 'the majority of [Muslim] philosophers'.

[27] Massignon, op. cit., p. 535. See a further discusion of this in relation to the *Mishkāt* in Hermann Landolt, 'Ghazali and "Religionswissenschaft"', *Asiatische Studien*, 45, 1991, pp. 19–72.

[28] Massignon, op. cit., p. 536.

[29] To reiterate: the category 'Docetic' is used in two senses in these pages. Here the term refers to the literal substitution of another person crucified in place of Jesus. There is also the important figurative-cum-poetic sense in which the term refers to two separate realities in the person of Jesus: the lower and comparatively ephemeral bodily reality, what the Brethren of Purity refer to (see) as the 'human dimension' – *nāsūt* – and the 'higher' eternal spiritual or divine reality, analogous to what they refer to as *lāhūt*.

was said with special reference to *al-Nafs al-Zakiyya*, the pretender to the Imamate, as early as 762 CE that, inasmuch as it were impossible for them to 'die before their time' and that the divine element had been removed from them and safeguarded unharmed, there was in reality nothing left of them but a human shell (*shibh* > *shubbiha*). And so the sufferings that they apparently experienced were actually transferred to one who deserved punishment, either a demon or a damned soul.[30] It is precisely this kind of teaching we find refuted in such 'orthodox' Twelver Shi'i narrations as the one ascribed to the eighth imam, 'Alī al-Riḍā, in which the Imam points out that it was only in the case of Jesus himself and no other imam or prophet, messenger or authority (*ḥujja*) that the matter was unclear to people. Al-Riḍā says that this confusion was intentional and allowed because, of all the prophets, messengers and authorities, only Jesus was born without a father (he does not mention Adam here) and 'Allah, the mighty and magnificent, only wanted to make his affair as a sign and mark for it to be known by this: that He has power over all things.'[31]

For the third imam, Ḥusayn (d. 61/680), a similar but more complex explanation was formulated: it was really the devoted disciple Ḥanẓala al-Shibāmī who assumed the physical resemblance of the apparently martyred imam, while the actual physical torment he appeared to suffer in place of the Imam had been visited upon one already damned, namely the second caliph, 'Umar ibn al-Khattāb. Massignon astutely compares the alternatives we have seen above in Sunni *tafsīr* – was it a disciple or an enemy who was actually crucified? – with this early Shi'i teaching.[32]

Thus the understanding of 4:157 has both inter- and intra-religious implications. During the post-Ṭabarī period we will see that there is a much greater variety of understanding within

[30] Massignon, op. cit., p. 535.

[31] Al-Majlisī, *Biḥār al-anwār*, vol. 25, p. 117, translated in *Jesus (Peace Be with Him) Through the Qur'an and Shi'ite Narrations*, ed. Mahdi Muntazir Qaim, trans. al-Hajj Muhammad Legenhausen with Muntazir Qaim (Elmhurst, NY: Tahrike Tarsile Qur'an, 2005), pp. 228–30.

[32] Massignon, op. cit., p. 535.

the greater Muslim umma than has heretofore been studied or discussed.[33]

## ABŪ ḤĀTIM AL-RĀZĪ (d. 322/933–4)

This contemporary of al-Ṭabarī was one of the most important early spokespersons for the Isma'ili intelligentsia. His debates with Abū Bakr Muḥammad ibn Zakariyya al-Rāzī, 'Rhazes' (d. ca. 313/925 or 323/935), are a seminal chapter in the history of Islamic thought. His controversies with Rhazes are preserved in his book *A'lām al-Nubuwwa* and it is because of this book that the latter's provocative, 'free-thinking' thoughts on prophets and religion are preserved for us. The problem of the crucifixion is encountered in the text when the Isma'ili philosopher responds to the great sceptic and physician, who in his *Kitāb makhāriq al-anbiyā'* had attacked the Qur'an precisely for denying the crucifixion and contradicting the unanimous view of both Christians and Jews (cf. above the argument of Ibn al-Rāwandī) as a proof that revealed religion is untrustworthy and probably causes more problems than it solves. How, he asks rhetorically, can we be expected to honour such books as holy and revealed if they cannot agree on a simple matter of history and, though not stated explicitly but in the context implied, one that is so pivotal in the respective identities of their followers. It is of extreme interest here that Abū Ḥātim, the Isma'ili missionary, does not invoke the easily available doctrine of textual corruption – *taḥrīf* – to explain the difference.[34] Rather, his response is based on a much more subtle

[33] Neal Robinson, in his excellent examinations of the issue, has not ventured into the subject of the intramural discussion indicated in the Isma'ili sources and the response to these sources, whether from representative Sunni thinkers such as al-Ghazali or from other Shi'i authors, whether explicit or not, that most certainly occurred. He does mention the article by Massignon, but his only interest is Masssignon's observations about the history of the substitution theory mentioned above. See Robinson, *Christ*, pp. 52, 141.

[34] Such arguments were well developed – though with characteristic differences and emphases – in both Sunni and Shi'i literature. See Lazarus-Yafeh, 'Taḥrīf (a.)', *EI²*, vol. 10, p. 111.

and radical hermeneutic. He holds that the key to understanding the verse is in its sequel, 4:158: AND THEY DID NOT REALLY (YAQĪNA) KILL HIM, GOD HAS RAISED HIM UP TO HIMSELF. This must be read in conjunction with two other important verses in which it is promised that martyrs do not die,but rather remain alive with God (Q. 2:149 and 3:169), inasmuch as Jesus died a martyr.[35]

He then points out to Rhazes that in fact both scriptures, the Qur'an and the Gospels, agree in letter and spirit. He refers to the Gospel of John (*Bushrā Yuḥannā*), which he quotes as 'the Messiah died in the body [*bi-al-jasad*], whereas he is alive in the spirit [*bi-al-rūḥ*]. So they thought that he who died in the body was delivered from sin.' He also quotes the Gospel of Luke (*Bushrā Lūqā*), where Jesus is quoted as follows: 'I say to you, oh my dear friends [*awliyā'ī*], do not fear those who kill the body, but cannot do more than that.' This is similar to his next quotation from the Gospel of Matthew (*Bushrā Matā*): 'Do not fear those who kill the body but are not able to kill the soul, and do fear the one who can [both] destroy the soul and cast the body into the fire [of hell].'[36] It is important to note that al-Rāzī also denies the crucifixion in another work. In that work al-Rāzī is arguing against another formidable Isma'ili scholar, al-Nasafī. While the exact details of this dispute need not detain us, it has been argued that al-Rāzī's apparent turnabout must be understood in the context of the particular *ad hominem* debate he is engaged in with his fellow Isma'ili disputant.[37] It is also important to observe that this

[35] Massignon, op. cit., p. 534.

[36] Shin Nomoto, 'Early Ismā'īlī Thought on Prophecy According to the Kitāb al-Iṣlāḥ by Abū Ḥātim al-Rāzī (d. ca. 322/934–5)', PhD thesis, McGill University, 1999, pp. 252–3. Two important articles by Antonella Straface on the Isma'ili interpretation of the phrase *shubbiha lahum* came to my attention as this book was going to press: 'An Ismā'īlī Interpretation of Shubbiha Lahum (Qur. IV, 157) in the Kitāb Šagarat al-yaqīn', *Authority, Privacy and Public Order in Islam, Proceedings of the 22nd Congress of L'Union Européenne des Arabisants et Islamisants*, ed. B. Michalak-Pikulska and A. Pikulski (Peeters: Leuven-Paris-Dudley, MA), pp. 95–100, and 'Influenze Neoplatoniche Nell'Interpretazione Ismā'īlita di *Shubbiha Lahum* (*Cor.* IV, 157)', *Pensiero e istituzioni del mondo classsico nelle culture del Vicino Oriente*, Atti del Seminario Nazionale di studio (Brescia, 14–15–16 ottobre 1999), a cura di Rosa Bianca Finazzi e Alfredo Valvo (Alessandria: Edizioni dell'Orso), pp. 265–75.

[37] The work is the *Kitāb al-Iṣlāḥ*. See Nomoto, *Early Ismā'īlī Thought*, pp. 253–6.

highlights the important fact that al-Nasafī himself believed in the historicity of the crucifixion. Unfortunately, the original work in which such an affirmation occurs is known only to us through quotation of select passages.

Quite apart from some minor discrepancies in the exact wording and numbering of verses from the Gospels, Abū Ḥātim demonstrates that both the Qur'an and the Gospels agree that Jesus was crucified when the problematic phrase *wa-lākin shubbiha lahum* is properly understood. That which APPEARED to be crucified was precisely the body, what others will refer to as 'the human dimension' (*al-nāsūt*), while the spirit or true reality of Jesus was 'raised' to his Lord. Thus, according to Abū Ḥātim, 'these passages from the Gospels are consistent with the Qur'an in terms of their actual meaning, since both the scriptures attest that Jesus could not be killed in the full sense, that is, in both body and soul'.[38]

## JA'FAR IBN MANṢŪR AL-YAMAN (d. ca. 349/960)

Another major figure in the Isma'ili mission or *da'wa*, though in the western regions, Ja'far ibn Manṣūr is credited with numerous works of great interest for the history of Islamic thought. One of these, the *Sarā'ir al-nuṭaqā'* has recently been studied.[39] It is now clear that the author agreed with the historicity of the crucifixion of Jesus.[40] We can assume that the author was likely to have held such a position on characteristic grounds: what might otherwise be thought an inordinate degree of attention to the symbolism of the cross. Thus there occur within this authentic text four brief chapters concerned with the proper interpretation of the cross: (1) a parable hidden within the cross; (2) the

[38] Ibid., p. 253.

[39] David Hollenberg, 'Interpretation after the End of Days: the Fāṭimid-Ismā'īlī Ta'wīl (Interpretation) of Ja'far ibn Manṣūr al-Yaman (d. ca. 960)', PhD dissertation, University of Pennsylvania, 2006. My thanks to Jamel Velji for this reference.

[40] 'A distinctive aspect of the life of Jesus in the *Sarā'ir* is the incorporation of Christological elements that were foreign or even anathema to Islam (*sic*). These include the Eucharist, the Trinity, the Cross, the Crucifixion, the institution of the Church, and replacing circumcision with the tonsure (as in Acts 21:21–24).' Hollenberg, op. cit., p. 328. See also pp. 329–32.

cross and its dimensions; (3) an explanation of the cross with its twelve positions and (4) a parable of the cross and the sunna of the prophets.[41] We will note concern with this again in the next author to be discussed, al-Sijistānī, a representative of 'eastern' Isma'ilism.

In another work ascribed to Ja'far ibn Manṣūr, the *Kitāb al-fatarāt wa-al-qirānāt*, analysed in this same recent study, we find an explicit affirmation of the crucifixion in the course of a discussion on cosmogony:

> [One] of the ancient wise ones said that the beginning of existence is two lines, one on the other in the middle, in this shape: † . Because of this, the Messiah (*al-masīḥ*) was erected on the cross to exemplify it, indicating the two sources.[42]

## AL-SIJISTĀNĪ (d. 360/971)

Abu Ya'qūb al-Sijistānī was first and foremost a member of the Isma'ili underground mission – the *da'wa*, as it is known in Arabic – that operated in the Iranian province of Khurasan and Sijistan during the tenth century. In the later part of his life, al-Sijistānī was a supporter of the Fāṭimid imams whose centre was Cairo in the west. Both al-Sijistānī and Abū Ḥātim al-Rāzī uphold the historicity of the crucifixion of Jesus. Abū Ḥātim does, as we saw above, on the basis of a hermeneutic strategy. It is the same with al-Sijistānī, except here the hermeneutic strategy employed is typological figuration. Al-Sijistānī, in his *Kitāb al-yanābī'*, says that the truth of the present Qā'im was foretold and predicted through the ministry of Jesus:

> Jesus – may peace be upon him! – gave his community to know that the master of the resurrection (*ṣāḥib al-qiyāmah*) is the one of whom he is the sign (*al-ladhī huwa 'alāmatu-hu*). For, [Jesus continued,] when he (i.e. the master of the Resurrection) unveils

[41] Ibid., p. 76.

[42] Ibid., pp. 123, 161–3, 165, and the reference to al-Rāzī's discussion of the two lines of the cross in the *Kitāb al-iṣlāḥ*.

> the structural realities of the sacred laws which are composed of the spiritual realities … the people will recognize them (i.e., the realities) and will not deny them, just as when all the people see a crucified one (*maṣlūb*), they recognize him and understand his form, although most of them would have been ignorant of him before that. Because of this meaning, his (i.e., the Qā'im's) day is called the 'day of baring' (*yawm al-kashf*), just as He said: *upon the day when the leg shall be bared ... and they shall be summoned to bow themselves* (Q 68:42). Thus the crucified one on the wood became an unveiled one (*makshūf*), although he was concealed before it (i.e., the crucifixion).[43]

Thus, Jesus' mission and status were made known to the people of his time primarily through the enormity of the crucifixion. Furthermore, his being crucified foreshadowed the Qā'im's mission of unveiling to all humanity the spiritual realities of the truths hidden in earlier religious law. Both figures are thus seen as unveilers and are therefore typological reflections of each other. Elsewhere al-Sijistānī speaks of Jesus as being the 'sign of resurrection' because he taught his disciples of things that would only be manifested at the time of the Lord of the Resurrection. Jesus' unveiling of hidden knowledge to his disciples was a typological prefiguration of the same act by the Lord of the Resurrection to his followers.

## THE BRETHREN OF PURITY (TENTH CENTURY)

The thought of the group of Arab philosophers of the fourth or fifth century AH (tenth or eleventh century CE) known as the *Ikhwān al-Ṣafa'* (the 'Brethren of Purity') is an intellectual synthesis of Greek philosophy and Islamic scripture. This group composed

[43] Slightly adapted from Nomoto, op. cit., pp. 249–50. See Abū Ya'qūb al-Sijistānī, *Kitāb al-yanābī',* ed. and partially trans. H. Corbin in his *Trilogie ismaelienne* (Tehran/Paris: Département d'iranologie de l'Institut franco-iranien, 1961). See also Paul E. Walker, *The Wellsprings of Wisdom: A Study of Abū Ya'qūb al-Sijistānī's* Kitāb al-Yanābī' *Including a Complete English Translation with Commentary and Notes on the Arabic Text*, trans. P.E. Walker (Salt Lake City: University of Utah Press, 1994).

fifty-two separate 'essays' (lit. 'epistles' from the Arabic *risāla*, pl. *rasā'il*) covering a wide diversity of topics: biology, geography, medicine, metaphysics, magic and so on. Their religious framework has long been considered, though not unanimously, to have been Isma'ili Shi'i. It is clear that their overall project was to demonstrate the inherent harmony between reason and revelation and to chart a programme for salvation that could satisfy the intellect. The teachings of the *Ikhwān al-Ṣafa'* on the problem of the historicity of the crucifixion of Jesus are quite uncompromising.

> So Jesus went the next day and appeared to the people and summoned them and preached to them until he was seized and taken to the king of the *banū isrā'īl*. The king ordered his crucifixion, so his *nāsūt* (physical reality) was crucified, and his hands were nailed to the wooden cross and he stayed crucified from morning till evening. And he asked for water but was given vinegar [to drink]. Then he was pierced with a lance and buried in a place near the cross while forty troops guarded the tomb. And all of this occurred in the presence of the disciples. When they saw him they knew that it was he CERTAINLY and that he had [not] commanded them to DIFFER ABOUT IT. Then they gathered three days later in a place. And Jesus did appear to them and they saw that mark which was known by them. The news was spread among the *banū isrā'īl* that the Messiah was not killed. So the tomb was opened and the *nāsūt* was not found. Thus the troops DIFFERED AMONG THEMSELVES and much idle chatter ensued, and the story was complicated.[44]

Although the passage from the *Rasā'il* is clearly not an example of 'official' *tafsīr*, it is obviously not quite so certain just how non-exegetical this passage is, even though it does not come from a work of *tafsīr*. Notice the terminological correspondences (e.g. 'certainly', 'appeared' and 'differed among themselves') to

[44] *Rasā'il ikhwān al-ṣafā' wa-khullān al-wafā'*, ed. Khayr al-Dīn al-Ziriklī (Cairo: al-Maktaba al-Tijārīya al-Kubrā, 1928) (facsimile reprint Frankfurt-am-Main: Ma'had Tārīkh al-'Ulūm al-'Arabīyah wa-al-Islāmīyah fī iṭār Jāmi'at Frānkfūrt, 1999), vol. 4, p. 97. See also Elder, op. cit., pp. 242–58 and Lootfy Levonian, 'The Ikhwān al-Ṣafā' and Christ', *Moslem World*, 35, 1945, pp. 27–31 for slightly varying translations of this passage. My thanks to Professor Abbas Hamdani for drawing my attention to Levonian's article.

4:157–8. Elder first noticed this passage in 1923. Why it has hardly figured in discussions of the crucifixion is difficult to determine.[45] But that it does exist, along with the other Isma'ili texts adduced here, encourages the interested student to persevere in the study of Shi'i-related materials for interesting new light on perennial problems in Islamic thought. These texts demonstrate that there is a serious difference between the Sunni and Shi'i understanding of Qur'an 4:157 and that this difference may not be immediately apparent in a comparison of just the so-called classical works of *tafsīr*.

The negative view – that Jesus most certainly was not crucified – is upheld in Twelver Shi'i exegetical literature. Thus a certain doctrinal rapprochement is achieved between the classical sources of Sunni and Imami Shi'i scriptural commentary, permitting agreement on an important topic between Sunni Islam and Ja'fari or Imami Shi'ism. It is certainly accurate, from one point of view, to assert, with Busse, that 'Shi'i exegsis does not differ substantially from the Sunni.'[46] But what needs to be emphasized is that this agreement appears to have been achieved as the consummation of a process that had begun much earlier – one that would succeed in virtually silencing and marginalizing the Isma'ili exegesis. The political power of the Fatimids was burgeoning at the time of the consolidation of those two Mesopotamian Islamicate identities. Al-Ṭūsi, who died in 1067 CE, lived to witness the humiliation, however brief, of the Abbasid polity when the above-mentioned Isma'ili leader, Mu'ayyad al-Shīrāzī, ordered the Turkish general Arsalān al-Basāsīrī to enter Baghdad with his troops in December 1058 CE. At this time the Fatimid Shi'i call to prayer was instituted and the *khuṭba* was said in the name of the Fatimid Imam, al-Mustanṣir. The Fatimid military presence remained a full year, apparently with the popular support of both Sunnis and Shi'ites, who were equally opposed to the erstwhile ruling Seljuks and their policies. The Fatimid presence was short-lived:

45 See also Robinson, *Christ*, pp. 55–7.

46 'Die schiitischen Exegese unterschiedet sich nicht wesentlich von der sunnitischen.' Busse, 'Jesu Errettung', p. 190.

> The Abbasid caliph, al-Qā'im, was forced to abdicate and was deported to 'Anā on the Euphrates. His cloak and other insignia were sent to Cairo. This was the greatest victory of the Faṭimids. At last they had realized the aim towards which they had so long aspired. The Abbasid dynasty of the 'usurper' had fallen [two hundred years before the Mongols], and Baghdad had become part of the Fatimid empire. The leader of the Ismaili *da'wa* in Iraq, al-Mu'ayyad al-Shirazi, rose to the office of chief *dā'ī*, thus crowning his career with a twofold victory. But this triumph was soon gambled away by Ibn al-Maghribī, the incompetent successor to the vizier al-Yāzūrī, who denied al-Basāsīrī urgently needed financial and military assisitance. And so in December 1059, when the Abbasid caliphate was restored with the help of the Turkish Saljuqs, the latter had to leave Baghdad again.[47]

Apart from doctrinal rapprochement between Twelver Shi'ism and Sunnism – what came to be known in a later period as *taqrīb al-madhāhib* – another reason that it was consistent for the Shi'ites to deny that Jesus was killed (Q. 4:157 says THEY DID NOT KILL HIM; it does not say 'he was not killed') is that his continued long life and his residence in occultation 'at the right hand of God' provide a compelling precedent and type for the central doctrinal feature of Twelver Shi'ism, namely that of the Hidden Imam. He also was not killed and he also resides in the unseen realm and he also will return to earth one day. Thus, in this instance the Hidden Imam is an anti-type of the Islamic Jesus. Massignon, as we saw, first theorized that the history of the so-called substitution legend in Islamic exegesis probably began in a Shi'i milieu.[48]

A perhaps much later anonymous Isma'ili text is equally confident about the understanding of Q. 4:157. The author compares this verse to a poem about the Prince of Martyrs, Ḥusayn ibn 'Alī:

> You are not killed, nay rather only the limbs visible (to the eyes of the enemy) that bear a likeness to yours were [killed].

[47] Halm, op. cit., pp. 80–1.
[48] Massignon, 'Le Christ dans les évangiles selon Ghazali'.

The author continues,

> The immaterial soul and the sublime temple of light cannot be killed or crucified, nor even die. [That which dies is] only the '[superficial] covers' of the body [made] of flesh and blood, which are nothing but an [outward] representation (*mithāl*) of the immaterial temple of light.[49]

The philosophical foundation for such a poetical view had long since been worked out by such Isma'ili thinkers as Ḥamīd al-Dīn Kirmānī (d. 411/1020). For Kirmānī, the prophets and imams are the physical manifestation and perfection of Intellect. At any given time it is the imam who most perfectly knows the truth and, according to the *Rāḥat al-'aql* (The Consolation of the Intellect) of Kirmānī, 'this is why God is said to have created Adam in his own image (*'alā mathal ṣūrat nafsihi*) and why Jesus reported that he was the son of heaven (*anā ibn min al-samā'*)'.[50]

## 'ABD AL-JABBĀR (d. 416/1025)

This Mu'tazili scholar's discussion of the problem is interesting because of the innovative way it deals with certain themes and issues already encountered. It also serves as something of an introduction to the next scholar inasmuch as it is well accepted that Mu'tazilism played a great role in the formation of what we may be tempted to refer to as 'orthodox' Twelver Shi'ism. In an article published in 1967, S.M. Stern drew attention to this influential thinker's ideas on the crucifixion and his explanation, though the work is not technically a *tafsīr*, of Q. 4:157–8.[51] 'Abd al-Jabbār explains that as a matter of fact it was Judas who was at the centre of the drama. As no one knew who Jesus was, the

[49] R. Strothmann, *Gnosis-Texte der Ismailiten: Ambrosiana Arabic Ms. H75* (Göttingen: Vandenhoeck & Ruprecht, 1943), Arabic p. 120, German p. 43.

[50] Kirmānī, *Raḥat al-'aql*, 146, cited in Paul Walker, *Ḥamīd al-Dīn al-Kirmānī* (London: I.B. Tauris/Institute of Ismaili Studies), p. 102.

[51] S.M. Stern, 'Quotations from Apocryphal Gospels in 'Abd al-Jabbar', *Journal of Theological Studies*, n.s., 18(1), 1967, 34–57, idem, 'New Light on Judaeo-Christianity? The Evidence of 'Abd al-Jabbar', *Encounter*, March 1968, pp. 53–7.

Romans asked Judas to identify him for them. Judas pointed out another, innocent man and identified him as Jesus. The Romans could not have known of the deception; otherwise, why would they have needed someone like Judas to identify Jesus in the first place? Thus when Judas laments that he has shed innocent blood, the meaning is clear: he caused a completely random and irrelevant death as a result of his desire to protect his master. Thus he hanged himself in despair. Stern's summary of 'Abd al-Jabbār is worth quoting in full:

> On the Thursday before the Passover, the Jews came to Herod and complained against Jesus. He ordered his attendants to go and arrest him, but when they were asked whether they knew him, they said no. Neither did the Jews know him, but they said they would surely find someone to point him out. They met Judas Iscariot who offered to indicate Jesus by kissing him and was paid thirty silver pieces. Judas after kissing a man disappeared in the crowd. The man, when arrested, showed great perturbation. When Herod saw his fright he had pity on him and interrogated him in a friendly manner. The man denied that he claimed to be the Messiah. Herod said to the Jews that the man denied the accusation, and washed his hands of his blood. Pilate asked Herod to send him the man who showed the same signs of fear before Pilate. Pilate returned him to Herod saying that he found in him no guilt but neither could he get anything reasonable out of him. Herod put the man into prison overnight. Next day he was mocked and whipped by the Jews and crucified in a field. His last words were: my God, why have you forsaken me, O God, why have you left me? Judas came to the Jews asking about the man arrested the day before. When he heard he was crucified he was greatly astonished and went to the field. Seeing the man he exclaimed: This is an innocent man, this is innocent blood. Throwing the thirty pieces of silver at the faces of the Jews, he went to his house and hanged himself.[52]

As Stern points out, 'Abd al-Jabbār is delighted to find such vindication for how he understood the Qur'anic account. He also points out that the general outline of the above story could just as

[52] Ibid., pp. 56–7. Note the obvious resonances here with the so-called Gospel of Judas.

easily come from the canonical gospels (cf. Matthew 27:4). In the context of the present study, this account is interesting because of the variation it introduces into the history of the exegesis. It is important to note that there are no miraculous interventions. What deception and confusion do occur are explained on perfectly understandable and rational grounds. Such is a mark of the Muʿtazila and we will see this expressed again in another narrative related by al-Ṭūsī, the first great Twelver Shiʿi exegete.

## AL-THAʿLABĪ (d. 427/1035)

New light has recently been cast on the form and contents, the importance and influence of the Qur'an commentary of Aḥmad b. Muḥammad b. Ibrāhīm Abū Isḥāq al-Nīsābūrī.[53] Among the more interesting aspects of his *tafsīr* is the discovery by Saleh of the possible reason for al-Thaʿlabī's marginalization in the history of the genre. It may come as no surprise in the context of the present discussion that this reason is none other than what came to be judged an excessive philo-Shiʿism on his part with regard to traditions and interpretations offered in his commentary. In light of this, it is more than a little disappointing that we find nothing unique in his commentary on the particular verses in question. However, his renowned *Lives of the Prophets* has several narratives touching the crucifixon, ascension and descent which merit serious study in connection with the information found in his *tafsīr.* One example is the variant on the substitution theory that depicts a Jew consciously pretending to be Jesus, who when his miracles fail is crucified by the angry crowd. Also worthy of notice is al-Thaʿlabī's account of how it was actually Pilate who was made to look like Jesus.[54]

[53] Saleh, op. cit., pp. 234–8. See also Isaiah Goldfeld, *Quranic Commentray in the Eastern Islamic Tradition of the First Four Centuries of the Hijra: An Annotated Edition of the Preface to al-Thaʿlabī's Kitāb al-kashf wa'l-bayān ʿan tafsīr al-Qur'ān* (Acre, Israel: Srugy, 1984). Many thanks to Professor Saleh for making available to me the manuscript of the *tafsīr.*

[54] Brinner, *'Arā'is*, pp. 662–72. See also the reference to al-Thaʿlabī in the Introduction.

## AL-ṬŪSĪ (d. 460/1067)

With this scholar, we now begin the examination of what has come to be known as classical Shi'i *tafsīr*. However, as we have seen, much exegetical effort had already been expended on this verse within the greater Shi'i community. With Abū Ja'far al-Ṭūsī, one of the founding fathers of Twelver Shi'i doctrine, there is considerable, and frequently original, commentary on our verse. He begins by citing the familiar tradition from Wahb we found in al-Ṭabarī's *tafsīr*, adding that Qatāda, al-Suddī, Ibn Isḥāq, Mujāhid and *Ibn Jurayj* all disagree about the number of disciples. Nor, he points out, do they mention the tradition, related by Wahb, in which the likeness was cast upon all of the disciples, and asserts that the likeness was cast upon only one. Al-Ṭūsī then goes on to say that one of the disciples, Būdis Zakariyya Būta (i.e. Judas), pointed Jesus out to the Jews, but later repented and hanged himself. He notes that some Christians say that this Būdis was the one on whom the likeness was cast and who was ultimately crucified. Al-Ṭūsī repeats al-Ṭabarī's assessment of Wahb's account: the likeness was cast upon all the disciples and thus the matter was obscured for everyone involved. However, he introduces a new element to this *tafsīr* by citing the famous Mu'tazilī, al-Jubbā'ī (probably *père*: Abū Hāshim 'Abd al-Salām, d. 303/915):

> The meaning of the error (*wajh al-tashbīh*) is that the leaders of the Jews took a man, killed him and crucified him on a hill. They prevented anyone from examining him until his body had decomposed beyond recognition. Then they claimed they had killed Jesus; thus they misled their people because they were afraid that if the Jews knew that Jesus had been raised by God from the house that they had entered in order to arrest him, that this divine intervention would cause the Jews to believe in Jesus. Those who crucified this man were not the ones who disagreed about it. (Ibid., p. 383)

The question is then posed – whether by al-Ṭūsī or al-Jubbā'ī it is difficult to determine – of whether it is possible for one's likeness to be cast upon another so that the two become indistinguishable. That such a question appears now is of obvious significance in the study of the history of the exegesis of this verse. It represents a development that we will have occasion to refer to below in the examination of the exegetical works of al-Zamakhsharī and Fakhr al-Dīn al-Rāzī. The answer al-Ṭūsī offers, though less important than the question he asks, is that such a thing is possible according to the Mu'tazila, but only through a prophet or during his time (*zamān*), and then only by the aid of God.

Next follows the familiar account of the disciples leaving Jesus and one companion in the house, such that the disciples were deprived of positive knowledge of the events. This is seen to be responsible for the Christians' confusion about the affair. Al-Ṭūsī agrees with al-Ṭabarī that the Christians cannot be called liars on account of this confusion; they simply have been deluded or deceived. Thus al-Ṭūsī propounds the traditional substitutionist theory. Any differences in interpretation, which might have been expected in view of his Shi'ism, are found only in the use of Mu'tazili dialectic. Like al-Ṭabarī, he employs no grammatical analysis or reference to poetry. This examination of al-Ṭūsī's *tafsīr* confirms the finding that the great Shi'i exegete was in general agreement with al-Ṭabarī. Indeed, much of his method and material offer a direct parallel.

The question naturally emerges as to why these two radically different religious orientations should find so much in common, especially at this highly fraught hermeneutic site. We have seen that Isma'ili Shi'i thinkers and exegetes found no difficulty in promoting a reading of the Qur'an text that agreed with Christianity.[55] The Fatimid Isma'ilis were at the height of their power during the lifetimes of Abū Ḥātim al-Rāzī and al-Sijistānī. Indeed, Fatimid ambitions towards the central Islamic lands are well known and were the cause of, among other things, the establishment of the vast network of madrasas founded to teach and propagate correct belief during the later Seljuk period. One of

[55] While it is certainly true that the Isma'ili scholars did not contribute to a genre of religious writing known technically as *tafsīr* the reasons for this have nothing to do with the fact that they did not interpret scripture, as has been abundantly demonstrated above. For a succinct and lucid discussion of this question, see Ismail K. Poonawala, 'Ismā'īlī *ta'wīl* of the Qur'ān', in *Approaches to the History of the Interpretation of the Qur'ān,* ed. A. Rippin (Oxford: Clarendon Press, 1988), pp. 199–222.

which, the Baghdad Niẓamiyya was famously presided over by Abū Ḥāmid al-Ghazālī, mentioned earlier in this chapter. The situation represented what would correspond today to a war of ideologies. During the tenth century it was possible to hear the distinctive Fatimid call to prayer in certain neighbourhoods of Baghdad.[56] If we bear in mind that such labels as 'Sunni', 'Shi'i' and 'Isma'ili' are – especially during this formative period – not mere doctrinal designators but also symbols of distinct, mutually exclusive religio-political aspirations and programmes, then it becomes easier to understand the otherwise somewhat anomalous Sunni–Twelver rapprochement vis-à-vis the crucifixion of Jesus. But other recent scholarship has pointed to what might be thought a 'Sunnification' of Shi'ism in the central Islamic lands during this period.[57] Nor has such a process been noticed only by outsiders. The famous Akhbari–Usuli debates of the seventeenth to ninteenth centuries also featured this argument. The Akhbari's ascribed the slow deterioration of the vigour of Shi'ism to its having become much too Sunni-like in its religious élan and praxis, especially with regard to legal thinking.

Isma'ili hermeneutic was by no means the only one in which the categories of 'outer and inner', 'exoteric and esoteric' (*bāṭin* and *ẓāhir*) were pressed into the service of understanding the Qur'an. But it is only among the Isma'ili authors that we find during this early period a reading of Q. 4:157 that can not only agree but bear explicit witness to the truth of Christian salvation history. We saw, of course, that such bearing witness is also a way of propagating their own typologically iterative view of salvation and eschatology.[58] And this points to another subtle difference between the two

[56] Farhad Daftary, *The Isma'ilis: Their History and Doctrines* (Cambridge, England: Cambridge University Press, 1990), pp. 63ff.

[57] Todd Lawson, 'Akhbari Shi'i Approaches to Tafsir', in *The Koran: Critical Concepts in Islamic Studies. Vol. IV: Translation and Exegesis*, ed. Colin Turner (London: RoutledgeCurzon, 2004), pp. 163–97.

[58] On the Isma'ili hermeneutic of typology, see the discussion in Nomoto, op. cit., pp. 248–52. It should be pointed out that the typological mode of discourse and interpretation in Islam is as old as the Qur'an itself. See Michael Zwettler, 'Mantic Manifesto: The Sūra of the Poets and the Qur'anic Foundations of Prophetic Authority', in *Poetry and Prophecy: The Beginnings of a Literary Tradition*, ed. James L. Kugel (Ithaca, NY/London: Cornell University Press), pp. 75–119 (notes 205–31). It also extends beyond the concerns of the Fatimids and other Isma'ili

Shi'i schools. While both rely on the persuasive power of typology in their understanding of the role of Jesus in history, they come to diametrically opposite conclusions with regard to the meaning of our verse. For Twelver Shi'i scholars, it is 'typologically crucial' that Jesus was not killed but rather raised to the invisible presence of God precisely because what may be thought a politically accommodationist doctrine of the occultation of the Imam entailed exactly the same process: unnaturally long life in a sacrosanct and protected unseen realm, viz. *al-ghayba* ('occultation').[59]

It remains a question why discussions of the Islamic Jesus have not heretofore stressed the importance of the thought of these Isma'ili scholars with regard to what is probably the greatest single obstacle in Muslim–Christian relations not to mention an extremely important feature of Muslim identity. There is no space to pursue this question now, but if, as some have argued, the Qur'an means everything Muslims have – over the centuries – said it means, it is difficult to also argue from a religious studies perspective, that according to Islam, the Qur'an denies the crucifixion of Jesus.[60] Rather, it is interpretation of the Qur'an that denies the crucifixion.

## ABŪ AL-FUTŪḤ AL-RĀZĪ (d. 525/1131)

He was the author of what is considered the oldest Shi'i *tafsīr* in Persian, the *Rawḍ al-jinān wa-rawḥ al-janān*. He quoted much

thinkers, as we have seen, to find an important niche in Twelver hermeneutics. This important topic is not properly broached in the standard work on early Shi'i scriptural commentary (Bar-Asher; see Bibliography) even though its vigorous revival in the works of the Shi'i school known as the Shaykhiyya has long been noted.

[59] Note, in this connection, the very interesting report transmitted by al-Ṣadūq from the fifth imam, al-Bāqir: 'As to [al-Qa'im's] similarity with Jesus, it is in the disagreement of those who differ about him, to the extent that one group from among them said: "He was [never] born"; another group said: "He didn't die"; and [still] another group said, "He was killed and crucified."' Al-Shaykh al-Ṣadūq, *Kamāl al-dīn wa tamām al-ni'ma* (Qum, Iran: Mu'assasat al-Nashr al-Islāmī al-Tābi'a li-Jimā'at al-Mudarrisayn bi Qum al-Musharrafa, 1405/1984), pp. 327–8. My thanks to Mr Omid Ghaemmaghami for this exceptionally suggestive reference.

[60] Wilfred Cantwell Smith, *What Is Scripture?: A Comparative Approach* (Philadelphia: Fortress Press, 1993).

from his contemporary, al-Zamakhsharī, though the statement of Massé that 'this would explain the Mu'tazilism of his commentary' is now somewhat obsolete in its formulation in light of recent research.[61] With regard to our verse, however, there is a rather interesting translation of MĀ QATALUHU WA MĀ ṢALABUHU WALĀKIN SHUBBIHA LAHUM: 'they did not kill him and did not hang him, but rather they disguised it [the event] by means of it'.[62] This is all that is offered on the issue. The language is sufficiently open to allow for what we have called a figurative Docetism without explicitly subscribing to it. It is also interesting that this language seems to echo New Testament terminology in passages where the death of Jesus is said to have been caused by his having been hung on a tree.[63] Such ambiguity and allusiveness are not unknown in the Persian mystical tradition after all. Thus we may have here a rather significant development in the understanding of the verse, one that suggests that a full study of the hermeneutic of al-Rāzī would repay the effort, particularly as a possible conduit of 'unorthodox' ideas for such later hybrid Iranian intellectual developments as the *Ḥikmat-i Ilāhī* movement dating from the seventeenth century. What is clear is that Abū'l-Futūḥ offers no Mu'tazili-influenced commentary on our verse.

## AL-ṬABRISĪ (d. 548–53/1153–8)

Some mention should be made here of the other renowned Twelver Shi'i *mufassir* of this general era. Abū 'Alī al-Faḍl al-Ṭabrisī (or al-Ṭabarsī) offers nothing new in interpreting our verse. The

[61] H. Massé, 'Abu'l-Futūḥ al-Rāzī', *EI*[2], vol. 1, p. 120. Andrew Lane has demonstrated that the actual commentary of al-Zamakhsharī is much less Mu'tazili than one might have expected from the widespread and notorious reputation of the author. See his *A Traditional Mutazilite Qur'an Commentary: The Kashshāf of Jar Allah al-Zamakhsharī (d. 538/1144)* (Leiden/Boston: E.J. Brill, 2006).

[62] 'va nakushtand ū rā va bardār nakardand ū rā va-lākin ū rādar ū pūshānīdand': Abū al-Futūḥ al-Rāzī, *Rawḍ al-Jinān w-Rawḍ al-Janān* (Qum, Iran: Intishārāt-i Kitābkhānah-yi Āyat Allāh al-Uẓmā Marashī-Najafī, 1404/1984), vol. 2, p. 165.

[63] Galatians 3:13. See also Acts 5:30, 10:39, 13:29 and 1 Peter 2:24. My thanks to Dr Stephen Lambden of Ohio University for pointing this out to me.

grammatical analysis one might have expected from reading his introduction to the commentary on this verse is absent. Al-Ṭabrisī simply repeats, in a condensed form, the *tafsīr* of al-Ṭūsī, including a quotation from al-Jubbā'ī, who is here positively identified as *père*. Al-Ṭabrisī does not repeat the 'rationalistic' questions of his counterpart. The reports of Wahb are the accepted accounts.

Before proceeding to the next section of this chapter in which Sufi commentary is presented, it will be helpful to take stock of what we have so far seen. Certain elements of the Shi'a, namely the Isma'ili philosophers and missionaries, held that Jesus did die and that what is meant by NAY, RATHER GOD RAISED HIM TO HIMSELF in 4:158 is in reality a modified or figurative Docetic process by means of which normal biological 'death' is in any case illusory. However, the fathers of Twelver Shi'i exegesis not only record no trace of having been influenced by or open to such interpretation; they did not even refer to it in order to refute it. The important 'hermeneutic' consideration is precisely the historical and political reality. The 'Abbasid (Sunni) establishment was surrounded on all sides by Shi'i elements, some more aggressive and some more cooperative. The 'Sunnification' of Shi'i exegesis as seen in the work of al-Ṭūsī is emblematic of the general process alluded to above. In the case of both Isma'ili and Twelver traditions, Jesus is a type of the Qā'im and other figures (including Muḥammad himself and 'Alī, the first imam). The robustness and utility of typological 'rhetoric' are borne witness here by the irony that while both Shi'i communities rely upon it, in this case they arrive at mutually exclusive and diametrically opposite conclusions. For the Isma'ilis, Jesus was crucified; for the Twelvers, he was not. That life of some form goes on, perhaps even more intensely (e.g. in the spiritual realm known after al-Suhrawardī [d. 587/1191] as the 'World of Images' [*'ālam al-mithāl*]), is something we see attested to in such verses as AND CALL NOT THOSE WHO ARE SLAIN [*yuqtalu*] IN THE WAY OF GOD 'DEAD' [*amwāt*]. NAY THEY ARE LIVING, ONLY YE PERCEIVE NOT (2:154, similar to 3:169).

So we have a serious cleavage between Sunni and Shi'i readings of the Qur'an texts. It is difficut to speculate on just how influential, in a negative way, the Isma'ili understanding of this verse (and of course many others) has been on the greater Islamic learned tradition. We have seen, in the case of al-Ghazālī, that their teaching about the crucifixion was actually influential in a positive sense.

## AL-QUSHAYRĪ (d. 465/1072)

This Ash'arī mystic is credited with several books; of interest here is his *Laṭā'if al-ishārāt*, a *tafsīr*.[64] He discusses 4:157 as part of an exegetical theme related to a section of the *sūra* that begins with 4:156 and ends with 4:158.

> Exceeding the limit (*ḥadd*) with regard to the truth is error; just as insufficiency and belittling with regard to the truth is error. They [Jews] arose speaking against Mary and slandering her with the charge of fornication. And others exceeded the limit in oppressing her – they said: 'Her son is the Son of God,' and all of the groups were in error.

The Christians, in other words, said too much and the Jews denigrated 'the truth'. This is the familiar theme of 'exaggeration' (*ghulūw*) and its opposite with regard to matters of religion. It is no surprise that it is being voiced by one of the 'orthodoxers' of the Islamic mystical tradition. It also continues the theme we saw above in my discussion of Ibn Isḥāq and one of the roles of the Prophet in the *sīra*, namely as one who points out a 'middle way' that both Jews and Christians can accept and unite upon.

> And it is said that Mary was the intimate friend (*walīya*) of God, and that He was troubled because of the two groups, the people of excess (*ifrāṭ*) and the people of neglect (*tafrīṭ*) who wronged

[64] Abū al-Qāsim 'Abd al-Karīm b. Hawāzin b. 'Abd al-Mālik b. Ṭalḥa b. Muḥammad al-Qushayrī (Imām al-Qushayrī), *Laṭā'if al-ishārāt tafsīr ṣūfī kāmil li-al-Qur'ān al-karīm*, ed. Ibrāhīm Baywānī, 5 vols (Cairo: Dār al-Kitāb al-'Arabī, n.d.). For a bibliography of his other works, see 'Abd al-Karīm ibn Hawāzin al-Qushayrī, *Das Sendschreiben al-Qusayris über das Sufitum*, ed. and trans. Richard Gramlich (Wiesbaden: Franz Steiner Verlag, 1989).

her. Their denial saddens by virtue of a lack of respect. And those who followed them did not have a right to do so; they troubled her exceedingly in their oppression. And most of their elders followed their [wrongful] example.

Again the characteristic theme of immoderation is emphasized.

It is said that God substituted a calumniator for Jesus, so he was killed and he was crucified in his place. And it has been said: 'He who digs a pit for his brother is put in it.'[65] And it is said that Jesus said: 'Whoever pleases may have my likeness cast upon him and be killed instead of me.' One of the disciples pleased to do this. Jesus warned him, saying: 'You will not be able to endure the suffering of this pain without faith in the God of creation!' He then recited, VERILY WE WILL NOT SUFFER TO PERISH THE REWARD OF ANY WHO DO A RIGHTEOUS DEED (18:30). Since the man freely offered, Jesus befriended him. Since Jesus was raised to the place of [spiritual] closeness (*zulfa*), the spirit of the one who was sacrificed was raised to the place of [spiritual] nearness (*qurba*).[66]

It is surprising that al-Qushayrī, a follower of al-Sulamī, offers nothing here comparable to the exegesis of Ja'far inasmuch as that *tafsīr* is preserved only in al-Sulamī's *tafsīr*, as was pointed out earlier.[67] What we have is simply the usual substitution legend painted in Sufi colours. The language is punctuated with such terms as *rūḥ*, *nafs*, *zulfa* and *qurba*. In the absence of a study of the author's use of these terms, it is difficult to guess their significance beyond their obvious designations as degrees of spiritual attainment.[68] One can discern, however, an apparent desire to justify Jesus' acceptance of a volunteer substitute. This is seen in

[65] Well-known Arab saying. It is probably an allusion to the story of Joseph.

[66] *Laṭā'if*, vol. 2, pp. 82–3. On *zulfa* and *qurba* as a near-synonymous tropic pair, see Bernd Radtke, 'Some Recent Research on al-Hakim al-Tirmidhi', *Der Islam*, 83, 2006, pp. 39–89.

[67] Assuming al-Sulamī transmitted Ja'far's *tafsīr*. See G. Böwering, 'The Major Sources of Sulamī's Minor Qur'an Commentary', *Oriens*, 35, 1996, pp. 35–56.

[68] Aloys Sprenger's edition of *'Abdur-Razzāq's Dictionary of the Technical Terms of the Ṣūfīs* (Calcutta: Asiatic Society of Bengal, 1845) offers no treatment of *zulfa* or *qurba*. See also R. Hartmann, *al-Kuscharīs Darstellung des Ṣūfītums* (Berlin: Mayer and Müller, 1914). See the new work on Sufi hermeneutics: Kristin Zahra Sands, *Sufi Commentaries on the Qur'an in Classical Islam* (London: Routledge, 2006).

the reference to 18:30. This fact tends to support the analysis of al-Ṭabarī's choice of traditions offered above.

## AL-ZAMAKHSHARĪ (d. 538/1144)

Widely recognized as one of the great exegetes of his time and indeed of the entire Islamic exegetical tradition, al-Zamakhsharī occupies a unique position in the science of *tafsīr*. Cognizant of this prestige, Goldziher devoted one-sixth of his pioneer study of *tafsīr* to this scholar.[69] Muslims have generally held his work in high esteem, even those who do not share his doctrines.[70] One of al-Zamakhsharī's outstanding achievements is his employment of grammatical and linguistic analysis in dealing with the holy text. This is considered by some to be his most valuable contribution to scholarship.[71]

This approach, combined with the author's rationalistic and non-traditional tendencies – usually labelled Mu'tazilī – produces a very different commentary from those which we have so far been studying. Thus we find al-Zamakhsharī going to great lengths to grapple with the sort of questions introduced by al-Ṭūsī, as we shall see below. Inasmuch as this represents a new departure in exegesis, the following detailed examination is presented.

Although no *asānīd* are used, al-Zamakhsharī does begin his commentary of this verse with a reference to tradition by introducing his discussion with the technical term *ruwiya* ('it is related'). First, the speakers of the phrase *rasūl Allāh* are said to be the Jews,

[69] Ignaz Goldziher, *Die Richtungen der Islamischen Koranauslegung,* 2nd edn (Leiden: E.J. Brill, 1952), pp. 117–77.

[70] Smith, op. cit., p. 92, citing James Heyworth-Dunne, *An Introduction to the History of Education in Modern Egypt* (London: Luzac, n.d.), pp. 45–6.

[71] In view of the report that al-Zamakhsharī was not only an exegete but also an accomplished scholar in as many as thirty disciplines, this is a rather spectacular assessment. Smith, op. cit., p. 90. Professor Lane, whose recent book, op. cit., replaces everything previously written on this figure and his *tafsīr*, thinks this number must be an exaggeration (personal communication, July 2007).

who uttered it in ridicule, in the same way that Pharaoh spoke of Moses at Q. 26:27: [PHARAOH] EXCLAIMED: 'BEHOLD, [THIS] YOUR "APOSTLE" WHO [CLAIMS THAT HE] HAS BEEN SENT UNTO YOU IS MAD INDEED!'[72] Then it is related that a group of Jews cursed Jesus and his mother, whereupon Jesus cried out against them and asked God to damn the cavillers. As a result, the Jews were changed into monkeys and swine.[73] The Jews then agreed to kill Jesus, and God informed Jesus that he would raise him to heaven and purify him of association with the offenders. Here al-Zamakhsarī refers to Q. 3:55 in order to confirm this narrative:

> LO! GOD SAID: 'O JESUS! VERILY, I SHALL CAUSE THEE TO DIE, AND SHALL EXALT THEE UNTO ME, AND CLEANSE THEE OF [THE PRESENCE OF] THOSE WHO ARE BENT ON DENYING THE TRUTH; AND I SHALL PLACE THOSE WHO FOLLOW THEE [FAR] ABOVE THOSE WHO ARE BENT ON DENYING THE TRUTH, UNTO THE DAY OF RESURRECTION. IN THE END, UNTO ME YOU ALL MUST RETURN, AND I SHALL JUDGE BETWEEN YOU WITH REGARD TO ALL ON WHICH YOU WERE WONT TO DIFFER.'

Al-Zamakhsharī then relates the familiar story of how Jesus asked his disciples for a volunteer to be killed in his stead. God cast the likeness of Jesus upon a disciple who was subsequently crucified and killed. The exegete mentions that some believe this to have been Judas, who was substituted for Jesus and crucified as a punishment for his betrayal.

That this account is unsatisfactory for al-Zamakhsharī is evident when he details the confusion of the witnesses of these events: 'Some said that Jesus was killed and crucified, and some said, "If that is Jesus, where is our companion, or if that is our companion, where is Jesus?" Some said he was raised to heaven and some said that the face is the face of Jesus, but the body is the body of our companion.'[74]

[72] He also cites Q. 43:9 in the same section.

[73] Maḥmūd b. 'Umar al-Zamakhsharī, *al-Kashshāf 'an ḥaqā'iq ghawāmid al-tanzīl*, 4 vols (Beirut: Dār al-Kitāb al-'Arabī, 1947), vol. 1, p. 396. Cf. Q. 5:60, 2:65, 7:166 and their similarity to Matthew 8:28–30. Cf. above the reference to Abū Hayyān's *Tafsīr*.

[74] *Pace* Robinson, *Christ*, p. 135. *Al-Kashshāf*, vol. 1, p. 396.

It is now that al-Zamakhsharī begins the grammatical discussion that distinguishes his *tafsīr.* A question, very simply posed, asks: to what subject does the verb *shubbiha*, as predicate, refer? We are already aware of the centrality of this word in the exegesis of the verse, having seen the results of previous attempts at its explication in the substitution theories. Al-Zamakhsharī states that if *shubbiha* has Jesus as its subject, then someone or something is likened to him – not the other way around. Since this someone or something is never specified in the Qur'an, such a reading is impossible – presumably because one of the purposes of the Book is to instruct the faithful and an allusion to the unknown cannot be considered instructive. The only alternative then is to read *shubbiha* as referring to the most readily available object at hand, namely the prepositional phrase *lahum.* Thus the understood subject of the verb is the impersonal pronoun, i.e. 'It [the affair of the crucifixion] was made obscure to them.' The gloss – perhaps an illustration from common parlance – *ḥuyyila ilayhi* is presented for *shubbiha lahum*. Thus, the following translation emerges: THEY KILLED HIM NOT NOR DID THEY CRUCIFY HIM, BUT THE AFFAIR WAS IMAGED SO TO THEM.[75]

It is certainly curious that no exegete before al-Zamakhsharī expressed an interest in this question. We have seen an interest in grammar before with al-Zajjāj. But it is still true that no one before al-Zamakhsharī went into such detail on grammatical problems in their *tafsīr.* If it is 'the affair' that is rendered obscure and not Jesus who is 'made similar' to someone else or someone else who is 'made similar' to Jesus, then this makes room for a break with the substitution legend and its use in solving the linguistic problem in the Qur'an. This amounts, in the event, to the 'grammatical acceptance' of the possibility of the Isma'ili *tafsīr* presented earlier, quite apart from what this author may have thought of the Shi'a. In the case of that exegesis, what appeared TO THEM was only the humanity (*nāsūt*) and not the divine eternality (*lāhūt*) of Jesus. Perhaps no need to broaden the understanding of the

[75] Ibid. See also Ayoub, op. cit., p. 13. It is interesting to note that here al-Zamakhsharī adds that *shubbiha* could be the predicate of the pronoun referring to the one killed, the position he seems to have just rejected (Andrew Lane, personal communication).

verse was felt in Sunni exegetical circles before al-Zamakhsharī. Whatever the reason, it is clear that this interpretation was the most significant development in the specific genre of *tafsīr* heretofore encountered, and, as will be seen, it could be questioned whether anything comparable has occurred since.

## AL-BAYḌĀWĪ (d. 685/1286)

As a sequel to our discussion of al-Zamakhsharī, it is appropriate to treat the later popularizer of his *tafsīr*, al-Bayḍāwī. For the most part, the latter simply repeats the former's exegesis, recounting the same traditions except for the inclusion of a name (Ṭaṭānūs) for the Jew who was crucified, and repeating the same grammatical analysis, adding (or perhaps clarifying) that the *tashbīh* that occured was 'between Jesus and the one who was killed [*bayna 'Īsā wa-l-maqtūl*]'.[76] Al-Bayḍāwī also mentions that such a substitution should be considered a miracle, possible only during the time of prophecy (*zamān al-nubuwwa*). God censured the Jews for their boasting and their intention to kill his prophet.

It is interesting that al-Bayḍāwī refutes the idea that the humanity (*nāsūt*) of Jesus was crucified whereas his divinity (*lāhūt*) was raised to heaven.[77] We are not told from where this rejected interpretation comes, but it is a familiar theme and needs no elaboration here. We will see later that the same terminology is stigmatized and ascribed to 'Christians' in the work of al-Ālūsī. That this scholar derived the statement from such a source is possible. It is also conceivable that his source was not so far afield.

[76] 'Abd Allāh b. 'Umar al-Bayḍāwī, *Anwār al-tanzīl wa-asrār al-ta'wīl*, 5 vols (Cairo: Dār al-Kitāb al-'Arabī 1330/1911), vol. 2, pp. 127–8. Cf. Helmut Gatje, *The Qur'an and Its Exegesis: Selected Texts with Classical and Modern Muslim Interpretations*, trans. and ed. Alford T. Welch (London: Routledge & Kegan Paul, 1976), pp. 127–9, where this tradition is translated but without indicating the kind of analysis that follows. This kind of representation is hardly just; indeed, the importance of the exegete's achievement is completely missed in this way, to say nothing of the opportunity to present an alternative Muslim view of the crucifixion.

[77] Al-Zamakhsharī, *Anwār al-tanzīl*, vol. 1, p. 128.

The *Ikhwān al-Ṣafā"*, as we saw above, taught an identical doctrine two centuries earlier.[78] It would be helpful to know with whom al-Bayḍāwī is quarrelling here.

Al-Bayḍāwī says that the Jews did not kill Jesus as they had claimed (*za'ama*), that is with certain knowledge. RATHER, GOD RAISED HIM TO HIMSELF, refuting and rejecting (*radda wa-ankara*) his killing, and verifying (*athbata*) his raising. Nothing is victorious against God's wish to protect Jesus. The terminology here is that of a theological debate and may be thought to reflect an abstraction of the issues rather than an allusion to actual events. Thus it is possible, particularly in light of the preceding grammatical discussion, that al-Bayḍāwī is suggesting a novel interpretation, one in which the Jews are confounded by more mysterious means than have elsewhere been understood.[79]

## AL-RĀZĪ (d. 606/1209)

Fakhr al-Dīn al-Rāzī was a man of diverse and monumental accomplishment. Known as a critic of the Mu'tazila, he produced several works in support of Ash'arite theology in which he freely employed the methods of the Aristotelians and the Mu'tazila. One of these, the *Mafātīḥ al-ghayb*, a commentary on the Qur'an, is considered 'the most comprehensive and inclusive commentary … ever composed'.[80] The *tafsīr* is truly a monument, composed

[78] Ikhwān al-Ṣafā", *Rasā'il* (Cairo: al-Maktaba al-Tijārīya al-Kubrā, 1347/1928). The following translation is from vol. 1, p. 98: 'So Jesus went on the morrow and appeared to the people and summoned them and preached to them until he was seized and taken to the king of the *Banū Isrā'īl*. The king ordered his crucifixion, so his *nāsūt* was crucified, and his hands were nailed to the wooden cross and he stayed crucified from morning.'

[79] Except of course al-Bayḍawī, *Anwār al-tanzīl*, vol. 1, p. 128. His treatment of *yaqīnan* is also worthy of notice. For the first time, verses of poetry are presented in an attempt to treat this *āya:*

> *ka-dhālika tukhbiru 'anhā l-'ālimātu bihā/ wa-qad qataltu bi-'ilmī dhālikum yaqīnan.*

Thus we understand the two worlds completely: 'And with my knowledge I have killed you certainly [*yaqīnan*].'

[80] Smith, op. cit., p. 105.

by one who may represent the high-water mark of Sunni scholarly achievement in the intellectual history of Islam. His role as philosopher, jurist and theologian combined with his vigorous defence of his faith against competing interpretations of Islam, whether Shi'i, Mu'tazili or Sufi, has formed the work as it has come down to us. It is a magisterial arrangement and coordination of all of the resources known and mastered by this exceptional scholar. Thus the work is complex and interconnected to a degree not encountered in earlier works of commentary. It is fair to say that such scholarship has not been encountered since, either. As Smith has observed,

> It is perhaps more difficult to select isolated verses and sections to consider (to dip down into the middle as it were) from this work than from any other of the commentaries considered in this essay. An entire thesis devoted to the *Mafātīḥ* could only begin to penetrate its depth.[81]

Al-Rāzī opens his discussion of 4:157 with a repetition of the tradition found in al-Zamakhsharī, although he does not name his source. He then cites two verses (26:27 and 15:16) to support his opinion that MESSENGER OF GOD was spoken by the Jews in ridicule. Al-Rāzī justifies the appearance of such a distasteful (*qabīḥ*) story because it EXALTS (*rafa'a*) the memory of Jesus. The commentator then observes that there are several questions about this verse that need answering. (Note here the subtly inserted explanation of the key Qur'anic verb *rafa'a* ['to raise'] from 4:158, RATHER GOD RAISED HIM TO HIMSELF.)

The first is the grammatical problem dealt with by al-Zamakhsharī (and later al-Bayḍāwī), which al-Rāzī answers in the same way. The second question pursues the problem introduced by al-Ṭūsī concerning the logical possibility of God transferring the identity of one man to another. Contrary to al-Ṭūsī's *tafsīr*, a detailed answer is presented. Claiming that such a possibility would 'open the door of sophistry', this argument runs,

[81] Smith, op. cit., p. 106. See now Tariq Jaffer, 'Fakhr al-Din al-Razi (d. 606/1210): Philosopher and Theologian as Exegete', PhD dissertation, Yale University, 2005.

> So that if we saw Zayd it would be possible that it was not really Zayd, but that the likeness of Zayd had been cast upon another. This would imply the nullification of social contracts such as marriage and ownership. Also it would lead to the impugning of the principle of *tawātur*, bringing into serious doubt all transmitted historical knowledge. This principle should be upheld as long as it is based on perceived phenomena (*al-maḥsūsāt*). Such confusion about perceived phenomena would threaten the foundations of all religious laws (*shar'īya*). Neither is it permissible to argue for such transference of identity by appealing to the tradition that allows for miracles during the time of prophecy. Such a provision would bring into question the identity of the prophets themselves, which in turn would call into question the probity of the sources of religious knowledge.[82]

In addition to raising the now familiar point about 'miracles during the time of prophecy', al-Rāzī's discussion of 4:158 does not go to the same length or depth as his discussion of the preceding verse. He offers a list of varying traditions (without *asānīd*), which call for the literal (i.e. dramatic) interpretation of Jesus being physically lifted to heaven. Al-Rāzī then adds that these are conflicting theories (*wujūh*) and that God knows best what happened.[83] However, reference to his commentary on 3:55 does offer some clues as to what he might have thought about verse 4:158.

Al-Rāzī's commentary on 3:55 is quite extensive,[84] but a summary of its highlights reveals that he met the issue with creativity and originality. After citing the several traditions referred to above, he says that the verse can mean several other things. One of these is that the deeds of Jesus were raised or accepted by God; the scholar cites 35:10, IT IS HE WHO EXALTS EACH DEED OF RIGHTEOUSNESS. This could mean that by enjoining obedience to Jesus' words upon the people, these words and works were sanctified or raised.[85]

[82] Fakhr al-Dīn al-Rāzī, *Mafātīḥ al-ghayb al-mushtahar bi-al-tafsīr al-kabīr*, 38 vols (Cairo: al-Maṭba'a al-Bahiyya, 1354–7/1935–8), vol. 11, pp. 99–100.
[83] Ibid., vol. 11, p. 100.
[84] Ibid., vol. 9, pp. 71–6.
[85] Ibid., vol. 9, p. 72.

Al-Rāzī dwells at some length on the implications this raising has for anthropomorphism. If Jesus were physically raised to God, then God would have to be located somewhere. Such a thing, for al-Rāzī, is clearly impossible. He then compares the verse with verse 37:99, I WILL GO TO MY LORD, which was spoken by Abraham in the face of opposition by his people. Another alternative is that Jesus was raised to a place ruled only by God, whereas in the world there are diverse peoples with various laws. In Jesus' case, some of these laws were invoked against him. Finally, al-Rāzī says that the raising is one of rank, attesting to Jesus' superiority (*fawqiyya*) – and not to a place.[86]

This review of al-Rāzī'*s tafsīr* has shown a refreshing attempt towards a new understanding of the problems presented in 4:157. Although he certainly stops short of actually affirming the usual Christian idea that Jesus was put on a cross and killed, al-Rāzī, in his criticism of the substitution legend, moves considerably towards such a position. In view of the enormous weight these traditions exerted, it is remarkable that this Ash'arite Shāfi'ī scholar went as far as he did. Our brief examination seems to confirm that his *tafsīr* is less a *tafsīr*, in the classical sense, than it is a philosophical treatise.[87] What is curious, however, is that his commentary on this verse has been virtually neglected by non-Muslims in their missionary efforts.[88] Likewise it is puzzling that this *tafsīr* has had so little influence on later Muslim exegetes.

86 Ibid., vol. 9, pp. 72–3.

87 See Gätje, op. cit., p. 37: '[F]rom the Muslim side, the objection has been raised, and not entirely unjustly, that al-Rāzī goes far beyond the realm of actual exegesis and in many instances misses the purpose.' If this purpose is simply to perpetuate tradition, it might well be asked what 'purpose' any post-Ṭabarī *tafsīr* might have had. Indeed, according to this criterion, the assessment of al-Rāzī is correct. In leaving this exegete, it is unavoidable to ask, as did Smith, op. cit., p. 105, just what his alleged opposition to the Mu'tazila means, particularly in light of his elaboration of themes first introduced with the name of al-Jubbā'ī. On the genre of *tafsīr* see Norman Calder, 'Tafsir from Ṭabarī to Ibn Kathīr: Problems in the Description of a Genre', in *Approaches to the Qur'an*, ed. G.R. Hawting and A.K. Shareef (London: Routledge, 1993), pp. 101–40.

88 Thus Elder, op. cit., p. 245, refers to both al-Bayḍāwī and al-Rāzī but only to quote the tradition translated by Gätje. Elder ignored the extensive criticism of this tradition offered by both exegetes. Such criticism might have been thought to aid the author's argument. Nor does this unfortunate tendency cease with Elder. See also Schedl, op. cit., p. 562. Cf. Robinson, 'Crucifixion'.

## RŪZBIHĀN AL-BAQLĪ (d. 606/1209)

This prolific, influential Sunni Sufi author has been the object of much scholarship in the last fifty years. He is probably best known for his collection of paradoxes and theopathic utterances. He, like al-Qushayri, was an Ash'arite in theology. Part of his enduring legacy is the result of his rehabilitation of al-Ḥallāj.[89] There is only space here to draw attention to his Qur'an commentary, *The Brides of Explanation of the Divine Realities in the Exegesis of the Qur'an.* He isolates only the phrase *wa-lākin shubbiha lahum* from the verse 4:157. His commentary is worth translating directly:

> [Jesus] was a divine spiritual spirit through whom the dead would be brought to life in as much as the light of the divine spirit (*nūr al-ulūhīya*) would come forth (*yabraz*) from him to them. [This is] because God, exalted be He, generously bestowed on him power. So, when God desired to raise him (*rafa'ahu*) to His vicinity, He lifted (*rafa'a*) the veil [i.e. of the body] from his spirit. Then, his spirit appeared (*ẓahara*) to one of his special followers, who became imprinted (lit. *manqūsha* = perhaps 'inscribed') with the spirit's image (*naqsh*). This is because the form (*ṣūra*) of Jesus was conditioned (*manqūsha*) by the character (*naqsh*) of his spirit. [This spirit], as it proceeds from him, is a divine power through which he was given divine support (*mu'ayyad*) to transform external individual existents (or perhaps: identities?; *qalb al-a'yān*). This can only occur from one who is far above (*munazzah*) mixing his divine character (*lāhūt*) with the human body (*nāsūt*). The finest indication of this is that God, exalted be He, knew of the avidity of the Jews and the Christians in their tendency toward anthropomorphism (*tashbīh*) and their shying away from what is holy and [away from the affirmation of] divine transcendence (*tanzīh*). For they are people of imaginary delusions (*aṣḥāb al-makhā'il*). Did you not see the worshipers of the [golden] calf, how [intense] was their love for it? [Cf. e.g. Q. 2:92–3] and the saying of the Christians that God is the Christ (*al-masīḥ*) [Cf. e.g. Qur'an 5:73]? But [the reality is] that He

[89] Carl W. Ernst, *Ruzbihan Baqli: Mysticism and the Rhetoric of Sainthood in Persian Sufism* (Richmond, England: Curzon Press, 1996).

> caused to appear to them the form of Jesus (*fa-shabbaha lahum ṣūrat ʿĪsā*) by means of the medium of [mystic] disguise (*bi-naʿt al-iltibās*) by means of which the self-manifestation of the light of divinity (*tajallī nūr al-lāhūt*) became [clothed/disguised – and therefore 'visible'] with the form of Jesus. Because of their lack of ability to recognize and distinguish the sanctity of the eternal from the characteristics of that which has been temporally generated some of them fell into error [reading *ghalaṭ* for *ghilaẓ*] and spoke of the divinity of Jesus and ʿUzayr, peace be on both of them. Jesus [tried to] apprise them of the place of deception in the [process of mystic] disguise. But they were luckless in [not] seeing it and intended to kill him. Thus God, praised be He, cast the reflection of this likeness on someone [else], as an enticement and a ruse, so that they killed [the latter]. [They did this] because they did not find in him what they found in Jesus [, namely] the sweetness of love and the joy of intense passion. And this loss [of theirs] was due to His raising him to heaven, with His statement, exalted is He, BUT HE RAISED HIM TO HIMSELF. In explaining this, it is said: When God raised him to Himself, He clothed him with feathers, endowed him with light, and severed [from him] the pleasure of food and drink; and [Jesus] then flew with the angels around the Throne, and was an angelic human, celestial and earthly.[90]

While we see here a continuation of the substitution motif, it is important to notice the new style and vocabulary that accompany this exegesis. The first significant development is in the generous use of those terms we encountered above with the Ismaʿili authors: *lāhūt* and *nāsūt*. It is important to note that such terms would become the object of pointed criticism in the exegesis of this verse by al-Bayḍawī (see above). This could indicate that the solution to the problem put forth by the Ismaʿili authors had acquired some popularity by the mid-thirteenth century, at least enough to have to be refuted in the pages of al-Bayḍawī's popularization of al-Zamakhsharī's *tafsīr*. It is also worth noting that it had apparently not been a problem deemed worth mentioning by al-Zamakhsharī himself.

[90] Rūzbihān Baqlī al-Shīrāzī, *ʿArāʾis al-bayān*, vol. 1, p. 166. My thanks to Professor M.E. Marmura for his learned advice on translating this passage.

In addition, we find here an important invocation of that distinctive theory of al-Baqlī – *iltibās* or 'spiritual disguise'. In the context of Rūzbihān's thought, Corbin preferred to translate this word as 'amphiboly' because he felt this best represented the kind of confusion in the 'grammar of perception' that the author was trying to analyse. Indeed, the theory itself would appear to anticipate the famous (or infamous) 'Oneness of Being' theory associated with Ibn al-'Arabī (d. 637/1240). For al-Baqlī, *iltibās* describes the process whereby the question 'emanation or transcendence?' is addressed. Through *iltibās*, God is made present in the world, but disguised by the identities of the various phenomena through which he is made present.[91] Al-Baqlī wants us to appreciate the problems of perception and recognition that he sees as the main subject of this verse. Thus, while the problem of the substitute still haunts the discoursee it is clear that the entire problematic has been elevated far above the 'comedy of errors' enshrined in earlier Sunni exegesis.

## IBN KATHĪR (d. 774/1373)

Abū al-Fidā' lsmā'īl b. 'Umar ibn Kathīr was born near Baṣra in 701/1301. Educated in Damascus, he became an authority on the Shāfi'ī legal method and composed a universal history for which he is best known. His *tafsīr* exhibits a strong reliance upon tradition and is considered by Muslims one of the most important works in the genre.[92] Although it is well known that this student of the influential revisionist-reformer Ibn Taymiyyah (d. 728/1328) was concerned mainly with reiterating the traditional themes of religious science, it is surprising that his *tafsīr* shows nothing of the rational approaches of al-Rāzī. Although it might appear infelicitous to mention such divergent temperaments in the same paragraph, it may be recalled that al-Rāzī carries the

[91] Henry Corbin, *En Islam iranien*, vol. 3, pp. 75–6. See also Carl Ernst, *Ruzbihan Baqli*, pp. 35–44: 'Unveiling and Clothing: The Fundamental Metaphor of Mystical Experience'.

[92] For a discussion of Ibn Kathīr and his work, see Smith, op. cit., pp. 127–30.

title of *mujaddid* for the sixth century, and was an exponent of the same legal school as Ibn Kathīr. We also know that the *tafsīr* of al-Zamakhsharī had by this time acquired wide fame.[93] It is therefore at least somewhat strange that an exegete writing in the fourteenth century could have avoided reference to such commentaries. Nonetheless, this is precisely the case with Ibn Kathīr. Ibn Kathīr's commentary is replete with vilification of the Jews, missing no opportunity to call down the curse of God on those who mocked and envied Jesus' ability to perform miracles (by God's will).

> They disobeyed Jesus and tried to harm him in every possible way, until God led His prophet away from them – Jesus and Mary traveled extensively to avoid such persecution. Ultimately, the Jews notified the King of Syria that there was a man in the holy house who was charming and subverting the people. The king wrote to his deputy in Jerusalem to be on guard against this. Moreover, the deputy was instructed to crucify the culprit (Jesus) and place thorns on his head to stop him from harming the flock. The deputy obeyed the order and led a group of Jews to where Jesus was staying with his twelve or thirteen followers. When Jesus was aware that they were after him, he asked for a volunteer to take his place. One stepped forward and was taken by the Jews and crucified, while Jesus was himself raised through the roof of the house. The Jews then announced that they had crucified Jesus and boasted about it. In their ignorance and lack of intellect, a number of Christians accepted this claim. The fact that the other disciples had seen Jesus raised was ignored. Everyone else thought that the Jews had crucified Jesus.[94]

There is really not much to be said here, except to remark once again how quickly the rationalistic endeavours of Ibn Kathīr's forbears were forgotten. Perhaps the political climate encouraged the anti-Jewish rhetoric – or perhaps it was necessary to assert some kind of uniquely Islamic position because of inter-confessional polemical activity. We must remember that barely a hundred years

[93] Carl Brockelmann, 'al-Zamakhsharī', *EI*[1], vol. 4, p. 1205.

[94] Ibn Kathīr, '*Umdat al-tafsīr*, ed. Aḥmad Muḥammad Shākir, 5 vols (Cairo: Dār al-Ma'ārif, 1376/1957), vol. 4, pp. 28–34. See also Ayoub, op. cit., pp. 12–13.

had elapsed since the cruel and stupendous shock of the fall of Baghdad. In his resort to tradition, Ibn Kathīr may have been seeking refuge in one of the only inviolable sanctuaries left to him.

## AL-SUYŪṬĪ (d. 911/1505)

It is appropriate that we end our study of classical and medieval *tafsīr* with reference to this illustrious student of the Qur'an. As the codifier of Qur'anic sciences, al-Suyūṭī deserves mention if only for the unflinching energy and thoroughness with which he pursued his task as a preserver of the traditional exegesis of the book. He composed two works of exegesis, the first was begun by his teacher Jalāl al-Dīn al-Maḥallī (d. 864/1459) and completed by al-Suyūṭī. This work, the so-called *Tafsīr al-Jalālayn* ('*Tafsīr* of the Two Jalāls') is in the nature of a *vade mecum* commentary. Because of its concision and brevity it is often found printed on the margins of a Qur'an and is thus a handy reference tool for the reader. The other much more extensive work, *al-Durr al-manthūr fī tafsīr bi-al-ma'thūr*, indicates by this title ('[A Collection of] the Scattered Pearls of Authoritative Traditional Exegesis [Based upon Sound *ḥadīth*]') that it will carry none of the philosophical and theological musings found in the work of, for example, Fakhr al-Dīn al-Rāzī. Thus it continues the emphasis on tradition found expressed in the *tafsīr* of Ibn Kathīr. It offers no exciting new interpretations for our verse. Rather, the author lists the usual traditions, complete with *asānīd*, which had by this time acquired new variations in detail.[95]

One variation is his 'History of Religions' attempt to trace the origin of Christian sects to the events surrounding the crucifixion

[95] Jalāl al-Dīn al-Suyūṭī, *al-Durr al-manthūr fi al-tafsīr bi-albi-al-ma'thūr*, 6 vols (Tehran: al-Maṭba'a al-Islāmiyya, 1377/1957), vol. 2, pp. 239–41. While there is nothing new here, an interesting study might compare the ordering of the traditions found here with the ordering, say, in al-Ṭabarī. Such a comparison would likely confirm the observation made above that, far from being a mere invocation of authority, such ordering and sequencing of *aḥādīth* reports represent a certain authorial perspective through deliberate arrangement producing something like an 'exegetical narrative'.

scene. Thus we are told, on the authority of none other than Ibn 'Abbās, that when Jesus asked for a volunteer to take his place on the cross three disciples stepped forward. Jesus rejected the first two for unspecified reasons and the third took his place. Jesus was then raised through the roof and the disciple was crucified. After the crucifixion, his disciples split into three groups: Jacobites, Nestorians and Muslims. The implication is of course that the three volunteers each represented one of these groups. All but the latter became *kāfirūn* and when God sent Muḥammad the Muslims who had existed, presumably on their own and largely unrecognized by the rest of the world since that time, accepted him.[96]

Al-Suyūṭī cites eleven traditions in all, most of which are already familiar to us. There are, however, three we have not encountered so far. These are presented on the authority of Abū Rāfi', Abū al-'Alīya and Ibn 'Abd Allāh b. Sulaymān, respectively.[97] The first two describe the manner in which Jesus ascended to heaven and are brief. The third contains a statement from 'Abd al-Jabbār that Jesus was raised to the place described in 54:55: IN AN ASSEMBLY OF TRUTH, IN THE PRESENCE OF SOVEREIGN OMNIPOTENT.[98]

Reference to his other major exegetical work, the *Tafsīr al-Jalālayn*,[99] simply reveals a restatement of the substitution legend. This commentary is quite short and it is not surprising that al-Suyūṭī wasted no space to identify the characters of the legend by name. In fact, there is not even a mention of the Jews. The speakers of WE KILLED THE MESSIAH are identified only as braggarts (*muftakhirīn*), thus perhaps focusing on the universality of the moral problem rather than the specificity of religious or ethnic community. The object of the divine deception is simply to change the braggarts' certainty (*mu'akkada*) to uncertainty by refuting (*nafā*) their claims (*za'ama*). With regard to 4:158, the only comment made is that God is MIGHTY in his sovereignty and

[96] Ibid., vol. 2, pp. 239–41.

[97] The text gives no biographical or other information for these figures.

[98] Yūsuf 'Alī's translation. Pickthall has: FIRMLY ESTABLISHED IN THE FAVOR OF A MIGHTY KING. For more on 'Abd al-Jabbār's reading of 4:157, see S.M. Stern, 'Quotations from the Apocryphal Gospels in 'Abd al-Jabbār', *Journal of Theological Studies*, 18, 1967, pp. 34–57.

[99] Al-Suyūṭī, *Tafsīr al-imāmayn al-jalālayn* (Damascus: Matkabat al-Milla, n.d.).

WISE in his design, that is, in the way he fooled or perhaps confounded the braggarts.[100]

Although al-Suyūṭī makes no mention in either of his works of the kind of *tafsīr* that culminated in the logical and systematic method of al-Rāzī, he does not find it necessary to castigate the Jews the way Ibn Kathīr did. Al-Suyūṭī is content with the early traditions because they affirm what is for him the most important dimension of the verse, namely that God is ever ready to protect the righteous and humiliate the disdainful. Obviously the importance of the crucifixion for al-Suyūṭī and his traditional ancestors is to be found in the way it illustrates this truth. To expect otherwise would involve a radical, perhaps artificial, change in the attitude of these Muslims towards their unique and profound understanding of the religious life.[101]

## SUMMARY

In summary, our study of classical and medieval exegesis has shown that a need was felt very early to absolve the Christians from spreading 'false' doctrines. Shortly thereafter, criticism of the principle of *mutawātir* ('overwhelmingly attested and continuously transmitted without a break' = a category of *ḥadīth*) was voiced in connection with the traditions. The Twelver Shi'a were the first to introduce rational criticism of the traditions, while the Sufi al-Qushayrī, neglecting Ja'far's method, chose to propagate a substitution theory. Yet, already in the tenth century, the *Ikhwān al-Ṣafā"* and several other Isma'ili authors were able to affirm the historical reality of the crucifixion of Jesus. Later, there appeared extensive criticism of traditions, centring on the problem of identity transfer. Subsequent commentators soon forgot this criticism.

[100] Ibid., p. 135.

[101] See above the lengthy quotation from Gibb in the Introduction.

# 4

## MODERN DEVELOPMENTS

It would be impossible to offer an exhaustive survey of modern exegesis. The number of *tafsīr* works produced in the twentieth century itself bears eloquent witness to the enduring vitality of the relation of Muslims to the Qur'an.[1] Unfortunately, some of the works that should have been included in this section were unavailable or inaccessible. The Urdu commentary of the so-called father of modern exegesis, Sayyid Aḥmad Khān (d. 1316/1898), is one example. While his *tafsīr* is unavailable to me, we do have some indication of his views on the question.

> Crucifixion itself does not cause the death of a man, because only the palms of his hands, or the palms of his hands and feet are pierced ... After three or four hours Christ was taken down from the cross, and it is certain that at that moment he was still alive. Then the disciples concealed him in a very secret place, out of fear of the enmity of the Jews.[2]

[1] For a partial list of modern Egyptian *tafāsīr*, see J.J.G. Jansen, *The Interpretation of the Koran in Modern Egypt* (Leiden: E.J. Brill, 1974), p. 13. As the title implies, the rest of the Muslim world is ignored. Baljon, op. cit., deals in a disappointing way with the exegesis of the Indian subcontinent. See also Charles J. Adams, 'Islamic Religion, II', *Middle East Studies Association Bulletin*, 5(1), 1976, p. 13.

[2] See J.M.S. Baljon, *Modern Muslim Koran Interpretation (1880–1960)* (Leiden: E.J. Brill, 1968), p. 4. This passage is quoted by Geoffrey Parrinder in *Jesus in the Qur'an* (London: Faber & Faber, 1965), p. 13. Al-Ṭabāṭabā'ī makes a similar statement (see below). For a brief discussion of the manner in which crucifixion causes death, see J. Jomier, *Le commentaire coranique du Manâr: tendances modernes de l'exégèse coranique en Egypte* (Paris: Maisonneuve, 1954), p. 130. A discussion of

The 'aesthetic' *tafsīr* of Muḥammad Abū Zayd is another.[3] The well-known *mufassira* Bint al-Shāṭi' might have been included had her *tafsīr* covered the relevant verses.[4]

Furthermore, much modern commentary is true to the exegetical tradition in that it is quite repetitive. A few exegetes are considered representative of a distinct approach to exegesis and an attempt has been made to select authors from this group. A number of major authors from different cultural and geographic areas has been chosen with the hope of indicating the kind of diversity one may expect to find in modern exegesis. The first authors are the 'pre-modern' al-Kāshānī and al-Ālūsī,[5] followed by Rashīd Riḍā, Sayyid Quṭb, Mawdūdī, al-Ṭabāṭabā'ī and others.

## AL-KĀSHĀNĪ (d. 1091/1680)

With this Shi'i author we are given the possibility of a confluence or rapprochement between the divided Shi'i exegsis we encountered earlier. Mullā Muḥammad Muḥsin Fayḍ al-Kāshānī was one of the more remarkable Muslim scholars of the last five hundred years. He produced innumerable works on law, theology and philosophy and also wrote poetry. His life, work and accomplishments still need to be critically assessed. But for our purposes here, there is more than enough available from two of his unique and noteworthy works. The first is his monumental *Tafsīr* written for the Safavid Shah, and the second is his brief handbook entitled *The Hidden Words* (*al-Kalimāt al-maknūna*).[6] The first is

Sir Sayyid's exegetical method is provided in Daud Rahbar, 'Sir Sayyid Aḥmad Khān's Principles of Exegesis', *Muslim World*, 46, 1956, pp. 104–12, 324–35.

[3] See Arthur Jeffery, 'The Suppressed Qur'ān Commentary of Muḥammad Abū Zaid', *Der Islam*, 20, 1932, pp. 301–8.

[4] See 'Ā'isha 'Abd al-Raḥmān, *al-Tafsīr al-bayānī lil-Qur'ān al-karīm*, 2 vols (Cairo: Dār al-Ma'ārif, 1962–9). A partial treatment of her thought is found in Issa J. Boullata, 'Modern Qur'an Exegesis: A Study of Bint al-Shāṭi''s Method', *Muslim World*, 64, 1974, pp. 103–13. For her rather candid remarks regarding the crucifixion, see below.

[5] Smith, op. cit., p. 174.

[6] Al-Kāshānī, *al-Ṣāfī*, vol. 2, p. 518.

entirely in Arabic, the second in equal parts Arabic and Persian. Al-Kāshānī is considered one of the founders and consolidators of post-Safavid Twelver Shi'ism and is ranked on a par with the earlier scholars, such al-Ṭūsī, examined above.

His views on the crucifixon continue the theme of typological figuration encountered earlier but with the added factor of a new cosmology and ontology that had been developing through the work of such influential scholars as Avicenna, al-Suhrawardī, Ibn al-'Arabī and al-Kāshānī's own teacher Mullā Ṣadrā (d. 1050/1640). This new cosmology and ontology include a dimension of reality called 'The World of Images' (*'ālam al-mithāl*). And though its reality seems to have been accepted at this time throughout the wider Muslim world, it had special importance within Shi'ism. As a philosophical and metaphysical postulate apparently beyond dispute, this World of Images supplied a rational answer to such questions arising from within Shi'ism as 'How could the Hidden Imam have lived so long?' It also provided a 'place' for the heretofore untenably irrational, or perhaps better, supra-rational dogma of bodily resurrection. The World of Images solved such problems as well as many others.[7]

In Al-Kāshānī's *tafsīr* we find the following:

> AND THEIR SAYING VERILY WE KILLED THE MESSIAH, JESUS SON OF MARY THE MESSENGER OF GOD
> BUT THEY DID NOT KILL HIM AND THEY DID NOT CRUCIFY HIM, RATHER IT APPEARED SO TO THEM

Al-Kāshāni says that the key to this episode is found in the understanding of Qur'an 3:55:

> LO! GOD SAID: 'O JESUS! VERILY, I SHALL CAUSE THEE TO DIE, AND SHALL EXALT THEE UNTO ME'

[7] Henry Corbin, *Spiritual Body and Celestial Earth: From Mazdean Iran to Shí'ite Iran*, trans. N. Pearson (Princeton, NJ: Princeton University Press, 1977), pp. 177–81. See also the same author's *The Man of Light in Iranian Sufism*, trans. Nancy Pearson (Boulder, CO/London: Shambhala, 1978), esp. pp. 125–8; and Todd Lawson, 'Ahmad Ahsa'i and the World of Images', in *Shi'ite Streams and Dynamics in Modern Times*, ed. D. Hermann and S. Mervin (Tehran/Paris: IFRI, Presses Universitaires d'Iran, in press).

Here the object is to demonstrate the great vanity and arrogance of those who claim to have killed Jesus.

> VERILY, THOSE WHO DISAGREE ABOUT IT ARE TRULY IN DOUBT ABOUT IT
>
> It is said that when this thing happened the people disagreed. One/some of the Jews lying said: 'We really killed him.' Others refuted this and one of them said: 'If this is Jesus, then where is our companion?' And another said 'The face is the face of Jesus, while the body is the body of our companion.' And he said 'Who has heard that God will raise me to heaven he raised to heaven.' And a group (*qawm*) said: 'His *nāsūt* was crucified and his *lāhūt* ascended.'
>
> AND THEY HAVE NO KNOWLEDGE EXCEPT THEY FOLLOW MERE CONJECTURE

They are followers of conjecture.

> AND THEY DID NOT KILL HIM CERTAINLY

as they claimed. This verse confirms the denial of killing, that it was not in reality (*ḥaqqan*).

> NAY, RATHER GOD EXALTED HIM UNTO HIMSELF – AND GOD IS INDEED ALMIGHTY, WISE.

Al-Kāshānī now cites several *ḥadīth* reports, one of which, from the *Ikmāl al-dīn* by the important Twelver founding father *Shaykh al-Ṣadūq* Ibn Bābawayh (d. 381/991), is of special interest here:

> In *al-Ikmāl* on the authority of the Prophet ... Jesus son of Mary came to the Holy House and he dwelt there calling them and wanting for them the things of God for 33 years until the Jews sought him, intent upon punishing him and they buried him alive. And some claimed that they killed him and crucified him. But God would not give them the authority and power (*salṭana*) to do such a thing against him. IT ONLY APPEARED TO THEM SO. They had no power to punish him and bury him not to mention KILL

HIM AND CRUCIFY HIM. They had no power to do that because it would go against (*takdhib*) His Word nay, God EXALTED him unto Himself after he had called him.

AND GOD IS INDEED ALMIGHTY

and will not be confounded with regard to his desire,

WISE

in what he disposes for his servants.[8]

In another work of al-Kāshānī's that impinges upon an understanding of this verse, we read that Jesus is alive in his reality in that realm mentioned earlier, the World of Images. This is also where the Hidden Imam may be thought to reside in his occultation and from where he will arise at the appointed time to make his appearance (*ẓuhūr*, a word Corbin typically and suggestively translates as 'parousia'). It is an event *of* the World of Images. He quotes Ibn Bābawayh again: 'The descent of Jesus to the Earth is his return to this world after being carried away from this world,' because God himself proclaims, 'IT IS I WHO RECEIVE YOU AND I WHO CARRY YOU OFF TOWARD MYSELF, AND DELIVER YOU FROM THOSE WHO DENY YOU ... UNTIL THE RESURRECTION DAY' (Q. 3:48). In addition, Corbin points out that Shi'i teaching includes the return of people who had died in earlier generations, at the time of the *ẓuhūr* or advent of the Hidden Imam. This includes both such people who are recognized to have been among the specially preferred disciples of the imams and also particularly virulent enemies. Thus the apocalyptic imagination of Shi'ism supplies a scenario for the eschaton; whether this scenario is to be read in purely gnostic terms or not is impossible to determine here. But this is how, according to al-Kāshānī, such verses as Q. 4:157 are to be understood, in their spiritual dimension.[9] Corbin elaborates:

[8] Fayḍ al-Kāshānī, *Tafsīr al-Ṣāfī*, vol. 1, p. 518.

[9] See the translation of al-Kāshāni's *Kalimāt al-maknūna* in Corbin, *Spiritual Body*, pp. 178–9. It should be stressed that it is far from clear that either al-Kāshānī or his teacher Mullā Ṣadrā taught that the Hidden Imam resided *only* in the World of Images. My thanks to Mr Omid Ghaemmaghami for making the problematic of this topic more precise. It is a topic that we shall return to in future.

> It is known that Qur'anic Christology is determinedly docetist (3:48, 4:156 [sic]). So, although the text of Muḥsin Fayḍ here says *ba'd mawtihi*, one should read *ba'd raf'ihi*, in keeping with all the Shi'ite traditions on this point ... Jesus was 'carried away' to Heaven like Khiẓr-Elijah, Idrīs-Enoch, and kept apart until the Resurrection. It is precisiely thanks to the world of Hūrqalyā [or World of Images] that the Christology of this Islamic prophetology is docetist, yet without turning the person of Christ, so to speak, into a phantasm. Later on, the reader will see the deep meaning which the idea of the hidden Imām acquires: it is men who have made themselves incapable of seeing him and have hidden him from themselves. In the same way, his enemies, in denying Jesus his prophetic message, have obscured him from themselves: he who they believed they had put to death was no longer here (4:157), and he is never there when one interprets events by historical materialism, under the guise of theology, instead of grasping the spiritual history 'in Hūrqalyā.'[10]

## AL-ĀLŪSĪ (d. 1270/1854)

Abū al-Thanā' al-Ālūsī was the son of a Sunni scholarly family of Baghdād. By the age of thirteen, he was already a teacher and author. Eventually, he came to be considered by his peers one of the most eminent scholars of Iraq. According to Smith, al-Ālūsī's *tafsīr* is important for its organized treatment of a great mass of earlier material, some of which is unavailable elsewhere. In this work, we find no analysis of *asānīd* – only the citation of traditions with some theological discussion. This method is later adopted and elaborated by the authors of the *Tafsīr al-manār*. Thus, al-Ālūsī is seen to be a link between the classical and modern commentators.[11]

Al-Ālūsī divides 4:157 into the usual exegetical units: The boastful statement of the Jews is compared with the taunt of the

[10] Ibid.

[11] For a more complete general discussion, see Smith, op. cit., pp. 174–5. A study of some aspects of his *tafsīr* is provided in Harris Birkeland, *The Lord Guideth: Studies on Primitive Islam* (Uppsala, Sweden: Almqvist & Wiksells, 1956), passim.

*kāfirūn* found in 15:6; MESSENGER OF GOD is said to be spoken by the Jews in ridicule;[12] and WA-LĀKIN SHUBBIHA LAHUM is God's counter-assertion (*i'tirāḍ*) against the perfidious claim. The familiar legends from Wahb are then offered. It is here that al-Ālūsī's Shi'i source is apparent,[13] for what follows is almost an exact quotation from al-Ṭūsī – including a statement from al-Jubbā'ī,[14] although the former's name is not mentioned. Surprisingly, although credit is not given to him by name, the grammatical analysis of al-Zamakhsharī is also included. However, al-Ālūsī does not dwell on the latter contribution at length, but simply characterizes it as one statement among many.[15]

At this point, al-Ālūsī digresses from the usual type of exegetical discussion to offer some criticism of the Christologies of two Christian groups. Beginning with 'Some of the Christians say his *nāsūt* was crucified but his *lāhūt* was not,' the exegete takes to task the Jacobites and the orthodox (*al-rūm*). He proves the inconsistency of their arguments by holding the Christians to their own doctrine of Jesus' unity of being.[16] It is also possible that his unspoken reference is to the Isma'ili ideas encountered earlier.

According to al-Ālūsī, the Christians and Jews are both said to be FULL OF DOUBT about the crucifixion. *Yaqīnan* has the obvious (*ẓāhir*) meaning that the Jews did not kill Jesus. He then cites Ibn Qutayba's discussion, but notes that Ibn Qutayba means the Jews did not know who Jesus was – rather than: the Jews did not kill their doubt about the matter. Here we find agreement with the views of 'Abd al-Jabbār. Al-Suddī is said to have connected *yaqīnan* to *rafa'a* in the following verse to mean that God

[12] This is in marked contrast to Riḍā.

[13] Abū al-Thanā' al-Ālūsī, *Ruḥ al-ma'ānī fī tafsīr al-Qur'ān al-'aẓīm*, 11 vols (Deoband: Idāra al-Ṭaba'āt al-Muṣṭafiyya, n.d.), vol. 4, p. 10.

[14] The material credited to al-Jubbā'ī is slightly different from that found in al-Ṭūsī and al-Ṭabarsī.

[15] *Ruḥ al-ma'ānī*, vol. 7, p. 10, here reads 'wa-yaqūl …'

[16] *Ruḥ al-ma'ānī*, vol. 7, p. 11. This concern with Christian sects in *tafsīr* – as distinct from classical heresiographies such as those of Ibn Ḥazm and Shahrastānī – was first encountered in al-Suyūṭī. Notice also the terminological similarity with the *Ikhwān al-Ṣafā'*, but here the source is positively identified as Christian. Cf. also Bayḍāwī, op. cit.

certainly raised Jesus in order to counter the Jewish boast.[17] Clearly, al-Ālūsī prefers the substitution interpretation, and, after some discussion, closes the subject with MIGHTY, WISE, that is, God is mighty and wise in having cast the likeness upon someone else.[18]

Although al-Ālūsī touches upon most of the exegetical history of the verse he makes no reference to the position articulated and presumably held by al-Rāzī. His selective and superficial treatment of the earlier exegetes depends for its success upon a lack of familiarity with their writings among al-Ālūsī's readership. The author himself must have been aware of other commentators, for he has culled from various exegetes those statements that either support or embellish his own thesis.[19] Such selectivity has the effect of making the author appear qualified for the prodigious demands of *tafsīr*, while at the same time allowing him to avoid ideas he does not choose to discuss. As we have seen, this trend towards selectivity began very early, but al-Ālūsī is here singled out because of his comparatively blatant employment of such tactics. As will become more apparent, this is one more feature that links this author to twentieth-century exegesis.

## TAFSĪR AL-MANĀR

A few words of introduction are in order before proceeding directly to the exegesis contained in this work. Although it was begun by Muḥammad 'Abduh (d. 1323/1905), the famous reformer was able only to comment up to verse 4:125. Rashīd Riḍā (d. 1354/1935) completed the work as it is available up to 12:25. The problem of a discrepancy of thought between the master and his disciple is

[17] This comment has not been met with before and confirms al-Ālūsī's value as a source for otherwise unavailable material. Smith, op. cit., p. 174.

[18] *Ruḥ al-ma'ānī*, vol. 6, p. 12.

[19] For example, his tacit allusion to al-Zamakhsharī. But the source could just as easily have been al-Rāzī. If this is the case, then the phenomenon is even more acute, inasmuch as the latter handily dispensed with the possibility of a transference of identity.

well known. Though it is quite beside the point of this study, some discussion of it will be seen to be relevant.[20] Following Smith, Rashīd Riḍā is considered the author of the *tafsīr*.

## RASHĪD RIḌĀ (d. 1354/1935)

Rashīd Riḍā, like his master Muḥammad ʻAbduh, was partly educated in Europe. However, he was not influenced positively by this education to the same degree as his teacher. Before founding the journal *al-Manār* in 1898, Riḍā had been a confirmed Syrian nationalist. Thus, it is possible to read some political concerns into his commentary. The outstanding feature of his exegesis of 4:157 is its polemical nature in which the argument is supported, in part, by appealing to the Qur'an in the light of 'scientific' statements from various sources. It should not be inferred from this that Riḍā indulged in so-called 'scientific exegesis'. In fact, he opposed this type of exegesis.[21]

His commentary on the crucifixion in *Tafsīr al-manār* is in two sections. The first is presented along the lines of traditional 'interlinear' exegesis. The second and much longer section is a detailed discussion of the soundness of the Christian creed (*ʻaqīda*) of the crucifixion. We begin with a detailed summary of the former.

The verse is divided into the usual five segments for the purpose of detailed explanation. Riḍā agrees with his predecessors that VERILY, WE KILLED THE MESSIAH, JESUS SON OF MARY is spoken by the Jews in extreme insolence (*bi-muntahā al-jur'a*) and boastful ridicule. It is interesting that the author reads MESSENGER OF GOD not as Jewish sarcasm but as the Qur'anic affirmation of Jesus' apostleship as opposed to the divinity ascribed to him by Christians.[22] AND THEY DID NOT KILL HIM, NOR DID THEY CRUCIFY

[20] Smith, op. cit., p. 187; Jansen, op. cit., pp. 18–34. The outstanding in-depth analysis of the commentary at hand is Jomier, op. cit.

[21] Jansen, op. cit., p. 53.

[22] Muḥammad Rashīd Riḍā, *Tafsīr al-Qur'ān al-karīm, al-shahīr bi-tafsīr al-manār*, 2nd edn, 12 vols (Cairo: Dār al-Manār, 1367–75/1948–56), vol. 6, p. 18. Here the author cites John 17:3, 'And this is eternal life, that they know thee the

HIM means that the Jews, contrary to their claims, which they had spread among the people, did not kill Jesus. WA-LĀKIN SHUBBIHA LAHUM signifies that what really happened was uncertain for them. They thought (*ẓannū*) they had crucified Jesus, whereas they had really crucified another (*ghayrahi*) – a double (*al-shabah*). This uncertainty is comparable to the doubt or confusion (*al-ishtibāh*) that happens in all periods of time. AND THOSE WHO DISAGREE ABOUT IT ARE FULL OF DOUBTS ABOUT IT. THEY HAVE NO KNOWLEDGE, ONLY CONJECTURE TO FOLLOW means that the 'People of the Book' who disagreed about the matter of Jesus' crucifixion are in doubt about the truth of the affair. They are in confusion (*ḥayra*), are unsure (*taraddud*), have no conclusive (*thābit qāṭi'*) knowledge, but simply follow conjecture (*ẓann*).

So far, Riḍā has done little more than repeat the Qur'anic language or derivations of Qur'anic roots. Other than this, the *tafsīr* is distinguished by the immediate introduction of polemics. This theme is greatly expanded in the second section, to be dealt with partially in due course. For now, let us return to the text. The DOUBT, Riḍā says, was complete. None of the witnesses was free of it. The account that reports that Jesus was crucified is simply one of a number of conflicting opinions that happened to gain ascendancy over others. Because of all these conflicting stories, it is not possible to say what really happened.[23] Those who followed CONJECTURE in this matter were individuals who glazed (*zajjajū*)[24] what actually occurred with DISAGREEMENT about the events or with their own fancy or desire. The true interpretation can be found in the conventional meaning of *shakk*. Its meaning is 'ignorance' (*jahl*), that is, to be deprived of clarity (*istibāna*) of mind concerning a given matter. Riḍā then cites two poets to support this definition and sums up his argument by

only true God, and Jesus Christ whom thou hast sent,' to argue against the divinity of Jesus by confounding the Christians with their own book (which incidentally he declares to be untrustworthy). Thus the commentary immediately assumes a polemical rather than a purely exegetical function. See also Ayoub, op. cit., p. 30.

[23] *Tafsīr al-manār*, vol. 6, p. 18. Riḍā draws support for this conclusion by claiming to use the methods of the logicians: '*kamā yaqūl 'ulamā' al-manṭiq*.' Thus he is able to be seen as a modern rationalist.

[24] Ibid. The text has *zaḥḥajū*, which is probably a misprint for *zajjajū*.

invoking the famous classical Arabic lexicon *Lisān al-'arab* as stating that *al-shakk* is the antonym (*ḍidd*) of *al-yaqīn* and thus implies CONJECTURE (*ẓann*). In other words, the doubt surrounding the crucifixion is indecision (*taraddud*) about whether Jesus or another was killed. None of the witnesses had certain knowledge (*'ilm yaqīnī*), since they were following CONJECTURE (*ẓann*). Riḍā then quotes Matthew 26:31: 'You will all fall away (lit. 'doubt') from me this night' (*kullikum tashukkūna fīya fī hādhihi al-layla*).[25] He concludes that if those who knew Jesus best were in doubt about the situation then it is not impossible that a mistake in identity occurred. In any case, the whole story is based upon an imperfectly transmitted historical account.

Riḍā goes on to say that *mā qatalūhu yaqīnan* means they did not kill Jesus with a certain killing (*qatlan yaqīnan*), nor were they sure (*mutayaqqinīn*) that the victim was none other than he because they (the Jews) did not really know who Jesus was. He then recounts the familiar story in which Judas was asked by the Jews to lead them to Jesus. Riḍā says that according to the *Gospel of Barnabas*, a mistake was made and the Jews took Judas. There was no disagreement about whom they had seized, even though none of the Jews knew who Jesus was to begin with.[26] Riḍā then refers to the treatment of the word *yaqīnan* first encountered as a lemma in Ibn Qutayba. He mentions no source here, his only comment coming in the introductory 'and it is also said'. The author cites the tradition (on the authority of Ibn 'Abbās) that interprets the statement as 'They did not kill their conjecture with certainty.' According to Riḍā, the accounts of the *mufassirūn bi-al-ma'thūr* are in disagreement on this point because their information came from Jews and Christians and neither group had certain knowledge about the affair. But, he adds, all of these

[25] Notice the presence of the Qur'anic root *sh-k-k*.

[26] Ibid., p. 19. *The Gospel of Barnabas* was first published in England by Lonsdale and Laura Ragg (Oxford: Clarendon Press, 1907). It was translated by the Raggs from an Italian manuscript and contained a critical introduction. This extensive assessment was deleted in the later Arabic translation, executed under the direction of Rashīd Riḍā, published by the Manār Press (see Jomier, op. cit., p. 128). The Ragg edition is quite rare and, as such, was unavailable to me. I have consulted instead L. Cirillo and M. Frémaux's edition (see n. 74). The relevant passage here is on pp. 545–6.

early exegetes agree that Jesus was saved and another was killed in his place.[27]

Rashīd Riḍā's treatment of 4:157 is a mixture of reference to philological discussion and tradition and his own critique of Christian scriptures and doctrine. Noticeably lacking is the grammatical analyses of the rationalists and the discussion about the acceptability of transference of identity. That discussion reached its highest development with al-Rāzī and becomes particularly conspicuous by its absence when this commentator is referred to in the treatment of 4:158. Riḍā cites al-Rāzī by name when he offers the latter's argument that Jesus was not raised to an actual place. It is thus obvious that Riḍā was extremely selective in what he chose to use from the works of early *mufassirūn.*

Riḍā refers the reader to the *tafsīr* of 3:55 for a better understanding of 4:158. This former verse was commented upon by 'Abdūh himself, but Riḍā takes the opportunity to offer an original comment. He argues quite strongly that Jesus was raised in both body and spirit, although it is not clear to whom this argument is addressed. Riḍā says that it is well known among the exegetes 'and others' that God raised Jesus because Muḥammad saw him in the second heaven during the *mi'rāj.* This means that not only Jesus but also the other prophets whom Muḥammad saw in the other heavens were raised in body and spirit. He ends his discussion of these two verses by admitting that some scholars reject his interpretation and he allows that *tafsīr is* not a proper place in which to find a solution because the Qur'an itself is not firm (*lam yathbut*) about these questions.[28]

The most significant development here is Riḍā's use of the *Gospel of Barnabas*.[29] Riḍā was the first exegete to rely upon the

[27] *Tafsīr al-manār*, vol. 6, p. 20.

[28] Riḍā's reference here to the *mi'rāj* is (except for the oblique allusion noticed in Muqātil above) indeed an original one. It is of course quite possible that the *mi'rāj* tradition was so firmly a part of their religious view that the earlier commentators thought direct reference to it redundant. It is clear that the tradition has influenced, at least partially, the acceptability of a substitution theory that required the physical ascension of Jesus. See Geo Widengren, *Muḥammad the Apostle of God, and His Ascension (King and Savior V)* (Uppsala, Sweden: Almqvist & Wiksells, 1955), esp. pp. 96–114.

[29] A most comprehensive discussion of *Barnabas* is Louis Cirillo and M. Frémaux, *Evangile de Barnabé* (Paris: Beauchesne, 1977). For Riḍā's use of *Barnabas*,

*Gospel of Barnabas* and this reliance is seen to be the cause of some of the inconsistencies in his argument. For example, Riḍā condemns the Christian canon as unreliable but is able to accept the apocryphal *Barnabas* at face value. Jomier has pointed out that because *Barnabas* agrees with the Qur'an, Riḍā had no reason to reject it.[30] Riḍā dispenses with the legends of the *mufassirūn bi-al-ma'thūr* because of their Christian and Jewish provenance and asserts, solely on the testimony of the *Gospel of Barnabas*, that Jesus was not crucified. This, of course, presents an illusory break with tradition. Riḍā is now a 'modern' exegete, but his intractability about the crucifixion raises the question of just how modern Riḍā would have been without *Barnabas*.

The second section of Riḍā's discussion of the crucifixion is far too lengthy to summarize in detail here. His basic task is to refute the crucifixion and attack the idea of redemption in Christianity. He repeats his criticism of the poorly transmitted gospels, arguing that many important sources have been lost or destroyed. He then goes on to argue at great length for the possibility of a substitution for Jesus on the cross, citing past judicial errors involving mistaken identity. He even uses the Ahmadiyya argument that Jesus went off like Moses to die alone and his tomb is now in Kashmir.[31]

see Jomier, op. cit., pp. 128–30. See also the excellent 'Exkurs' on the crucifixion in the major work on *Barnabas* by Christine Schirrmacher, *Mit den Waffen des Gegners: christlich–muslimische Kontroversen im 19. und 20. Jahrhundert, dargestellt am Beispiel der Auseinandersetzung um Karl Gottlieb Pfanders 'Mîzân al-ḥaqq' und Raḥmatullâh ibn Ḫalîl al-'Uṯmânî al-Kairânawîs 'Iẓhâr al-ḥaqq' und der Diskussion über das Barnabasevangelium* (Berlin: K. Schwarz Verlag, 1992), pp. 357–83.

[30] See Jomier, op. cit., p. 128. It is, I think, a matter of opinion whether the two agree.

[31] This reference raises the subject of the Aḥmadiyya interpretation of this verse. As is well known, this version of Islam teaches that Jesus was certainly not killed on the cross, but remained alive and eventually made his way to Kashmir, where his tomb is now an object of pilgrimage and veneration. The interested reader is referred to Yohanan Friedmann, *Prophecy Continuous: Aspects of Ahmadi Religous Thought and Its Medieval Background* (Berkeley: University of California Press, 1989), pp. 6, 28–9, 112–16, 156. Similarly, another nineteenth-century modernist development, the Bahā'ī Faith, is interesting for the opposite reason that it finds no difficulty in affirming the historicity of the crucifixion of Jesus. The roots of this may go back to thinkers like Fayḍ al-Kāshānī and the much earlier Abū al-Futūḥ al-Rāzī who provided, as we have seen, 'hermeneutic space' for such an interpretation

Riḍā, ultimately dependent upon the *Gospel of Barnabas*, says that Judas was the one crucified.

The commentary offered in the *Tafsīr al-manār* raises questions that continue to confine the discussion of the crucifixion in modern exegesis. It is interesting to note that even Rashīd Riḍā confesses that the Qur'an itself is not definitive on this question. It appears, however, that even at this early period of the twentieth century the problem was complicated by the appearance of the *Gospel of Barnabas* and the rise of the Ahmadiyya movement. That these factors gained such importance is the result of the pressures of the Christian missionary effort. Ayoub, speaking of Riḍā and 'Abduh, writes, 'their polemical arguments against Christianity must be seen in the context of Christian polemics against Islamic tradition, both in its religion and culture'.[32] Riḍā himself tells us of his experience in a Cairo church when he was asked to leave because he'd interrupted the sermon with questions pertaining to Christian doctrine.[33] It is therefore possible that such an atmosphere of confrontation would tend to emphasize the differences – rather than similarities – of the two religious groups. Thus, Riḍā willingly dispenses with the evidence that might undermine the reliability of sources such as the *Gospel of Barnabas*, in order to assert what he perceives to be the Islamic view of Jesus' prophethood and mission.

## SAYYID QUṬB (d. 1386/1966)

This author of a complete *tafsīr* was born in Egypt in 1906. He was educated in the traditional manner and graduated from the

from within Islam. There seems to be little doubt that this also depended on the earlier work of those Isma'ili scholars we looked at earlier. A recent discussion of the problem is Mina Yazdani, 'The Death of Jesus as Reflected in the Bahá'í Writings', presentation to American Academy of Religion (AAR) Regional Conference, McGill University, Montreal, Summer 2006. See also Juan R. Cole, 'Behold the Man: Baha'u'llah on the Life of Jesus', *Journal of the American Academy of Religion*, 65(1), 1997, pp. 47–71.

32 Ayoub, op. cit., p. 32. For a good account of the non-exegetical section of the *tafsīr*, see Jomier, op. cit., pp. 311–13.

33 *Tafsīr al-manār*, vol. 6, p. 25.

*Dār al-'ulūm* in 1933. He appears to be the only commentator discussed in these pages, other than Mawdūdī, to have visited North America. After a two-year stay in the United States, he returned to Egypt in 1945 and became very active in the popular Muslim Brotherhood. His duties in the movement included the editorship of its official organ, the *Majallat al-ikhwān al-muslimīn*, along with other writing projects. After an attempt on the life of 'Abd al-Nāṣir, Sayyid Quṭb was imprisoned for nine years. Released, he quickly took up his political activities and was returned to prison. The publication of his critical *Ma'ālim al-ṭarīq* brought the government's wrath upon him. The author's refusal to moderate his activities caused him to be hanged in 1966.[34]

Among his non-political writings (although it may be reasonably questioned to what extent any of this dedicated man's work could be considered non-political), this *tafsīr* is accepted as a valid contribution to Qur'anic science.[35] The work has been characterized as an 'enormous collection of sermons'[36] rather than a strict commentary. Nonetheless, given its wide circulation and influence among Muslims,[37] it must be treated here.

Quṭb sees verses 4:157–8 in the general context of the divine reprimand of the Jews, although the Christians are also singled out by these verses for their conjectures about the crucifixion. Contrary to Riḍā, he maintains that MESSENGER OF GOD is spoken by the Jews in ridicule. According to Quṭb, since 'history' is silent on the details of Jesus' birth and death (*nihāya*), these things cannot be terribly important.[38] In any case, no one has spoken of the crucifixion in certainty. It is very difficult to determine exactly what happened because the events happened very fast and were confused by contradictory reports. We have only the word of God to properly guide us in this question.[39]

[34] Smith, op. cit., pp. 203–7.
[35] Smith, op. cit., p. 205.
[36] Jansen, op. cit., p. 79, n. 15.
[37] The *tafsīr* has been translated into Turkish and Persian and Urdu. It is quite possibly the most widely read Qur'an commentary of our time.
[38] Sayyid Quṭb, *Fī ẓilāl al-Qur'ān*, 7th edn, 8 vols (Beirut: Dār Iḥyā' al-Turāth al-'Arabī, 1391/1971), vol. 4, pp. 586–7.
[39] Ibid., vol. 4, p. 587.

Quṭb goes on to say that the fourth gospel that recounts the spiritually disgusting (*qabīḥ*) story of Jesus' crucifixion, death and resurrection was written after the weakening (*fatra*) of Jesus' covenant (*'ahd*). The whole story was suppressed (*iḍṭihād*) in his religion (*diyāna*) and for his followers. Therefore, it is difficult to ascertain what really happened in such an environment of secrecy and fear.[40] Many other gospels had also been written, but this fourth gospel was chosen officially near the end of the second century CE. For this reason it is not above suspicion (*al-shubuhāt*[!]).[41]

One of the gospels that was written before the fourth gospel and received official sanction was the *Gospel of Barnabas* (*injīl barnābā*). It disagrees with the canonical gospels about the crucifixion and death of Jesus. Quṭb then inserts a lengthy quotation from *Barnabas* that tells of Judas leading the Jews and Roman soldiers to arrest Jesus. According to this account, it was late at night and Jesus and the disciples were sleeping. When Judas entered the house, Jesus was carried to heaven by angels and his image and voice were cast upon Judas. Unaware that this had happened, Judas awakened the disciples to ask them where Jesus had gone. The disciples, recognizing Jesus, thought he was merely disturbed with the fear of death. Although the quotation stops here, the gospel goes on to add that Judas was seized by the Jews and Romans, his protests were considered the ravings of a madman and he was crucified. Jesus appeared three days later to his mother and the rest of his followers to reassure them and announce the coming of Muḥammad, who was to fulfil all that Jesus had taught.[42]

Sayyid Quṭb then says that we cannot be certain about these events which occurred in the darkness of night; nor can we determine exactly who DISAGREED about them in choosing one story over another. The Qur'an does not offer details about Jesus' being raised to God – whether it was in body or in spirit – or when and where his death occurred. 'But they did not kill him and they did not crucify him, but the killing and crucifixion happened to

[40] Ibid. This comment could be seen as an indictment of Quṭb's Egypt, thereby calling into question the 'apolitical' nature of his *tafsīr*.
[41] Ibid.
[42] Ibid., vol. 4, pp. 587–8. Cf. Cirillo and Frémaux, op. cit., pp. 539–45.

one who was made to look like him exactly' (*'alā man shubbiha lahum siwāhu*). The Qur'an does not offer details about this other person. We have only the statement in 3:55. But this gives no details about the death, its nature or its date. Quṭb says that he chooses to take refuge 'in the shade of the Qur'an' (*fī ẓilāl al-Qur'an*, the title of his commentary), and therefore does not refer to (untrusworthy) sayings and fables (*asāṭīr*) (presumably the traditions from Wahb et al.). In closing his discussion of these two verses, the author excuses himself for what he considers to be a digression from the general and all-important theme of this section of the Qur'an, namely 'redress' (*istidrāk*).[43]

## MAWDŪDĪ (d. 1399/1979)

The name of Abū al-A'lā Mawdūdī requires no introduction. For those interested in his revivalist and politico-religious activities, a sizable bibliography exists.[44] Unfortunately, this is not the case with Mawdūdī the exegete.[45] Some indication of what is to be expected in the *tafsīr* is found in Mawdūdī's statement of his religio-political philosophy: 'What was uppermost in my mind was to keep alive in the Muslims a sense of their separate entity and prevent their absorption into a non-Muslim community.'[46] Although there is no reason to believe that the author was here thinking of a Christian 'community', it is nonetheless significant, as the following will show, that this separatism was a personal

[43] Ibid., vol. 4, p. 588.

[44] For example, the one available in Kalīm Bahādur, *The Jama'at-i-Islāmī of Pakistan: Political Thought and Political Action* (New Delhi: Chetana, 1977), pp. 215–23.

[45] Charles J. Adams, 'Mawdudi's Qur'an Commentary', *Approaches to the History of the Interpretation of the Qur'an*, ed. A. Rippin (Oxford: Clarendon Press, 1988), pp. 199–222. See also references in Baljon, op. cit., and Jansen, op. cit., and see Freeland Abbot, 'Maulana Maudūdī on Qur'anic Interpretation', *Muslim World*, 48, 1958, pp. 6–19. There is also Mawdūdī's own introduction to the English edition of his Urdu *tafsīr*, *The Meaning of the Qur'an*, trans. Muḥammad Akbar, 6 vols published (Delhi: Markazi Maktaba Jamaat-E-Islami Hind, 1968); see vol. 1, pp. 5–28.

[46] Bahādur, op. cit., p. 12 and reference.

credo of the *mufassir*. Mawdūdī has spoken more directly about Qur'an interpretation, and although these words are of a very general nature, they may help to understand his work.

> In order to understand the Qur'an thoroughly, it is essential to know the nature of the Book, its central idea and its aim and object ... The aim and object of the revelation is to invite Man to that Right Way taught by all the previous prophets and to present clearly the guidance which he has lost ... The only thing with which it is concerned is to expound the Reality ... That is why it states or discusses or cites a thing only to that extent which is relevant to its aims and objects and leaves out unnecessary and irrelevant details.[47]

Ultimately for Mawdūdī, the only way to comprehend the theme of the Book is to try to live a life according to it, and above all to invite others to accept this way of life.[48]

Mawdūdī's treatment of 4:157–8 is seen to be in line with this general view. The Jews had no doubt that Jesus was a true prophet and Mawdūdī argues quite extensively to support the idea that their boast to have killed such a prophet is simply emblematic of the degradation to which this blighted people had sunk by this time in their history.

> Though it appears very strange that any community should slay a person whom they know to be and acknowledge as a Prophet of Allah, yet it is so, for the ways of wicked communities are strange. They cannot and do not tolerate that person who criticizes their evil ways and prohibits unlawful things. Such people, even though they are Prophets of Allah, have always been persecuted, imprisoned and slain by their own wicked people.

As a proof of this the following is quoted from the Talmud: 'When the city had been captured, [Nebuchadnezzar] with the princes

[47] Mawdūdī, *Meaning*, vol. 1, pp. 7, 9–10.
[48] Ibid., vol. 1, p. 27. It should be stated here that it is sometimes difficult to determine the author of the 'Explanatory Notes': whether it was Mawdūdī or his translator.

and officers of the Temple … found the mark of an arrow's head as though someone had been killed or hit nearby, and he asked "Who was killed here?"'

> 'Zachariah, the son of Yehoyadah, the high priest,' answered the people. 'He rebuked us incessantly on account of our transgressions and we were tired of his words and put him to death.' We learn also from the Bible that, when Prophet Jeremiah rebuked the Jews on account of their transgressions, they sent him to prison. Likewise John the Baptist was beheaded because he criticized them for their evil ways. It is therefore, obvious from their record, that when they presumed that they had crucified Jesus Christ, they would have most surely bragged, 'We have slain a Messenger of Allāh.'[49]

Mawdūdī distinguishes himself here from the other exegetes in this study with his use of the Talmud (though he gives no other reference) and the Hebrew Bible. His explanation of *shubbiha lahum* is equally unique:

> This verse is quite explicit on the point that Prophet Jesus Christ was rescued from crucifixion and that the Christians and the Jews are both wrong in believing that he expired on the cross. A comparative study of the Qur'an and the Bible shows that most probably it was Jesus himself who stood his trial in the court of Pilate, but they could not kill or crucify him, for Allāh raised him to Himself.
>
> This is what happened. Pilate knew quite well that Christ was innocent and had been brought in his court out of jealousy. So he asked the crowd whether Jesus Christ should be released on the occasion of the Festival, or Barabbas, a notorious robber. But the high priests and elders persuaded the crowd to ask for the release of Barabbas and for the crucifixion of Jesus. After this, God, Who can do any and everything He wills, raised Jesus to Himself and rescued him from crucifixion and the one who was crucified afterwards was somehow or other taken for Christ … As regards how, IT WAS MADE DOUBTFUL FOR THEM that they had crucified Jesus, we have no means of ascertaining this matter.

[49] Ibid., vol. 2, p. 389.

> Therefore, it is not right to base on mere guesswork and rumours an answer to the questions of how the Jews were made to believe that they had crucified him whereas in fact, Jesus the son of Mary had escaped from them.[50]

It is enough here for Mawdūdī that the Jews were bent upon wickedness and were duly foiled by God in their plot. There is no reference to any previous exegesis, rationalistic or otherwise, but it is clear that the author assigns special significance to the events described in the verse. Neither is he in need of the *Gospel of Barnabas* for an explanation of the mystery. He simply says that there are many versions of the crucifixion and that the existence of such variants proves that no one had definite knowledge about it. Without naming his sources, he gives the essence of these stories, some of obvious gnostic origin[51] and others reflecting other Christological disputes. It is curious that he does not mention the story found in *Barnabas* as one among these several conflicting accounts.

Mawdūdī's discussion of 4:158 is quite extensive. Although it is equally barren of reference to earlier exegetes, it is nonetheless significant in its attempt to find meaning in the cryptic assertion that God raised Jesus to himself. Mawdūdī's explanation begins,

> Here God has related the facts of the matter. The Qur'an explicitly says that the Jews did not succeed in putting Jesus to death and that God raised him to Himself, but it is silent about the nature and the details of the matter and does neither say explicitly whether God raised him bodily from the earth to some place in heaven; nor does it say that he died like other mortals and only his soul was raised to heaven. It has been couched in such a language that nothing can be said definitely about the incident except that it was uncommon and extraordinary.[52]

[50] Ibid., vol. 2, pp. 389–90.

[51] For example, Jesus was said to be watching the Romans crucify someone else and laughing at their folly. Cf. Elaine Pagels, *The Gnostic Gospels* (New York: Random House, 1979), pp. 70–101. Cf. also Wahb's second account as discussed above.

[52] Mawdūdī, *Meaning*, vol. 2, p. 390.

These words are suggestive of Sayyid Quṭb's commentary but it is not known if they reflect a direct influence.[53] Mawdūdī goes beyond Quṭb in his explanation of why the event must be so extraordinary. He says that the Qur'anic language is ambiguous and could even be interpreted to support the Christian 'Doctrine of Ascension'.

> Had it not factually been an extraordinary incident, the Qur'an would never have used such ambiguous words as helped support a doctrine of the God-head of Christ which the Qur'an refutes so strongly.
>
> Second, had God meant by the words (in v. 158) used in the Text that (a) 'Allāh caused his death' or that (b) 'God raised him in rank,' more explicit words would have been used.[54]
>
> In the case of (a) words to this effect would have been used: 'No doubt they did not slay him nor did they crucify him but God rescued him alive from them and afterwards he died a natural death,' and in the case of (b), 'They intended to dishonour him by the crucifixion but God [paradoxically/ironically] raised him very high in rank [precisely through this same act of crucifixion],' as in the case of Prophet Īdrīs: 'AND WE HAD RAISED HIM TO A HIGH POSITION.' (Q. 19:57)[55]

Mawdūdī is confident in his position to such a degree that he is able to speculate how the Qur'an would have been worded to derive an opposing interpretation. This is the first time we have encountered this kind of speculation. In addition to the possible oblique allusion to al-Rāzī, we find a similar refutation of the Ahmadiyya teaching that Jesus died a natural death in Kashmir. Mawdūdī is extremely careful, however, not to mention any names. Inasmuch as his work is directed to an English-speaking audience (one presumably non-Muslim as well), it may be that he desires to present Islam as a unified religion in the hope of attracting converts. Or,

[53] Cf. also Riḍā above.

[54] This is perhaps a veiled allusion to al-Rāzī's *tafsīr*, or to those later exegetes such as al-Ālūsī and Riḍā who cited relevant passages from it. Mawdūdī, *Meaning*, vol. 2, p. 391.

[55] Ibid.

it may be that he quite rightly judged that such direct references would have little meaning for most of his readers. Whatever the reason, he continues his discussion of 4:158, presenting a unique interpretation:

> Third, if the incident that has been related here meant merely the natural death of Christ, the use of the words, AND GOD IS ALL-POWERFUL, AND ALL-WISE (*'azīzan ḥakīman*) in connection with it, would have been quite meaningless. These words can appropriately be used only in connection with some extraordinary manifestations of the power and wisdom of God. The only thing that can be cited in support of this interpretation of v. 158 that Jesus died a natural death is the use of the word (*mutawaffīka*) in v. 55 of Sura Al 'Imran (3), in connection with this incident, but it has been made clear ... that the word (*mutawaffī*) does not literally mean 'to seize the soul' but merely 'to take and to receive' the body or the soul or both together. As there is a scope for both interpretations in this word, its use cannot refute the above mentioned arguments against the meaning, 'God caused his death.' Those who insist on this interpretation argue that there is no other instance in which *mutawaffī* has been used for the seizure of both body and soul together. This is meaningless, because this is the only incident of its kind in the whole of human history. The only thing to be considered is whether this word may lexically be used in this sense or not. If there is scope in the lexical meaning of the word for such a use, as there is, we have to face the question: Why does the Qur'an not use a direct word for each, instead of such a word as this which is liable to support the Doctrine of Ascension, which in its turn, has given rise to the Doctrine of the Divinity of Jesus? The use of this word is clear proof of the fact that there was something extraordinary about the incident. Above all, the doctrine of Ascension is further strengthened by the Traditions according to which Prophet Christ, son of Mary, will come again to the Earth and fight [the] Dajjal ... These [Traditions] clearly and categorically prove the Second Coming of Christ to the Earth. Therefore it would be more rational to believe that he must be living somewhere in the universe before his Second Coming than that he might be lying dead somewhere.[56]

[56] Ibid., vol. 2, pp. 391–2.

Mawdūdī's reading of MIGHTY, WISE is certainly unique; it is also obliquely reminiscent of certain aspects of Shi'i exegesis. As we have seen, these adjectives are usually construed to affirm God's wisdom in the way he countered the Jewish assertions, either by casting the likeness of Jesus on another or in a more general way. Again, Mawdūdī's only references to these verses' exegetical history are anonymous or general ('Traditions'). His effort at explanation is ingenious in its use of 'lexical' meaning, and may be thought to represent a distinct development in the *tafsīr* of the verse. In the above excerpt, it becomes even more tempting to identify at least one of his opponents as the Ahmadiyya.

In summary, although Mawdūdī emphasizes the 'extraordinary' nature of the event, he affirms that someone else was crucified. Like other modern exegetes, he is not able to speculate on who, or on how the ultimate confusion occurred. It is obvious that here, as in the case of Riḍā, it is of utmost importance to argue the error of Christian doctrine. In so doing, Mawdūdī has stripped away from his exegesis much of the early traditions while still maintaining a substitution theory. One may question how necessary, if the crucifixion of Jesus were a doctrinally neutral issue, it would have been for Mawdūdī and others to deny it. For example, it would seem that a simple crucifixion, which did not carry with it such un-Islamic concepts as vicarious atonement, could easily be accepted. In light of the almost universal acceptance that *someone* was crucified, it appears that the problem faced by the exegetes is not so much Jesus' death on the cross as their inability to accept this and at the same time maintain their Islamic understanding of prophecy. Mawdūdī's final question – how could Jesus return in the last days if he were not living somewhere in the universe? – could, for instance, be answered by reference to the verses that discuss those who have died in the path of God: THINK NOT OF THOSE WHO ARE SLAIN IN GOD'S WAY AS DEAD. NAY, THEY LIVE, FINDING THEIR SUSTENANCE IN THE PRESENCE OF THEIR LORD.[57]

That these verses are rarely, at least in the material surveyed for this study, cited in connection with 4:157–8 is symptomatic of what al-Fārūqī identified as a major shortcoming of modern

[57] Qur'an 3:169. See also the other verses referred to in Chapter One.

exegesis. The Qur'anic notion of death, particularly of the righteous – among whom the Qur'anic Jesus holds an indisputable rank – is a paradox. As such, it lends itself to discussion under the principles al-Fārūqī enunciated in an article published in 1962.[58] The historical roots may also go back to the period of 'orthodoxization' referred to above, when various Sunni and Shi'i groups were in the process of consolidating their identities. In this connection, it will not be impertinent to revisit here the Nuṣayrī understanding of our verse, in the form of a catechism that was quoted at the beginning of this study.

> Question 75: Was Christ crucified and killed as the Christians say in their account of him?
>
> Answer: Know that there is no truth in that, for the Jews (Q. 4:157–8) 'DID NOT SLAY HIM, NEITHER CRUCIFIED HIM, ONLY A LIKENESS OF THAT WAS SHOWN TO THEM ... BUT GOD RAISED HIM UP TO HIM' AS GOD SAYS (Q. 3:169) COUNT NOT THOSE WHO WERE SLAIN IN GOD'S WAY AS DEAD, BUT RATHER LIVING WITH THE LORD, BY HIM PROVIDED.[59]

As mentioned earlier, though al-Fārūqī's major concern here is with the derivation from the Qur'an of an ethical code that has meaning for modern Islam, his thesis is applicable to the Book as a whole. Inasmuch as this notion of 'death' represents an apparent contradiction in the Qur'an, the following quotation is especially pertinent.

> In the methodology we are suggesting, we may surmount the limitations under which Suyūṭī, al-Rāzī and Shāh Waliy Allāh have laboured. Every contradiction or variance in either the Holy Qur'an or the Sunnah is apparent, including the cases of *naskh* which to their minds have seemed obdurate. The differentiation of the levels of meaning, the distinction of categorical real-existents from ideally-existent values and of higher and lower orders of rank among the latter makes possible the removal of all ambiguities, equivocations, variations and contradictions without

[58] Ismā'īl Rāgī al-Fārūqī, 'Towards a New Methodology for Qur'anic Exegesis', *Islamic Studies*, 1(1), 1962, pp. 35–52.
[59] Meir M. Bar-Asher and Aryeh Kofsky, *The Nuṣayrī-'Alawī Religion: an Enquiry into Its Theology and Liturgy* (Leiden/Boston: E.J. Brill, 2002), p. 191.

> repudiating a single letter of the Holy Writ ... What is, therefore, paramountly imperative upon all Muslims at this state of their history ... is a systematic restatement of the Holy Qur'an's valuation content.[60]

Al-Fārūqī calls this process an 'axiological systemization' of values. Admittedly, his main concern is with the ethical content of the Book, but the re-examination of scripture that is called for here is bound to have implications for questions of theology and metaphysics.

## AL-ṬABĀṬABĀ'Ī (d. 1402/1981)

'Allamah Sayyid Muḥammad Ḥusayn al-Ṭabāṭabā'ī was a highly respected exponent of the classical Iranian intellectual tradition. The author of an authoritative introduction to Shi'ism,[61] he began teaching in the holy city of Qum in 1945, expounding such subjects as philosophy and theosophy to students of various backgrounds and interests, including the late Henry Corbin. According to Seyyed Hossein Nasr, al-Ṭabāṭabā'ī has 'exercised a profound influence in both the traditional and modern circles in Persia ... and tried to create a new intellectual elite among the modern educated classes'.[62] His most important work is a Qur'anic commentary whose title may be translated 'The Just Balance in the Explanation of the Qur'an', a title that has definite eschatological if not messianic overtones for a Shi'i audience who expect the return of their Hidden Imam with a number of other apocalyptic relics and sacred symbols, among which the scales with which to weigh good and evil figure prominently.[63] On the other hand, his discussion of this verse is similar to Sunni exegesis of the modern period in that very little traditional material is used to explain 4:157–8.

[60] Ibid., p. 45.

[61] Muḥammad Ḥusayn Ṭabāṭabā'ī, *Shī'ite Islam*, trans. and ed. Seyyed Hossein Nasr (Albany: State University of New York Press, 1975).

[62] Ibid., pp. 24–5.

[63] Ibid., p. 239.

According to al-Ṭabāṭabā'ī, the main purpose of 4:157–8 is to refute the Jews' claim that they had killed Jesus.[64] Pointing out that there is so much disagreement about the matter that it is difficult to determine what really happened, al-Ṭabāṭabā'ī says one possible interpretation (*ta'wīl*) is that 'they' did not kill him in the usual (*'ādīyan*) way.[65] The statement THEY DID NOT KILL HIM AND THEY DID NOT CRUCIFY HIM supports this in unambiguous terms, inasmuch as crucifixion was a customary punishment at that time. The meaning is that Jesus did not die by 'their' hands, but the matter appeared so to them (*bal shubbiha lahum amruhu*).[66]

They took someone other than Jesus and killed or crucified him in his place. And it was customary that such killings took place in a gathering of savage and brutal rabble. Perhaps the true criminal was mistaken for Jesus, the Roman soldiers killing him without knowing who he was. We have many accounts (*riwāyāt*) of how God cast the likeness on someone else.[67]

The author, striving towards a historically acceptable explanation, emphasizes the importance of the customs current at that time, what modern scholarship elsewhere refers to as a *Sitz im Leben*.[68] It is also interesting that he draws attention to the fact that the 'Romans' as opposed to the Jews were responsible for the killing. This argument has been used extensively by modern Christian writers in their attempts to accommodate the Qur'anic and the Gospel accounts of the crucifixion.[69] The author then offers the following curious comment:

[64] Al-Sayyid Muḥammad Ḥusayn al-Ṭabāṭabā'ī, *al-Mizān fī tafsīr al-Qur'ān*, 14 vols (Beirut: al-A'lamī lil-Maṭbū'āt, 1390/1970), vol. 5, p. 131.

[65] Ibid., vol. 5, p. 132.

[66] Ibid.

[67] Ibid.

[68] Could this be an example of 'influence' flowing in the opposite direction? It is frequently pointed out that al-Ṭabāṭabā'ī had a great effect on such important Western scholars of Islam as Corbin. But it may be that Corbin's own distinctive and rigorous approach to history of religions left an impression on the master himself.

[69] For example, Elder, op. cit., pp. 256–8; Parrinder, op. cit., p. 119. But see the difference in Giulio Basetti-Sani, *The Koran in the Light of Christ: A Christian Interpretation of the Sacred Book of Islam* (Chicago: Franciscan Herald Press, 1977), pp. 171–2.

> Perhaps [it is as] some historians have mentioned, that the stories relating to Jesus, his mission and the historical events of the rulers and other preachers of his time refer to two men called Christ. The two may have lived five hundred years or more apart. The earlier was the true Messiah, neither killed nor crucified, and the later, the false Messiah, was crucified. Thus what the Qur'an mentions concerning *tashbīh* ('confusion') is that of Jesus, son of Mary, with the [later] crucified [individual who was also known as] Christ.[70]

It should be mentioned that al-Ṭabāṭabā'ī's exegesis is replete with conditional statements. Thus, it is difficult to ascertain exactly what he wishes to convey. The above quotation is an example, par excellence, of this problem. It is obvious that the author himself is unsure about the Qur'anic teaching, in that he appears to accept *a* historical crucifixion of someone named Christ. His only source for this arresting bit of information is the vague 'Perhaps (*rubbamā*) [it is as] some historians have mentioned' which introduces the comment. Who these historians are, we are not informed. Obviously aware of this problem, the exegete ends this section with a simple 'God knows best.'[71]

The remainder of al-Ṭabāṭabā'ī's treatment of the subject differs little from the usual exegesis except that THOSE WHO DISAGREED are never identified, perhaps because it was assumed that their identity was common knowledge. However, given the lack of direct reference to Christians or Jews, together with the singling out of the polemically neutral Roman soldiers, it seems that al-Ṭabāṭabā'ī does not wish to confront either of these religious communities. His only comment here is that 'they' disagreed in ignorance (*jahl*) of the events, and their choice of one account over others was a mere guess (*takhmīn*).

The author then presents a discussion of *yaqīnan* in which he speculates on the antecedent of the pronoun of *qatalūhu* (THEY [DID NOT] KILL HIM), but admits that it is very difficult to determine in this context. It cannot refer to CONJECTURE (*ẓann*), according to the Book (*lafẓ al-Qur'an*), but might refer to knowledge

[70] Ayoub's translation, op. cit., p. 26.
[71] See Chapter Two.

(as Ibn Qutayba held, although his name is not mentioned), 'killing knowledge' being an Arabic idiom for indicating the obliteration of doubt and uncertainty, along the lines of 'mastering knowledge'.[72]

Al-Ṭabāṭabā'ī's discussion of 4:158 relies heavily on the *tafsīr* of 3:55. The main idea here is that Jesus was spiritually (*ma'nawī*) raised, 'because the Exalted One has no place of the kind occupied by bodies'.[73] As Ayoub points out, al-Ṭabāṭabā'ī is in line here with the Mu'tazilī and Shi'i exegetical traditions. The author does not refer to other exegetes in this discussion of 4:158. Likewise, such references are absent from his treatment of the previous verse. This, as we have seen, is consistent with the general trend of twentieth-century *tafsīr*. Al-Ṭabāṭabā'ī does not go to great lengths to refute the idea of identity transfer the way al-Rāzī did. However, it is clear from his understanding of *shubbiha lahum* (i.e. that the Romans merely picked the wrong man) that the author is a confirmed rationalist.

This review of modern exegetes has shown a general departure from the use of *ḥadīth* in the explanation of the Book. In its place has emerged a pronounced appeal to reason, whether this be by way of theological debate or lexical discussions. The *tafāsīr* in this section have offered some new and imaginative answers to old questions, and have also been affected by the appearance of the *Gospel of Barnabas*. It is interesting to note, however, that the last two authors make no mention of this work, demonstrating that it is possible, even without the use of it or the exegetical traditions of the type surveyed in Chapter Two, to deny the crucifixion of Jesus solely on the strength of 4:157–8. However, this denial seems to be a rejection of Christian soteriology more than a disclaimer of the event of the crucifixion of Jesus.

[72] See above, pp. 65–6 and 72–3.

[73] Ayoub's translation, op. cit., p. 25.

# CONCLUSION

Chapter One was an attempt to correct the assertion of modern non-Muslim students of the Qur'an that the Book denies the crucifixion of Jesus. In a brief discussion of the semantics of 4:157–8, it was also suggested that the Qur'an itself is neutral on the subject of the historicity of the crucifixion and may indeed be read to affirm it. Chapter Two made clear that the early exegetes were dependent upon sources other than the Qur'an for their interpretations. These sources were seen to be of either Jewish or Christian origin. Moreover, the early interpretations – often taking the form of substitution legends – were the source for the type of exegesis that denies that Jesus was crucified. Chapter Three described a trend in *tafsīr* that sought to free the Qur'anic text from interpretations based on the extra-Islamic substitution legends. This variation from the more usual patterns of exegesis is one of the principal arguments of the conclusion offered in this book that Muslims have not all agreed on the interpretation of the verses in question. This trend of disagreement about the meaning of these verses was seen to have ended abruptly in the fourteenth century. Chapter Four witnessed to the persistence of modern exegetes in denying the crucifixion, even though many of them disclaimed the utility of early traditions for purposes of exegesis. Some authors supported this denial with the *Gospel of Barnabas*. Others depended on different arguments in order to maintain their conclusions. In both instances, this persistence in denying the crucifixion indicated that the real issue was something other than the historicity of the crucifixion of Jesus. Specifically, the issue was Christian theories of salvation.

A few observations about the complicated problem of the origins of the substitution legend are now in order. As was mentioned at the beginning of this book, the earliest writer to have charged the Qur'an with a denial of the crucifixion was a Christian – John of Damascus. This fact, along with the disposition among certain non-Muslim scholars to view Islam and its revelation as a reiterated form of a previous religion, has moved some to posit a Docetic (Christian) precedent for 4:157–8.[1] Although a thorough discussion of Docetism would be out of place here, it certainly is not inaccurate to say that Docetic elements are discernible in many widely disparate periods and cultures as 'a peculiar feature of religious typology'.[2] Indeed, the fact that these elements

[1] It is not clear whether John Wansbrough, *Sectarian Milieu: Content and Composition of Islamic Salvation History* (Oxford: Oxford University Press, 1978), p. 108, was alluding to a direct borrowing, in the case of 4:157–8, of 'so-called "Docetic"' elements, but his statement on p. 128 indicates as much: 'The translation of word, and with it concept, into Arabic exhibits the one, perhaps only, class of "fact" unambiguously attested in the earliest literature. Some impression of the awkwardness occasioned by such "facts" can be seen in the Islamic accommodation (or, rather non-accommodation) of Christological concepts like messiah, virgin birth, and docetism.' See also Heribert Busse, 'Jesu Errettung vom Kreuz in der islamischen Koranexegese von Sure 4:157', *Oriens*, 36, 2001, pp. 160–95. Other authors, less opaque in their expression, who are disposed to read into our verse direct Docetic influences are: Henry Grègoire, 'Mohammed et le Monophysisme', *Etudes sur l'histoire et sur l'art Byzance: Mélanges Charles Diehl* (Paris: Ernest Leroux, 1930), pp. 107–19, and his transmitter, Henri Michaud, *Jésus selon le Coran* (Neuchâtel, Switzerland: Delachaux & Niestle, 1960), esp. p. 66. This thesis is in turn approved by Georges Anawati, "Īsā', *EI*², vol. 4, p. 84. See also Geoffrey Parrinder, op. cit., pp. 109–11. Such a position presents little advance over the theory of Richard Bell, *The Origins of Islam in Its Christian Environment* (London: Macmillan, 1926), p. 154, which supported the argument of Erdmann Fritsch, *Islam und Christentum in Mittelalter* (Breslau: Verlag Muller & Seiffert, 1930), pp. 66–70, echoes of which are heard in Claus Schedl, *Muḥammad and Jesus* (Vienna: Herder, n.d.), pp. 563–6. See also Henry Corbin, 'La Gnose Ismaélienne', *Eranos-Jahr Buch*, 23, 1954, pp. 142–244, esp. pp. 193–210; translated into English by Ralph Manheim as 'Divine Epiphany and Spiritual Birth in Ismailian Gnosisi, in *Man and Transformation: Papers from the Eranos Yearbooks*, ed. Joseph Campbell, 2nd edn (Princeton, NJ: Princeton University Press, 1972), pp. 69–160, esp. pp. 113–27.

[2] Ugo Bianchi, 'Docetism: A Peculiar Theory about the Ambivalence of the Presence of the Divine', *Selected Essays on Gnosticism, Dualism and Mysteriosophy* (Leiden: E.J. Brill, 1978), p. 265.

are not restricted to non-orthodox religion[3] might be expected to shed light on the relationship between Islamic orthodoxy and the so-called heterodox authors of the *Rasā'il Ikhwān al-Ṣafā"* and the other Isma'ili material quoted in Chapter Three. Or, more precisely, this fact might help define more clearly what the correct application of such terms as 'orthodoxy' and 'heterodoxy' should be, if indeed they can be used at all in the case of Islam. According to Bianchi's thesis, it is quite unnecessary, and may possibly be a hindrance to an appreciation of the general genius of Islam, to read into 4:157–8 direct influences from previous 'heterodox' religions. At the same time, the fact that John of Damascus could have done this is not only possible but also probable.

There is also sufficient evidence to suggest that any influence present in the verses need not be 'religious' (i.e. Jewish, Christian, Manichaean, etc.) in origin. As early as 1890, Goldziher drew attention to a belief shared by some of Muḥammad's 'pagan' contemporaries, who, upon hearing of the Prophet's death, renounced Islam 'under the pretext that a man who is subject to death like all other men cannot have been a prophet'.[4] The implication here is that a real prophet could not be 'defeated' by such an unworthy 'opponent' as (mere) death. Such an attitude may also be seen in the critique and analysis of the so-called Muslim denial of the crucifixion which says that the triumphalism of (Sunni) Islam does not allow for a prophet to have been defeated at the hands of such an obviously blighted people as 'the Jews'.[5] In this connection, the substitution legends may reflect a prevailing 'unconscious tendency' in early Islam 'to draw a picture of Muḥammad that should not be inferior to the Christian picture of Jesus'.[6] In other words, the lives and careers of the two prophets are

[3] Ibid. See A.L. Tibawi, 'Ikhwān as-Ṣafā and Their Rasā'il: A Critical Review of a Century and a Half of Research', in *Arabic and Islamic Themes: Historical, Educational and Literary Studies* (London: Luzac, 1976), pp. 161–86, esp. p. 174. An interesting analysis of this author's anti-Orientalist posture is Donald P. Little, 'Three Arab Critiques of Orientalism', *Muslim World*, 69(2), 1979, pp. 110–31, esp. pp. 111–15.

[4] Ignaz Goldziher, *Muslim Studies*, vol. 2, trans. S.M. Stern and C.R. Barber, ed. S.M. Stern (London: George Allen & Unwin, 1971), p. 261.

[5] This is the gist of the discussion in Anawati, 'Isa'.

[6] Goldziher, *Die Richtungen*, p. 346. See also p. 122.

'homogenized' so they become homologations or types of each other. In this instance, neither prophet can be seen to have fallen to their enemies. And, although none could claim for Muḥammad a parallel to the passion of the death and resurrection of Jesus, through exegesis inherent in the popular *qiṣaṣ al-anbiyā'* literature, the Christian account could be transformed into something more palatable to the soteriological and prophetological tastes of Muslims. Thus, to infuse the events surrounding the crucifixion with themes and motifs that parallel the attested 'facts' of Muḥammad's career, such as the *mi'rāj*, would serve to harmonize the lives and ministries of the two prophets of God.

Another dimension to a possible history of the ideas embodied in the substitution legends appears in the variegated motifs of Jewish messianism. For example, one may see in these legends a reflection of the Jewish idea that the Messiah 'would be defeated, hide, and eventually reappear'.[7] It is possible that the early exegesis of this verse (as a product of the Islamic preacher) represents the tailoring of the Revelation to suit the messianic expectations of prospective Jewish converts. In these legends, Jesus is 'defeated' by the authorities (either Roman or Jewish) in their sentencing him to death. Jesus is then 'hidden' by God and expected to 'reappear' sometime in the future.[8] A Jesus who thus conformed to the messianic beliefs of possible Jewish converts would make their acceptance of his Qur'anic title *al-masīḥ* much easier for them than would a Jesus who had died an inglorious and despised death on the cross.[9] This, of course, is only speculation, but I have found very little in the pertinent literature that makes even an initial attempt to trace the origins of the substitution legends.

[7] Solomon D. Goiten, *Jews and Arabs: Their Contacts through the Ages* (New York: Schocken, 1970), p. 168. One should also refer to Gershom Scholem, *The Messianic Idea in Judaism, and Other Essays on Jewish Spirituality* (New York: Schocken, 1971) and Joseph Kalusner, *The Messianic Idea in Israel from Its Beginning to the Completion of the Mishnah*, trans. W.F. Stinespring (New York: Macmillan, 1955), pp. 325–7.

[8] Cf. the divinely ordained occultation/advent (*ghayba/ẓuhūr*) of the Twelfth Imam in Shi'ism.

[9] For example, Deuteronomy 21:22–23; Joshua 8:29, 10:26; Isaiah 53; 2 Corinthians 21:6–9; possibly Numbers 25:4.

One exception is the solution posited by Massignon, referred to already above in our examination of post-Ṭabari exegesis. The great French student and scholar of Islam theorized that this legend, which was incorporated into Sunni exegesis from a very early period, around 765 CE, probably had a Shi'i origin. What we are really seeing here, according to Massignon, is the retrospective application to the life and death of Jesus certain explanations found in Kufa for the violent death of the legitimate imams of the Shi'a. According, especially, to the views of those who had 'divinized' their imams, God would never make them 'die before their time'. He would, however, 'rescue' the divine spark that was deposited within them during the assaults on them by their enemies. Thus, the only spiritless 'shell' (*loque*) of the imam was left.[10] This hollow identity then 'was put on' – at the command of God, by either a demon or a condemned one during the agonies of torture suffered by the imam. Massignon points out, basing his argument on Baghdadi, that such readings of tragic events were used to explain the failure of the revolt led against the Abbassids by the Shi'i Mahdi *al-Nafs al-Zakiyya* (d. 145/760). For the third imam (d. 61/680), a more complex theory was adopted. It was thought that only his physical identity was assumed by a devoted follower, one Hanzala Shibami while the agonies of what appeared to be his murder at Karbala by the forces of Yazīd were actually redirected by God to an invisible 'Umar ibn al-Khaṭṭāb (d. 23/644), the second so-called 'rightly guided caliph', who was condemned by the Shi'a as the arch-enemy of 'Alī. Massignon adds the astute observation that we see the same equivocation in Sunni *tafsīr:* sometimes the substitute was a faithful disciple and sometimes an enemy of Jesus.[11]

[10] The original French is *loque*, which is used to translate the extremely important Arabic word *shabḥ/shabaḥ*. Note the clear connection between this word and the root of the problematic verb, *shubbiha*, from which is dervied the near homonym *shabah* with the non-velarized 'h'. It was a word used very early (around 140/757) by the extremist sect al-Khaṭṭābiyya (Kulayni, *al-Kāfī*, vol. 1, p. 78). Both this early group and after them the Isma'ilis frequently sacrificed their lives in the belief that a martyr's outward suffering was in reality ecstasy. See Louis Massignon, 'Le Christ dans les évangiles selon Ghazali', *Revue des études Islamiques*, 1932, pp. 523–6.

[11] Ibid., p. 525.

If, as Massignon suggests, it is possible to see a Shi'i origin for the substitution legends, then it must be asked why early Shi'i commentators felt it necessary to uphold the substitution theory. That is, if the Shi'a would accept the violent deaths of their imams and all of the suffering that went along with such deaths, why were they unable to accept the traditional Christian account of Jesus' death? This question becomes more pressing in light of Ayoub's treatment of the positive role of the idea of redemptive suffering in Islam,[12] which attempts to revise and correct the general assumption that redemptive suffering is a concept foreign to Muslim thinking. An answer to the question has been suggested in the preceding pages in light of Isma'ili acceptance of the crucifixon of Jesus. Whether this acceptance was based on purely philosophico-theological grounds or on the basis of typological figuration, it became mandatory for the fledgling Twelver movement to distinguish and differentiate itself from such 'Fatimid' associations. So, the Twelvers here, as in other instances, adopted a more 'Sunni'/Baghdadi/'Abbāsid stance. That in both cases typological exegesis was used to achieve diametrically and mutually exclusive results is a testimony to the power of the figure for what might be thought the Shi'i apocalyptic imagination.

Whatever the original impulse may have been, the substitution legend has been a popular exegetical device ever since the second Islamic century. Kamel Hussein, author of *City of Wrong*, assesses the legend by saying, 'The idea of a substitute for Christ is a very crude way of explaining the Qur'anic text. The exegetes, we assume, had to explain a lot to the masses.'[13]

Hussein's statement is in line with the modern trend to minimize the value of traditions, especially of the *Isrā'īliyyāt*, for exegesis. We have also seen that some versions of the substitution legend fall into the category of *Isrā'īliyyāt* inasmuch as they were related on

[12] Mahmoud Ayoub, *Redemptive Suffering In Islam: A Study of the Devotional Aspects of 'Āshūrā' in Twelver Shī'ism* (The Hague: Mouton, 1978).

[13] Kamel Hussein, *City of Wrong*, trans. Kenneth Cragg (Amsterdam: Djambatan, 1959), p. 222. The passage continues, 'No cultured Muslim believes this nowadays. The text is taken to mean that the Jews thought they killed Christ but God raised him unto Him in a way we can leave unexplained among the several mysteries we have taken for granted on faith alone.'

the authority of either Christians or Jews. Although it is true that one might mistake this modern rejection of tradition for a function of 'revivalist' or so-called 'fundamentalist' exegesis, it is also clear certain contemporary modern Muslim religious scholars of a different stamp share these ideas. For example, Dr 'Ā'isha 'Abd al-Raḥmān (*Bint al-Shāṭi'*) is a widely published Muslim Qur'anic scholar whose informed and earnest approach to *tafsīr* has been discussed in detail by Boullata. Of the four guidelines for exegesis to which *Bint al-Shāṭi'* subscribes, one is of immediate interest:

> To understand the subtleties of expression, the text in its Qur'anic setting is studied for what it may mean, both the letter and the spirit of the text being considered. The sayings of exegetes are then examined in relation to the text thus studied, and only what agrees with the text may be accepted. To be avoided are all sectarian interpretations and all intrusive *Isrā'īliyyāt* (Jewish–Christian materials) that were forced on the books of *Tafsīr*.[14]

The integrity of this principle has recently been substantiated in an independent analysis of early exegesis. The results of that study by Wansbrough have already been mentioned, but I refer to them again here for the purpose of drawing attention to what is perceived to be significant, if unlikely, correspondence between modern and contemporary scholars of the Qur'an.[15] Such a general consensus has continued to be expressed in recent years by what may be considered a new approach to the Qur'an. This approach is distinguished by a concern for literary, social and anthropological factors as much as it is historical, philological scholarship. A recent, fascinating study of the image of Jesus and the crucifixion in the contemporary Arab novel is a clear demonstration of how what otherwise might be thought 'merely theological' concerns are not only bound up with literary history but are constitutive of cultural identity.[16] The remarkable

[14] Issa J. Boulatta, 'Modern Qur'an Exegesis, A Study of Bint al-Shāṭi''s Method', *Muslim World*, 64, 1974, p. 105.

[15] This should not imply, of course, that either scholar would completely subscribe to the views of the other.

[16] Maher Jarrah, 'The Arabic Novel Carries Its Cross ... Iconography of Jesus in Some Modern Arabic Novels', in *Poetry's Voice – Society's Norms: Forms of*

*Encyclopaedia of the Qur'an* is emblematic, representative and generative of such developments.[17] That all conclusions are temporary, however, is axiomatic of the life of the mind and intellectual history. Thus, in the substantial and deeply learned article on 'Shi'ism' in this monumental reference work, scant attention is paid to the internal debate and polemics within the greater Shi'i community between representatives of the various subdivisions on the concerns of exegesis and thought in general.[18] It is hoped that the foregoing has offered ample evidence why such problems should not be ignored. They are keys to gaining a better understanding of the eventual doctrinal and perhaps even social history of these 'minoritarian orthodoxies'.[19] But they are also keys to understanding how such discussions have influenced the entire religious history of Islam. It is possible to hear the tonalities and themes of those ancient debates today in the following words of the Sunni scholar Bint al-Shaṭi', whose *tafsīr*, as we have noted, does not explicitly address the problem in the crucifixion verse, but who has left us with a strong indication of how she might have interpreted it in the following excerpt from a book review entitled 'Easter Impressions of the *City of Wrong*'. It seems a fitting place to conclude.

> I listened to the bells tolling out the triumph of Right and Good, blessing the name of the Lord Christ (on him peace). The city of wrong supposed that it had put an end to him when it condemned him to crucifixion. But he lived on to fill all history and life, and the agonies he endured because of his message were blessed.[20]

*Interaction between Middle Eastern Writers and Their Societies,* ed. A. Pflitsch and B. Winckler (Wiesbaden: Reichert Verlag, 2006), pp. 61–92.

[17] *The Encyclopaedia of the Qur'ān*, ed. J.D. McAuliffe (Leiden: E.J. Brill, 2005).

[18] Meir M. Bar-Asher, 'Shī'ism and the Qur'ān', in *The Encyclopaedia of the Qur'ān* (Leiden: E.J. Brill, 2001–6), vol. 6, pp. 593–604.

[19] See in this connection the very interesting discussion in which it is also pointed out that another representative of the Islamic tradition, Qāsim ibn Ibrāhīm, also 'accepted the crucifixion at face value', in Tobias ('Alī Mūsā) Mayer, 'A Muslim Speaks to Christians', *Priests and People*, January 2003, pp. 9–13, esp. p. 11.

[20] *Muslim World*, 51, 1961, p. 149.

# APPENDIX

## BALLAD OF THE GOODLY FERE

Simon Zelotes speaking after the crucifixion
(fere = mate, companion)

Ha' we lost the goodliest fere o' all
For the priests and the gallows tree?
Aye lover he was of brawny men,
O' ships and the open sea.

When they came wi' a host to take Our Man
His smile was good to see,
'First let these go!' quo' our Goodly Fere,
'Or I'll see ye damned,' says he.

Aye he sent us out through the crossed high spears
And the scorn of his laugh rang free,
'Why took ye not me when I walked about
Alone in the town?' says he.

Oh we drank his 'Hale' in the good red wine
When we last made company,
No capon priest was the Goodly Fere
But a man o' men was he.

I ha' seen him drive a hundred men
Wi' a bundle o' cords swung free,
That they took the high and holy house
For their pawn and treasury.

They'll no' get him a' in a book I think
Though they write it cunningly;
No mouse of the scrolls was the Goodly Fere
But aye loved the open sea.

If they think they ha' snared our Goodly Fere
They are fools to the last degree.
'I'll go to the feast,' quo' our Goodly Fere,
'Though I go to the gallows tree.'

'Ye ha' seen me heal the lame and blind,
And wake the dead,' says he,
'Ye shall see one thing to master all:
'Tis how a brave man dies on the tree.'

A son of God was the Goodly Fere
That bade us his brothers be.
I ha' seen him cow a thousand men.
I have seen him upon the tree.

He cried no cry when they drave the nails
And the blood gushed hot and free,
The hounds of the crimson sky gave tongue
But never a cry cried he.

I ha' seen him cow a thousand men
On the hills o' Galilee,
They whined as he walked out calm between,
Wi' his eyes like the grey o' the sea,

Like the sea that brooks no voyaging
With the winds unleashed and free,
Like the sea that he cowed at Genseret
Wi' twey words spoke' suddently.

A master of men was the Goodly Fere,
A mate of the wind and sea,
If they think they ha' slain our Goodly Fere
They are fools eternally.

I ha' seen him eat o' the honey-comb
Sin' they nailed him to the tree.

Ezra Pound[1]

# BIBLIOGRAPHY

## WORKS IN WESTERN LANGUAGES, INCLUDING TRANSLATIONS OF THE QUR'AN

*The following authors, their works, and publication information appear as they are found on the title pages of the works cited. No attempt is made to standardize the spellings or transliterations.*


Abbot, Freeland. 'Maulana Maududi on Qur'anic Interpretation.' *Muslim World* 48 (1958): 6–19.

Abbott, Nabia. *Studies in Arabic Literary Papyri II: Qur'anic Commentary and Tradition*. Chicago: University of Chicago Press, 1967.

'Abd al-Tafāhum (aka Kenneth Cragg). 'City of Wrong.' *Muslim World* 46 (1956): 132–46, 225–36.

'Abd al-Tafāhum (aka Kenneth Cragg). 'The Qur'ān and the Holy Communion.' *Muslim World* 46 (1956): 239–48.

Abdel Haleem, M.A.S. (trans.). *The Qur'an: A New Translation*. Oxford: Oxford University Press, 2004.

Abdul Haqq, Akbar Abdiyah. 'Christologies in Early Christian Thought and in the Qur'an: Being a Critical Analysis and Comparison of Selected Christological Views in Christian Writings to 785 A.D. and Those of the Qur'an.' PhD dissertation, Northwestern University, 1953.

Abdul, Musa O.A. 'The Historical Development of Tafsīr.' *Islamic Culture* 50 (1976): 141–53.

Abdul, Musa O.A. *The Qur'an: Shaykh Tabarsi's Commentary*. Lahore: Sh. Muhammad Ashraf, 1977.

Abel, Armand. *Le Coran*. Brussels: Office de Publicité, 1951.

Abraham, Mihdat. 'Mahmud Shaltut (1863–1963), A Muslim Reformist: His Life, Works, and Religious Thought.' PhD thesis, Hartford Seminary, 1976.

Abrahamov, Binyamin (ed. and trans.). *Anthropomorphism and Interpretation of the Qur'an in the Theology of al-Qasim ibn Ibrahim [(785–860)]: Kitab al-Mustarshid*. Leiden: E.J. Brill, 1996.

Adams, Charles J. 'Mawdudi's Qur'an Commentary.' In *Approaches to the History of the Interpretation of the Qur'ān*, ed. A. Rippin. Oxford: Clarendon Press, 1988, 199–222.

Adams, Charles J. 'Islamic Religion, II.' *Middle East Studies Association Bulletin* 5(1) (1976): 9–25.

Adams, Charles J. 'Islam and Christianity: The Opposition of Similarities.' In *Logos Islamikos: Studia Islamica in Honorem Georgii Michaelis Wickens*, ed. Roger M. Savory and Dionisius A. Agius. Toronto: Pontifical Institute of Mediaeval Studies, 1984, 287–306.

Addison, James Thayer. *The Christian Approach to the Moslem: A Historical Study*. New York: AMS Press, 1966.

Ahmad Khan, Sayyid. *The Mohomedan Commentary on the Holy Bible*. Ghazeepore, 1865.

Ahrens, K. 'Christliches im Qoran.' *Zeitschrift der Deutschen Morgenländischen Gesellschaft* 84 (1930): 15–68.

Algar, Hamid. *Jesus in the Qur'an: His Reality Expounded in the Qur'an*. Oneonta, NY: Islamic Publications International, 1999.

Anawati, Georges C. "Īsā.' *EI*², vol. 4, 81–6.

Anawati, Georges C. 'Jésus et ses juges d'aprés "La Cité inique" du Dr. Kamel Hussein.' *Mélanges de l'Institut Dominicaine des Études Orientales du Caire* 2 (1959): 71–134.

Anderson, J.N.D. (ed.). *The World's Religions*. Grand Rapids: W.M.B. Eerdmans, 1972.

Andrae, Tor. *Mohammed: The Man and His Faith*, trans. Theophil Menzel. New York: Harper, 1960.

Arberry, Arthur J. *The Koran Interpreted*. London: Oxford University Press, 1964.

Arnaldez, Roger. *Hallâj ou la religion de la croix*. Paris: Plon, 1964.

Ayoub, Mahmoud. 'Towards an Islamic Christology: An Image of Jesus in Early Shi'i Muslim Literature', *Muslim World* 66 (1976): 163–88.

Ayoub, Mahmoud. 'Towards an Islamic Christology, II: The Death of Jesus, Reality or Delusion?' *Muslim World* 70 (1980): 91–121.

Ayoub, Mahmoud. *Jesus the Son of God: A Study of the Terms Ibn and*

*Walad in the Qur'an and Tafsīr Tradition*. Gainesville: University Press of Florida, 1995.

Azmi, Mohammad Mustafa. *Studies in Early Hadith Literature with a Critical Edition of Some Early Texts*. Beirut: al-Maktab al-Islami, 1968.

Bahadur, Kalim. *The Jama'at-i-Islami of Pakistan: Political Thought and Political Action*. New Delhi: Chetana, 1977.

Baljon, J.M.S. *Modern Muslim Koran Interpreters (1880–1960)*. Leiden: E.J. Brill, 1968.

Bar-Asher, Meir M. *Scripture and Exegesis in Early Imami Shiism*. Leiden: E.J. Brill, 1999.

Bar-Asher, Meir M. 'Shī'ism and the Qur'ān.' In *Encyclopaedia of the Qur'ān*, ed. J.D. McAuliffe. Leiden: E.J. Brill, 2001–6, vol. 5, 593–604.

Bar-Asher, Meir Mikhael and Aryeh Kofsky. *The Nuṣayrī-'Alawī Religion: An Enquiry into Its Theology and Liturgy*. Leiden/Boston: E.J. Brill, 2002.

Basetti-Sani, Giuilio, O.F.M. *The Koran in the Light of Christ: A Christian Interpretation of the Sacred Book of Islam*. Chicago: Franciscan Herald Press, 1977.

Bausani, Alessandro. *Il Corano*. Trans. Alessandro Bausani. Bologna: Sansoni-Firenze, 1955.

Bauschke, Martin. *Jesus im Koran*. Cologne: Böhlau, 2001.

Becker, Carl Heinrich. 'Christliche Polemik und Islamische Dogmabild.' *Islamstudien: vom warden und Wesen der Islamicshen Welt*, vol. 1. Leipzig: Quelle & Meyer, 1932, 432–49.

Bell, Richard. *The Origins of Islam in Its Christian Environment*. London: Macmillan, 1926.

Bell, Richard. *The Qur'ān Translated, with a Critical Rearrangement of the Surahs*. 2 vols. Edinburgh: T. & T. Clark, 1937.

Beskow, P. *Strange Tales about Jesus: A Survey of Unfamiliar Gospels, 1985*. Philadelphia: Fortress Press, 1983.

Bianchi, Ugo. 'Docetism: A Peculiar Theory about the Presence of the Divine.' In *Selected Essays on Gnosticism, Dualism, and Mysterisophy*. Leiden: E.J. Brill, 1978, pp. 265–73.

Birkeland, Harris. *The Lord Guideth: Studies on Primitive Islam*. Uppsala, Sweden: Almqvist & Wiksells, 1956.

Birkeland, Harris. *Old Muslim Opposition against Interpretation of the Koran*. Uppsala, Sweden: Almqvist & Wiksells, 1956.

Bishop, E.F.F. 'Shubbiha lahum: A Suggestion from the New Testament.' *Muslim World* 30 (1940): 67–75.

Björkman, W. 'Kāfir', *EI*², vol. 4, 407.
Blachère, Régis. 'al- Farrā'.' *EI*², vol. 2, p. 806.
Blachère, Régis. *Introduction au Coran*, 2nd edn. Paris: G.P. Maisonneuve, 1959.
Blachère, Régis. *Le Coran: traduction nouvelle*. Paris: G.P. Maisonneuve, 1950.
Boullata, Issa J. 'Modern Qur'ān Exegesis: A Study of Bint al-Shāṭi''s Method.' *Muslim World* 64(2) (1974): 103–13.
Böwering, Gerhard. 'Ghazālī.' *Encyclopaedia Iranica*, vol. 10, 358–63.
Böwering, Gerhard. 'The Major Sources of Sulamī's Minor Qur'ān Commentary.' *Oriens* 35 (1996): 35–56.
Böwering, Gerhard. *The Mystical Vision of Existence in Classical Islam: The Qur'ānic Hermeneutics of the Ṣūfī, Sahl At-Tusṭarī* (d. 238/896). Berlin: Walter de Gruyter, 1980.
Brinner, William M. *'Arā'is al-majālis fī qiṣaṣ al-anbiyā' or 'Lives of the Prophets' as Recounted by Abū Isḥāq Aḥmad ibn Muḥammad ibn Ibrāhīm al-Tha'labī.* Leiden: E.J. Brill, 2002.
Brown, David. *The Cross of the Messiah*. London: Sheldon Press, 1969.
Buhl, Frants. 'Ḳur'ān.' *EI*¹, vol. 2., 1065–76.
Burton, John. *The Collection of the Qur'ān*. Cambridge, England: Cambridge University Press, 1977.
Busse, Heribert. 'Jesu Errettung vom Kreuz in der islamischen Koranexegese von Sure 4:157.' *Oriens* 36 (2001): 160–95.
Busse, Heribert. *Islam, Judaism, and Christianity: Theological and Historical Affiliations*, trans. Allison Brown. Princeton, NJ: Markus Wiener, 1998 [1988].
Butt, Muhammad Yahya. *Jesus Christus in Koran und Bibel: zwei Vorträge anlässlich der Feier des Geburtstages des Propheten Jesu*. Berlin/Wilmersdorf: Die Moschee, die Muslim Mission, ca. 1980.
Cirillo, Luigi and Michael Frémaux. *Evangile de Barnabé: Recherches sur la composition et l'origine*. Paris: Beauchesne, 1977.
Cole, J.R.I. 'Behold the Man: Baha'u'llah on the Life of Jesus.' *Journal of the American Academy of Religion* 65(1) (1997): 47–71.
Cook, David, *Martyrdom in Islam.* Cambridge, England: Cambridge University Press, 2007.
Corbin, Henry. *Cyclical Time and Isma'ili Gnosis*, trans. Ralph Mannheim and James W. Morris. London: Routledge & Kegan Paul International/Islamic Publications, 1983.
Corbin, Henry. 'Divine Epiphany and Spiritual Birth in Ismailian Gnosis', trans. Ralph Manheim. In *Man and Transformation:*

*Papers from the Eranos Yearbooks,* ed. Joseph Campbell, 2nd edn. Princeton, NJ: Princeton University Press, 1972 [1954], 69–160.

Corbin, Henry. 'L'Ismaélisme et le symbole de la Croix.' *La Revue La Table Ronde: Un Sommaire sur Le Signe de la Croix* 120 (1957): 123–34.

Corbin, Henry. *The Man of Light in Iranian Sufism*, trans. Nancy Pearson. Boulder, CO: Shambhala, 1978.

Corbin, Henry. *Spiritual Body and Celestial Earth: From Mazdean Iran to Shi'ite Iran*, trans. Nancy Pearson. Princeton, NJ: Princeton University Press, 1977.

Corbin, Henry. ed. *Trilogie ismaelienne. Textes édités avec traduction française et commentaires.* Tehran: Département d'iranologie de l'Institut franco-iranien, 1961.

Corbin, Henry. *Swedenborg and Esoteric Islam*, trans. Leonard Fox. West Chester, PA: Swedenborg Foundation, 1999.

Cragg, K. *Jesus and the Muslim: An Exploration.* London: Allen & Unwin, 1985.

Cragg, Kenneth. *The Call of the Minaret*. New York: Oxford University Press, 1964.

Daftary, Farhad. *The Isma'ilis: Their History and Doctrines*. Cambridge, England: Cambridge University Press, 1990.

Din, Maulvi Muhammad. 'The Crucifixion in the Koran.' *Muslim World* 14 (1924): 23–9.

Elder, Earl E. 'The Crucifixion in the Koran.' *Muslim World* 13 (1923): 242–58.

Ernst, C.W. *Ruzbihan Baqli: Mysticism and the Rhetoric of Sainthood in Persian Sufism.* Richmond, England: Curzon Press, 1996.

Esack, Farid. *The Qur'an: A User's Guide.* Oxford: Oneworld, 2005.

Ess, J. van and P. Heinegg. *Islam and the Other Religions: Jesus in the Qur'an. Islamic Perspectives.* London: SCM Press, 1993.

Fārūqī, Ismā'īl Rāgī al-. 'Towards a New Methodology for Qur'ānic Exegesis.' *Islamic Studies* 1(1) (1962): 35–52.

Fisher, Humphrey J. *Aḥmadiyyah: A Study in Contemporary Islām on the West African Coast*. London: Oxford University Press/Nigerian Institute of Social and Economic Research, 1963.

Fitzgerald, M.L. *Jesus in a Shî`ite commentary.* Rome: Pontificio Istituto di Studi Arabi e d'Islamistica, 1996.

Fitzgerald, M.L. 'Jesus in a Shi'ite Commentary.' In *Recueil d'articles offert à Maurice Borrmans par ses collègues et amis.* Rome: Pontificio Istituto di Studi Arabi e d'Islamistica, 1996, 77–91.

Flusser, David. *Judaism and the Origins of Christianity*. Jerusalem: Magnes, 1988.

Flusser, David. *Jesus*. Jerusalem: Magnes, 1997.

Friedmann, Yohanan. *Prophecy Continuous: Aspects of Ahmadi Religous Thought and Its Medieval Background.* Berkeley: University of California Press, 1989.

Friemuth, Maha El-Kaisy. '*Al-Radd al-Jamīl:* al-Ghazālī's or Pseudo-Ghazālī's?' In *The Bible in Arab Christianity*, ed. David Thomas. Leiden: E.J. Brill, 2007, 275–94.

Fritsch, Erdmann. *Islam und Christentum im Mittelalter: Beiträge zur Geschichte der Muslimischen Polemik Gegen das Christentum in Arabischer Sprache*. Breslau: Müller & Seiffert, 1930.

Fudge, Bruce. 'Qur'ānic Exegesis in Medieval Islam and Modern Orientalism.' *Die Welt des Islams* 46 (2006): 115–47.

Fyzee, Asaf A.A. (trans.). *A Shī'ite Creed: A Translation of* I'tiqādātu'l-Imamiyyah *(The Beliefs of the Imamiyyah) of Abū Ja'far, Muḥ ammad ibn 'Alī ibn al-Husayn, Ibn Bābawayh al-Qummī Known as ash-Shaykh as-Sadūq (306/919-381/991)*. Tehran: World Organization for Islamic Services, 1402/1982.

Gardner, Iain. 'Docetism.' In *Encyclopedia of Religion*, 2nd edn, ed. Lindsay Jones. Detroit: Macmillan, 2005, vol. 4, 2381.

Gätje, Helmut. *The Qur'ān and Its Exegesis*, trans. and ed. Alford T. Welch. London: Routledge & Kegan Paul, 1976.

Gibb, Sir Hamilton A.R. *Mohammedanism: An Historical Survey*. New York: Mentor Books, 1958.

Gilliot, Claude. *Exégèse, langue et théologie en Islam: l'éxègese coranique de Ṭabari (m. 311/923)*. Paris: J. Vrin, 1990.

Ginaidi, Ahmed. *Jesus Christus und Maria aus koranisch-islamischer Perspektive: Grundlagen eines interreligiösen Dialogs*. Stuttgart: Ibidem, 2002.

Glassé, C. *Jesus, Son of Mary: An Islamic Perspective*. London: Altajir World of Islam Trust, 1998.

Goitein, Solomon D. *Jews and Arabs: Their Contacts through the Ages*. New York: Schocken, 1970.

Goldfeld, Isaiah. *Quranic Commentray in the Eastern Islamic Tradition of the First Four Centuries of the Hijra: An Annotated Edition of the Preface to al-Tha'labī's Kitāb al-kashf wa'l-bayān 'an tafsīr al-Qur'ān*. Acre, Israel: Srugy, 1984.

Goldstein, Ronnie and Guy S. Stroumsa. 'The Greek and Jewish Origins of Docetism: A New Proposal.' *Zeitschrift für Antikes Christentum* 10(3) (2007): 423–41.

Goldziher, Ignaz. *History of Classical Arabic Literature*, trans. and revised Joseph Desomogyi. Hildesheim, Germany: George Olms, 1966.

Goldziher, Ignaz. *Muslim Studies*, vol. 1, ed. S.M. Stern, trans. C.R. Barber and S.M. Stern. London: George Allen & Unwin, 1971.

Goldziher, Ignaz. *Die Richtungen der Islamischen Koranauslegung*. Leiden: E.J. Brill, 1952.

Goldziher, Ignaz. *Streitschrift des Ġazālī gegen die Bāṭinijja-Sekte*. Leiden: E.J. Brill, 1916.

[Gramlich, Richard.] *Das Sendschreiben al-Qusayris über das Sufitum* [see below in Arabic bibliography].

Grégoire, Henri. 'Mahomet et le Monophysisme.' In *Etudes sur l'histoire et sur l'art Byzance: Mélanges Charles Diehl*. Paris: Ernest Leroux, 1930, 107–19.

Guillaume, Alfred. *The Life of Muḥammad: A Translation of Ishaq's Sirat Rasul Allah*, ed. Alfred Guillaume. Karachi: Oxford University Press, 1974.

Gwynne, Rosalind Ward. *Logic, Rhetoric, and Legal Reasoning in the Qur'an: God's Arguments*. London/New York: RoutledgeCurzon, 2004.

Gwynne, Rosalind Ward. 'The "*Tafsīr*" of Abu Ali al-Jubbai: First Steps Toward a Reconstruction, with Texts, Translation, Biographical Introduction and Analytical Essay.' PhD thesis, University of Washington, 1981.

Halm, Heinz. *The Fatimids and Their Traditions of Learning*. London/ New York : I.B. Tauris/Institute of Ismaili Studies, 1997.

Hamidullah, Muhammad. *Le Saint Coran: Traduction Integrale et Notes*, ed. Hadji Mohamed Noureddine Ben Mahmoud. Paris: Club Français du Livre, 1959.

Haqq, Akbar Abdiyah Abdul. 'Christologies in Early Christian Thought and in the Qur'an (Being a Critical Analysis and Comparison of Selected Christological Views in Christian Writings to 785 A.D. and those of the Qur'an).' Doctoral Dissertation Series. Pub. 6200. Ann Arbor University Microfilms, 1979 (Northwestern University, 1953).

[Hartmann, Richard.] *Al-Kuschairîs Darstellung des Sûfitums; mit Ûbersetzungs-Beilageund Indices von Richard Hartmann*. Berlin: Mayer & Müller, 1914.

Hayat, Khan. 'Messiah, Jesus Son of Mary (His Ascension and Return) as Confirmed by the Qur'an.' *Bulletin of Christian Institutes of Islamic Studies* 1(3) (1978): 2–13.

Hayek, Michael, 'L'origine des termes 'Isâ-al-Masîh (Jésus-Christ) dans le Coran.' *Orient syrien* 7 (1962): 223–54, 365–82.

Hayek, Michael. *Le Christ de l'Islam*. Paris: Editions de Seuil. 1959.

Hein, David. 'Farrer on Friendship, Sainthood, and the Will of God.' In *Captured by the Crucified: The Practical Theology of Austin Farrer*, ed. David Hein and Edward Hugh Henderson. New York/London: Continuum/T. & T. Clark, 2004, 119–48.

Hennecke, Edgar. *New Testament Apocrypha*, ed. W. Schneemelcher, trans. A.J.B. Higgins et al., ed. R.McL. Wilson. 2 vols. Philadelphia: Westminster Press, n.d.

Herbert, F.W. Von. 'The Moslem Tradition of Jesus' Second Visit on Earth.' *Hibbert Journal* 7 (1909): 27–48.

Hirschfeld, Hartwig. *New Researches into the Composition and Exegesis of the Qoran*. London: Royal Asiatic Society, 1902.

Hodgson, Marshall G.S. *The Venture of Islam: Conscience and History in a World Civilization*. 3 vols. Chicago: University of Chicago Press, 1975.

Hollenberg, David. 'Interpretation after the End of Days: the Fatimid–Isma'ili Ta'wil (Interpretation) of Ja'far ibn Manṣūr al-Yaman (d. ca. 960).' PhD dissertation, University of Pennsylvania, 2006.

Horst, Heribert. 'Zur Überlieferung im Korankommentar aṭ-Ṭabarīs.' *Zeitschrift der Deutschen Morgenländischen Gesellschaft* 53 (1953): 290–307.

Hussein, Kamel. *City of Wrong*, trans. Kenneth Cragg. Amsterdam: Djambatan, 1959.

Ismail, Mohammed Nour Eldin. *Christus im Koran: Verse des Korans, die über die Offenbarung Allahs über Jesus und das Judentum berichten*. Vienna: Europ. Verlag, 1996.

Izutsu, Toshihiko. *God and Man in the Koran: Semantics of the Koranic Weltanschauung*. Tokyo: Keio Institute of Cultural and Linguistic Studies, 1964.

Izutsu, Toshihiko. *Ethico-religious Concepts in the Qur'ān*. Montreal: McGill University Press, 1966.

Jansen, J.J.G. *The Interpretation of the Koran in Modern Egypt*. Leiden: E.J. Brill, 1974.

Jarrar, Maher. 'The Arabic Novel Carries Its Cross and Asks the Son of Man. Iconography of Jesus in Some Modern Arabic Novels.' In *Poetry's Voice – Society's Norms: Forms of Interaction between Middle Eastern Writers and their Societies*, ed. A. Pflitsch and B. Winckler. Wiesbaden: Reichert Verlag, 2006, 61–92.

Jeffery, Arthur. *The Foreign Vocabulary of the Qur'ān*. Baroda: Oriental Institute, 1938.

Jeffery, Arthur. *Materials for the History of the Text of the Qur'ān*. Leiden: E.J. Brill, 1937.

Jeffery, Arthur. 'The Present Status of Qur'ānic Studies.' In *Report on Current Research Spring 1957: Survey of Current Research on the Middle East*, dir. William Sands, ed. John Hartley. Washington: Middle East Institute, 1957, 1–16

Jeffery, Arthur. *The Qur'ān as Scripture*. New York: Russel F. Moore, 1952.

Jenkinson, E.J. 'Jesus in Moslem Tradition.' *Moslem World* 18 (1928): 263–9.

*Jesus (Peace Be with Him) through the Qur'an and Shi'ite Narrations*, ed. Mahdi Muntazir Qáim, trans. al-Hajj Muhammad Legenhausen with Muntazir Qáim. Elmhurst, NY: Tahrike Tarsile Qur'an, 2005.

Jomier, Jacques. *Les grands thèmes du Coran*. Paris: Centurion, 1978.

Jomier, Jacques. *Le commentaire coranique du Manar*. Paris: Maisonneuve, 1954.

Jones, Alan (trans.). *The Qur'ān*. Cambridge, England: E.J.W. Gibb Memorial Trust, 2007.

Jullandri, Rashid Ahmad. 'Qur'ānic Exegesis and Classical Tafsīr.' *Islamic Quarterly* 12 (1968): 71–119.

Juynboll, Theodore W. 'Crimes and Punishment (Muḥammadan).' In *Encyclopedia of Religion and Ethics*, ed. James Hastings. Edinburgh: T. & T. Clark, 1908–26, vol. 4, 290–4.

Keeler, Annabel. *Sufi Hermeneutics: The Qur'an Commentary of Rashid al-Din Maybudi*. Oxford/New York: Oxford University Press/Institute of Ismaili Studies, 2006.

Kesler, M. Fatih. 'Prophetic Solidarity in the Qur'ân and the Gospels: The Model of Muḥammad and Jesus.' *Akademik Araştırmalar Dergisi. Journal of Academic Studies* 6 (2004): 149–60.

Khalidi, Tarif. *The Muslim Jesus: Sayings and Stories in Islamic Literature*. Cambridge, MA: Harvard University Press, 2001.

Khoury, Raif Georges. *Wahb b. Munnabih Pt. I: Leben und Werk des Dichters*. Wiesbaden: Otto Harrassowitz, 1972.

Küng, H. and P. Heinegg. *Islam and the Other Religions: Jesus in the Qur'an. A Christian Response*. London: SCM Press, 1993.

Küng, Hans. *Islam: Past, Present and Future*, trans. John Bowden. Oxford: Oneworld, 2007 [2004].

Lane, Andrew J. *A Traditional Mutazilite Qur'an Commentary: The*

*Kashshaf of Jar Allah al-Zamakhshari (d. 538/1144)*. Leiden/Boston: E.J. Brill, 2006.

Lawson, Benjamin T. 'The Crucifixion of Jesus in the Qur'ân and Qur'ânic Commentary: A Historical Survey, Part I.' *Bulletin of Henry Martyn Institute of Islamic Studies* 10(2) (1991): 34–62.

Lawson, Benjamin T. 'The Crucifixion of Jesus in the Qur'ân and Qur'ânic Commentary; A Historical Survey, Part II.' *Bulletin of the Henry Martyn Institute of Islamic Studies* 10(3) (1991): 6–40.

Lawson, Todd. 'Akhbari Shi'i Approaches to Tafsir.' In *The Koran: Critical Concepts in Islamic Studies. vol. IV: Translation and Exegesis*, ed. Colin Turner. London: RoutledgeCurzon, 2004, 163–97.

Lawson, Todd. 'Martyrdom.' In *The Oxford Encyclopaedia of the Modern Islamic World*, ed. J. Esposito. New York: Oxford University Press, 1995, vol. 3, 54–9.

Lecomte, Gérard. *Ibn Qutayba (mort en 276/889): L'Homme, Son Oeuvre, Ses Idées*. Damascus: Institut Français de Damas, 1965.

Leirvik, O. *Images of Jesus Christ in Islam*. Uppsala, Sweden: Swedish Institute of Missionary Research, 1999.

Levonian, Lootfy. 'The Ikhwān al-Safā' and Christ.' *Moslem World* 35 (1945): 27–31.

Madelung, Wilferd. 'al- Rassī , al-Ḳāsim b. Ibrāhīm b. Ismā'īl Ibrāhīm b. al-Ḥasan b. al-Ḥasan b. 'Alī b. Abī Ṭālib.' In *Encyclopaedia of Islam*, ed. P. Bearman, Th. Bianquis , C.E. Bosworth , E. van Donzel and W.P. Heinrichs. Leiden: E.J. Brill, 2008. <http://www.brillonline.nl/subscriber/entry?entry=islam_SIM-6247> (accessed 8 May 2008).

Marshall, D. *The Resurrection of Jesus and the Qur'an*. Oxford: Oneworld, 1996.

Martin, Malachi. *The Encounter.* New York: Farrar, Straus & Giroux, 1970.

Massignon, Louis. 'Le Christ dans les évangiles selon Ghazali.' *Revue des études Islamiques* 6 (1932): 523–36.

Masson, Denise. *Le Coran et la Révélation Judéo-Chrétienne: Etudes Comparées*. 2 vols. Paris: Librairie d'Amérique et d'Orient Adrien-Maisonneuve, 1958.

Mawdudi, Abu 'Ala'. *The Meaning of the Qur'ān*, trans. Muhammad Akbar. 16 vols. Lahore: Islamic Publications, 1982–8.

Mayer, Tobias (Alí Músá). 'A Muslim Speaks to Christians.' *Priests and People: Pastoral Theology for the Modern World*, January 2003, 9–13.

McAuliffe, Jane Dammen. *Qur'anic Christians: An Analysis of*

*Classical and Modern Exegesis*. New York: Cambridge University Press, 1991.

McLean, William Paul. 'Jesus in the Qur'ān and the Literature.' MA thesis, McGill University, 1970.

Michaud, Henri. *Jésus selon le Coran*. Neuchâtel, Switzerland: Editions Delachaux & Niestle, 1960.

Monferrer Sala, J.P. 'Algo más acerca de 'Īsà, el nombre de Jesús en el Islam.' *Miscelánea de Estudios Arabes y Hebraicos: Sección Arabe–Islam* 47 (1998): 399–404.

Mourad, Suleiman A. 'On the Qur'anic Stories about Mary and Jesus.' *Bulletin of the Royal Institute for Inter-faith Studies* 1(2) (1999): 13–24.

Muhammad Ali, Maulvi. *The Holy Qur'ān: Containing the Arabic Text with English Translation and Commentary*, 3rd edn. Lahore: Ahmadiyya Anjuman-i-Ishaat-i-Islam, 1935.

Nagel, Tilman. *Islam: die Heilsbotschaft des Korans und ihre Konsequenzen*. Westhofen, Germany: WVA, 2001.

Nomoto, Shin. 'Early Ismā'īlī Thought on Prophecy According to the Kitāb al-Iṣlāḥ by Abū Ḥātim al-Rāzī (d. ca. 322 / 934–5).' PhD thesis, McGill University, 1999.

Nwyia, Paul. *Exégèse coranique et langage mystique: Nouvel essai sur le lexique technique des mystiques muslumans*. Beirut: Imprimerie Catholique, 1970.

Nwyia, Paul. 'Le tafsīr mystique attribué a Ǧa'far Ṣādiq: Edition Critique.' *Mélanges de l'université Saint-Joseph*, 43(4) (1968): 182–230.

O'Shaughnessy, Thomas S.J. *Muḥammad's Thoughts on Death: A Thematic Study of the Qur'ānic Data*. Leiden: E.J. Brill, 1969.

Paret, Rudi. 'Islam and Christianity', trans. Rafīq Aḥmad. *Islamic Studies* 3 (1964): 83–95.

Parrinder, Geoffrey. *Jesus in the Qur'ān*. London: Faber & Faber, 1965.

Pedersen, J. 'The Islamic Preacher: Wa'Iz, Mudhakkir, Qass.' In *Goldziher Memorial Volume*, vol. 1, ed. Samuel Lowinger and Joseph Desomogyi. Budapest: Globus Nyomdai Munitezet, 1948, 226–51.

Poonawala, Ismail K. 'Ismā'īlī *Ta'wīl* of the Qur'ān.' In *Approaches to the History of the Interpretation of the Qur'ān*, ed. A. Rippin. Oxford: Clarendon Press, 1988, 199–222.

Radtke, Bernd. 'Some Recent Research on al-Hakim al-Tirmidhi.' *Der Islam* 83 (2006): 39–89.

Räisänen, Heikki. *Das Koranische Jesusbild: Ein Beitrag zur Theologie des Korans*. Helsinki: Savon Sanomain Kirjapaino Oy Kuopio, 1971.

Räisänen, H. 'The Portrait of Jesus in the Qur'ān: Reflections of a Biblical Scholar.' *Muslim World* 70 (1980): 122–33.

Reynolds, Gabriel S. 'The Ends of *Al-radd al-jamīl* and Its Portrayal of Christian Sects.' *Islamochristiana* 25 (1999): 45–65.

Risse, Günter. *'Gott ist Christus, der Sohn der Maria': eine Studie zum Christusbild im Koran.* Bonn: Borengässer, 1989.

Robinson, Neal. 'Jesus and Mary in the Qur'ān: Some Neglected Affinities.' In *The Qur'an: Style and Contents*, ed. Andrew Rippin. Aldershot, England: Ashgate, 2001, 21–35.

Robinson, Neal. *Christian and Muslim Perspectives on Jesus in the Qur'ân*. London: Bellew, 1991.

Robinson, Neal. 'Creating Birds from Clay: A Miracle of Jesus in the Qur'ān and in Classical Muslim Exegesis.' *Muslim World* 79(1) (1989): 1–13.

Robinson, Neal. *Christ in Islam and Christianity*. Albany: State University of New York Press, 1991.

Robinson, Neal. 'Jesus.' In *Encyclopaedia of the Qur'an*, ed. Jane McAuliffe, vol. 3. Leiden: Brill Academic Publishers, 2003, 7–21.

Robinson, Neal. 'Crucifixion.' In *Encyclopaedia of the Qur'an*, ed. Jane McAuliffe, vol. 1. Leiden: Brill Academic Publishers, 2001, 487–9.

Robson, James. 'Stories of Jesus and Mary.' *Muslim World* 40 (1950): 236–43.

Robson, James. 'Muḥammadan Teachings about Jesus.' *Moslem World* 29 (1939): 37–54.

Rodwell, J.M. *The Koran*. London: J.M. Dent, 1971.

Rosenthal, Franz. 'The Influence of the Biblical Tradition on Muslim Historiography.' In *Historians of the Middle East*, ed. Bernard Lewis and P.M. Holt. London: Oxford University Press, 1962, 35–45.

Sahas, Daniel J. *John of Damascus on Islam: The 'Heresy of the Ishmaelites'*. Leiden: E.J. Brill, 1972.

Sale, George. *The Koran: With Explanatory Notes from the Most Approved Commentators*. London: Frederick Warne, n.d.

Saleh, Walid. *The Formation of the Classical* Tafsīr *Tradition: The Qur'ān Commentary of al-Tha'labi (d. 427/1035).* Leiden: E.J. Brill, 2004.

Sands, Kristin Zahra. *Sufi Commentaries on the Qur'an in Classical Islam*. London: Routledge, 2006.

Ṣawwāf, Mujāhid Muḥammad al-. 'Early Tafsīr – a Survey of Qur'ānic Commentary up to 150 A.H.' In *Islamic Perspectives: Studies in*

*Honor of Mawlana Abul-'Ala Mawdudi*, ed. Kurshid Ahmad and Zafar Ishaq Ansari. Jeddah, Saudi Arabia: Islamic Foundation UK/ Saudi Publishing House, 1979, 135–45.

Schedl, Claus. *Muḥammad und Jesus: Die Christologisch Relevanten Texte des Korans Neu übersetz und Erklärt*. Vienna: Herder, 1978.

Schimmel, Annemarie. 'Dreams of Jesus in the Islamic Tradition.' *Bulletin of the Royal Institute for Interfaith Studies* 1(1) (1999): 207–12.

Schirrmacher, Christine. *Mit den Waffen des Gegners: christlich–muslimische Kontroversen im 19. und 20. Jahrhundert, dargestellt am Beispiel der Auseinandersetzung um Karl Gottlieb Pfanders 'Mîzân al-ḥaqq' und Raḥmatullâh ibn Ḥalîl al-'Uṭmânî al-Kairânawîs 'Iẓhâr al-ḥaqq' und der Diskussion über das Barnabasevangelium*. Berlin: Klaus Schwarz Verlag, 1992.

Schumann, O. 'Present-Day Muslim Writers on Christ.' *Al-Mushir* 19(1) (1977): 31–43.

Seale, Morris. *Muslim Theology: A Study of Origins with Reference to the Church Fathers*. London: Luzac, 1964.

Seale, Morris. *Qur'ān and Bible: Studies in Interpretation and Dialogue*. London: Croon Helm, 1978.

Shah-Kazemi, Reza. Jesus in the Qur'an: Selfhood and Compassion. An Akbari Perspective.' *Journal of the Muhyiddin Ibn 'Arabi Society* 29 (2001): 57–75.

Shaltout, Mahmoud. '[The "Ascension" of Jesus].' *Majallat al-Azhar* 31 (1960): 189–93.

Shoemaker, Stephen J. 'Christmas in the Qur'ān: The Qur'ānic Account of Jesus' Nativity and Palestinian Local Tradition.' *Jerusalem Studies in Arabic and Islam* 28 (2003): 11–39.

Siddiqui, Mona. 'The Image of Christ in Islam: Scripture and Sentiment.' In *Images of Christ: Ancient and Modern*. Sheffield: Sheffield Academic Press, 1997, 159–72.

Smith, Jane I. *An Historical and Semantic Study of the Term 'Islām' as Seen in a Sequence of Qur'ān Commentaries*. Missoula, MT: Missoula Scholars Press, 1975.

Smith, Jane Idleman and Yvonne Yazbeck Haddad. *The Islamic Understanding of Death and Resurrection*. New York: Oxford University Press, 2002 [1981].

Smith, Wilfred Cantwell. *Islam in Modern History*. New York: New American Library, 1959.

Smith, Wilfred Cantwell. *What Is Scripture?: A Comparative Approach.* Philadelphia: Fortress Press, 1993.

Stern, Samuel M. 'Quotations from Apocryphal Gospels in 'Abd al-Jabbār.' *Journal of Theological Studies* 18 (April 1967): 34–57.

Stowasser, Barbara Freyer. *Women in the Qur'an, Traditions, and Interpretation.* New York: Oxford University Press, 1996.

Strothmann, Richard. *Gnosis-Texte der Ismailiten: AmbrosianaArabic Ms. H75.* Göttingen: Vandenhoeck & Ruprecht, 1943.

Swanson, Mark N. 'Folly to the Hunafa: The Crucifixion in Early Christian–Muslim Controversy.' In *The Encounter of Eastern Christianity with Early Islam*, ed. E. Grypeou, M. Swanson and D. Thomas. Leiden: E.J. Brill, 2006, 237–56.

Sweetman, J.W. *Islam and Christian Theology.* 2 vols. London: Lutterworth Press, 1947.

Ṭabāṭabā'ī, Muḥammad Ḥusayn. *Shī'ite Islam*, trans. Seyyed Hossein Nasr. Albany: State University of New York Press, 1975.

Tartar, G. 'Le Coran confère la "primauté" à Jésus-Christ: exégèse du verset coranique 2/254.' In *Actes du Deuxième Congrès International d'Études Arabes Chrétiennes (Oosterhesselen ... 1984)*, ed. Khalil Samir. Rome: Pontificium Institutum Studiorum Orientalium, 1986, 247–58.

Tartar, George. *Connaître Jésus-Christ: lire le Coran à la lumière de l'Evangile: texte arabe des versets coraniques et des commentaires des exégètes sunnites Baydawi, Razi, Tabari et Zamakhshari.* Combs la Ville, France: Centre évangèlique de témoignage et de dialogue, 1985.

Tibawi, A.L. *Arabic and Islamic Themes: Historical, Educational and Literary Studies.* London: Luzac, 1976.

Troll, C.W. 'Jesus Christ and Christianity in Abdullah Yusuf Ali's English Interpretation of the Qur'an.' *Islamochristiana/Dirāsāt Islāmīya Masīḥīya* 24 (1998): 77–101.

Vajda, Georges. 'Isrā'īliyyāt.' *EI²*, vol. 4, 211.

Veccia Vaglieri, Laura. "Abd Allāh ibn al-'Abbās', *EI²*, vol. 1, 40–1.

Vogel, F.E. 'Ṣalb.' In *Encyclopaedia of Islam*, ed. P. Bearman, Th. Bianquis, C.E. Bosworth, E. van Donzel and W.P. Heinrichs. Leiden: E.J. Brill, 2008. <http://www.brillonline.nl/subscriber/entry?entry=islam_SIM-6530> (accessed 8 May 2008).

Waardenburg, Jean-Jacques. *L'Islam dans le miroir de l'occident: comment quelques orientalistes occidentaux se sont penchés sur l'Islam et se sont formé une image de cette religion.* The Hague: Mouton, 1962.

Walker, Paul E. *Ḥamīd al-Dīn al-Kirmānī: Ismaili Thought in the Age of al-Ḥākim.* London: I.B. Tauris/Institute of Ismaili Studies, 1999.

Walker, Paul E. *Abū Ya'qūb al-Sijistānī: Intellectual Missionary.* London: I.B. Tauris in association with The Institute of Ismaili Studies, 1996.

Walker, Paul E. *The Wellsprings of Wisdom: A Study of Abū Ya'qūb al-Sijistānī's* Kitāb al-Yanābi' *Including a Complete English Translation with Commentary and Notes on the Arabic Text.* Salt Lake City: University of Utah Press, 1994.

Wansbrough, John. *The Sectarian Milieu: Content and Composition of Islamic Salvation History*. Oxford: Oxford University Press, 1978.

Wansbrough, John. *Qur'anic Studies: Sources and Methods of Scriptural Interpretation*. Oxford: Oxford University Press, 1977.

Watt, Montgomery. *Bell's Introduction to the Qur'ān*. Edinburgh: Edinburgh University Press, 1970.

Watt, Montgomery. 'The Christianity Criticized in the Qur'ān.' *Muslim World* 57 (1967): 197–201.

Watt, Montgomery. *The Formative Period of Islamic Theology.* Edinburgh: Edinburgh University Press, 1973.

Watt, Montgomery. 'The Materials Used by Ibn Ishaq.' In *Historians of the Middle East*, ed. Bernard Lewis and P.M. Holt. London: Oxford University Press, 1962, 23–34.

Welch, Alford T. 'The Pneumatology of the Qur'ān: A Study in Phenomenology.' Dissertation, Edinburgh University, 1970.

Wensinck, A.J. [D. Thomas] 'al- Ṣalīb.' *Encyclopaedia of Islam*, ed. P. Bearman, Th. Bianquis, C.E. Bosworth, E. van Donzel and W.P. Heinrichs. Leiden: E.J. Brill, 2008. <http://www.brillonline.nl/subscriber/entry?entry=islam_SIM-6533> (accessed 8 May 2008).

Whittingham, Martin. 'How Could So Many Christians Be Wrong? The Role of *Tawātur* (Recurrent Transmission of Reports) in Understanding Muslim Views of the Crucifixion.' *Islam and Christian–Muslim Relations* 19(2) (2008): 167–78.

Widengren, Geo. *Muḥammad the Apostle of God, and His Ascension (King and Saviour V)*. Uppsala, Sweden: Almqvist & Wiksells, 1955.

Wismer, Don. *The Islamic Jesus: An Annotated Bibliography of Sources in English and French*. New York: Garland, 1977.

Yahya, Osman. *Histoire et classification de l'oeuvre d'Ibn 'Arabi, étude critique*. 2 vols. Damascus: Institut français de Damas, 1964.

Yazdani, Mina. 'The Death of Jesus as Reflected in the Bahá'í Writings.' Presentation to AAR Regional Conference, McGill University, Montreal, Summer 2006.

Yusuf Ali, Abdullah. *The Holy Qur'ān: Text, Translation and Commentary*. Washington: American International Printing Company, 1946.
Zebiri, Kate. 'Contemporary Muslim Understanding of the Miracles of Jesus.' *Muslim World* 90(1) (2000): 71–90.
Zwemer, Samuel M. *The Moslem Christ: An Essay on the Life, Character, and Teachings of Jesus Christ According to the Koran and Orthodox Tradition*. New York: American Tract Society, 1912.

## ARABIC AND PERSIAN WORKS

'Abd al-Raḥmān, 'Ā'isha. *Bint al-Shāṭi*. *Al-Tafsīr al-bayānī l'il-Qur'ān al-karīm*, 2nd edn. Cairo: Dar al-Ma'ārif, 1966.
Abū Ḥātim al-Rāzī, Aḥmad ibn Ḥamdān. *A'lām al-nubūwah: al-radd 'alā al-mulḥid Abī Bakrin al-Rāzī.* Beirut: Al-Mu'assasah al-'Arabīya lil-taḥdīth al-Fikrī, 2003.
Abū Ḥātim al-Rāzī, Aḥmad ibn Ḥamdān. *Kitāb al-Iṣlāh*, ed. Ḥasan Manuchihr and Mehdi Mohaghegh, trans. Jalāl al-Dīn Mujtabvī. Tehran: Mu'assasah-'i Muṭāla'āt-i Islāmī, Dānishgāh-i Tihrān, Dānishgāh-i Mak'gīl, 1377/1998.
Abū Ḥayyān, Muḥammad ibn Yūsuf. *Al-Tafsīr al-kabir al-musammá bi-al-Baḥr al-muḥīt*. Cairo: Maṭba'at al-Sa'ādah, 1328/1910.
Abū 'Ubaydah. *Majāz al-Qur'ān*, ed. Fuad Sezgin. 2 vols. Cairo: Muḥ ammad Sāmī Amīn al-Khanjī, 1374–81/1954–62.
Al-Ālūsī, Abū al-Thanā'. *Rūh al-ma'ānī fī tafsīr al-Qur'ān al-'aẓīm wa al-sab' al-mathānī.* 11 vols. Deoband, India: Idārat al-Ṭibā'at al-Muṣṭafā'iya, n.d.
Al-Baḥrānī, Hāshim, al-Shī'ī. *Al-Burhān fī tafsīr al-Qur'ān*, 2nd edn. 4 vols. Tehran: Chapkhāna-yi Āftāb, 1375/1956.
Al-Bayḍāwī, 'Abd Allāh b. 'Umar. *Anwār al-tanzīl wa asrār al-ta'wīl*. 5 vols. Cairo: Dār al-Kutub al-'Arabīya al-Kubrā, 1330/1911.
Dhahabī, Muḥammad Ḥusayn. *Al-Tafsīr wa-al-mufassirun*. 3 vols. Cairo: Dār al-Kutub al-ḥadīthah, 1961–2.
Al-Farrā', Abū Zakariyyā' Yaḥyā ibn Ziyād, *Ma'ānī al-Qur'ān.* bi-taḥ qīq Aḥmad Yūsuf Najātī & Muḥammad 'Alī al-Najjār, 3 vols. Beirut: Dār al-Surūr, 1988.
Al-Fīrūzābādī, Abū Ṭāhīr Muḥammad b. Ya'qūb. *Tanwīr al-miqbās min tafsīr Ibn 'Abbās*, 2nd edn. Cairo: al-Bābī al-Ḥalabī, 1370/1951.
Ibn Abī Hātim, 'Abd al-Rahmān ibn Muhammas. *Tafsīr Ibn Abi Hatim*

*al-Rāzī: al-musammā, al-Tafsīr bi-al-ma'thūr*. Beirut: Dar al-Kutub al-'Ilmiya, 2006.

Ibn Isḥāq, Muḥammad. *Al-Sīra al-nabawīya li ibn Hishām*, ed. Muṣ ṭafā al-Saqqā and Ibrāhīm al-Ubyarī 'Abd al-Ḥāfiẓ Shalabī. 2 vols. Cairo: al-Bābī al-Halabī, 1375/1955.

Ibn Kathīr, Ismā'īl ibn 'Uthmān. *'Umdat al-tafsīr*, ed. Aḥamd Muḥ ammad Shākir. 5 vols. Cairo: Dār al-Ma'ārif, 1376/1957.

Ibn Qutayba = Ibn Muṭarrif al-Kinānī, Muḥammad ibn Aḥmad. *Al-Qurtayn 'aw kitāb mushkil al-Qur'ān wa gharīb li Ibn Qutayba*, ed. 'Abd al-'Azīz al-Khanābī. 2 pts in 1 vol. Cairo: al-Khanābī, 1355/1936.

Taqī al-Dīn Aḥmad ibn Taymiyya. *Al-Muqaddima fi uṣūl al-tafsir.* Beirut: Dār al-Qur'ān al-Karīm, 1399/1979.

Ikhwān al-Ṣafā". *Rasā'il*. 4 vols. Cairo: al-Maktaba al-Tijārīya al-Kubrā, 1347/1928.

Ja'far al-Ṣādiq. *Tafsīr*. Chester Beatty MS 5253.

Jassas, Ahmas ibn 'Ali. *Kitab ahkam al-Qur'an*. Al-Qustatiniya: Dar al-Khilafa al-'Aliya, Matba, 1971.

Al-Kāshānī, 'Abd al-Razzāq. *Tafsīr al-Qur'ān al-karīm li al-shaykh al-akbar al-'ārif bi Allāh al-'allāma Muḥyī al-Dīn bin 'Arabī*. 2 vols. Beirut: Dār al-Yaqaẓat al-'Arabīya, 1387/1968.

Khoury, Raif Georges. 'Wahb b. Munabbih. Abū 'Abd Allāh.' *EI*², vol. 11, 34–6.

Al-Kirmānī, Ḥamīd al-Dīn. *Kitāb rāḥat al-'aql*, ed. Kāmil Ḥusayn and M.M. Ḥilmī. Cairo, 1953.

Lazarus-Yafeh, Hava. *Studies in al-Ghazzali*. Jerusalem: Magnes Press, Hebrew University, 1975.

Lazarus-Yafeh, Hava. 'Taḥrīf (a.).' *EI*², vol. 10, 111.

Majlisī, Muḥammad Bāqir. *Biḥar al-anwār: al-jāmi'ah li-durar akhbār al-A'immah al-Aṭhār.* 111 vols. Beirut: Mu'assasat al-Wafā', 1983.

Al-Māturīdī, Abū Manṣūr. *Ta'wīlāt*. Haled Effendi MS 22.

Mujāhid b. Jabr. *Tafsīr Mujāhid*, ed. 'Abd al-Raḥmān al-Ṭāhir b. Muḥ ammad al-Surtī. Qatar: Maṭābi'al-Duḥa al-Ḥadītha, 1395/1976.

Muqātil b. Sulaymān. *Tafsīr*. Beyazit Umumi MS 561.

Nahhas, Ahmad ibn Muḥammad. *Ma'ani al-Qur'án al-karim*. Mecca: Jami'at Umm al-Qura, 1988.

Nakhjavani, Nimat Allah Mahmud. *Al-Fawatih al-ilahiyah wa-al-mafatih al-ghaybiyah: al-mawdihah lil-kalam al-Quraniyah wa-al-hukm al-furqaniyah.* 2 vols. Istanbul: al-Matbaah al-Uthmaniyah, 1325/1907.

Al-Qummī, 'Alī ibn Ibrāhīm b. Hāshim. *Tafsīr al-Qummī*. 2 vols. Najaf, Iraq: Maktabat al-Amīn, 1387/1976.

Al-Qushayrī, *Laṭā'if al-ishārāt*, ed. Ibrāhīm Basyūnī. 5 vols. Cairo: Dār al-Kitāb al-'Arabī, n.d.

Al-Qushayrī, 'Abd al-Karīm ibn Hawāzin. *Laṭā'if al-ishārāt: tafsīr ṣūfī kāmil li-l-Qur'ān al-Karīm*, ed. Ibrāhīm Basyūnī, 2nd edn. 6 vols. Cairo: Markaz Taḥqīq al-Turāth, 1981.

Al-Qushayri, 'Abd al-Karim ibn Hawazin. *Das Sendschreiben al-Qusayris über das Sufitum*, ed. and trans. Richard Gramlich. Wiesbaden: Franz Steiner Verlag, 1989.

Quṭb, Sayyid. *Fī ẓilāl al-Qur'ān*, 7th edn. 8 vols. Beirut: Dār Iḥyā' al-Turāth al-'Arabī, 1391/1971.

*Rasā'il ikhwān al-ṣafā' wa-khullān al-wafā'*, ed. Khayr al-Dīn al-Ziriklī. Frankfurt-am-Main: Ma'had Tārīkh al-'Ulūm al-'Arabīyah wa-al-Islāmīyah fī iṭār Jāmi'at Frānkfūrt, 1999 [1928].

Al-Rāzī, Abū al-Futūḥ . *Rawḍ al-Jinān w-Rawḥ al-Janān*. Qum, Iran: Intishārāt-i Kitābkhānah-yi Āyat Allāh al-Uẓmā Marashī-Najafī, 1404/1984.

Al-Rāzī, Fakhr al-Dīn. *Mafātīḥ al-ghayb al-mushtahar bi al-tafsīr al-kabīr*. 32 vols. Cairo: al-Maṭba'at al-Bahīya, 1354–7/1935–8.

Sā'ātī, 'Abd al-Raḥmān. *Minḥat al-ma'būd fī tartīb musnad al-Ṭayālisī Abī Dā'ūd*. 2 vols. Cairo: Maṭba'at al-Munīrīya, 1372/1952.

Ṣadūq, al-Shaykh al-. *I'tiqādāt fī dīn al-Imāmīya*. Beirut: Dār al-Mufīd lil-Ṭibā'a wa al-Nashr wa al-Tawzī', 1414/1993.

Ṣadūq, al-Shaykh al-. *Kamāl al-dīn wa tamām al-ni'ma*. Qum, Iran: Mu'assasat al-Nashr al-Islāmī al-Ṭābi'a li-Jamā'at al-Mudarrisayn bi Qum al-Musharrafa, 1405/1984.

Ṣalībī, Kamāl S. *al-Baḥth 'an Yasū ': qirā'ah jadīdah fī al-Anājīl*. Ammān: Dār al-Shurūq, 1999.

Shahrastani, Muḥammad ibn Abd al-Karim. *Tafsīr al-Shahrastani al-musammá Mafātiḥ al-asrār wa-maṣābiḥ al-abrār.* 2 vols. Miras-i Maktub, 1997.

Shīrāzī-Kazarūnī, Rūzbihān Baqlī. *Arā'is al-bayān fī ḥaqā'iq al-Qur'ān*. 2 vols in 1. Kanpur, India: Nawal Kishawr, 1315/1897.

Al-Sijistānī, Abū Bakr Muḥammad. *Gharīb al-Qur'ān*. Cairo: Muḥ ammad 'Alī Ṣabīḥ, 1372/1952.

Sufyān al-Thawrī. *Tafsīr al-Qur'ān al-karīm*. Rambūr: Hindūstān Brintink Wurks, 1385/1965.

Al-Suyūṭī, Jalāl al-Dīn. *Al-Durr al-manthūr fi al-tafsīr bi al-ma'thūr*. 6 vols. Tehran: al-Maṭba'a al-Islāmīya, 1377/1957.

Al-Suyūṭī, Jalāl al-Dīn. *Al-Itqān fī 'ulūm al-Qur'ān*. Cairo: Maṭba'at Ḥijāzī, 1328/1950.

Al-Suyūṭī, Jalāl al-Dīn. *Tafsīr al-jalālayn*. Damascus: Maktabat al-Milla, n.d.

Al-Ṭabarī, Abu Ja'far. *Jāmi' al-bayān 'an ta'wīl āy al-Qur'ān*, ed. Maḥ mūd Muḥammad Shākir and Aḥmad Muḥammad Shākir, vols 1–15. Cairo: Dār al-Ma'ārif, 1374/1954.

Ṭabāṭabā'ī, Muḥammad Ḥusayn. *Shī'ite Islam*, trans. and ed. Seyyed Hossein Nasr. Albany: State University of New York Press, 1975.

Al-Ṭabrisī/Ṭabarsī, Abū 'Alī. *Majma' al-bayān fī tafsīr al-Qur'ān al-karīm*, ed. Ibrāhīm Basyūnī. 30 vols. Beirut: Dār al-Fikr wa Dār al-Kitāb al-Lubnānī, 1377/1957.

Al-Ṭabāṭabā'ī, Muḥammad Ḥusayn. *al-Mīzān fī tafsīr al-Qur'ān*. 21 vols. Beirut: al-Maṭba'a al-Tijārīya al-Maktab al-'Ālamī, 1390–1405/1970–85.

Al-Ṭūsī, Abū Ja'far. *Shaykh al-Ṭā'ifa. Al-Tibyān fī tafsīr al-Qur'ān*. 10 vols. Najaf, Iraq: Maktabat al-Amīn, 1376–83/1957–63.

Versteegh, C.M.H. 'al-Zadjdjādj, Abū Isḥāḳ Ibrāhīm b. al- Sarī.' *EI*[2], vol. 11, 377.

Al-Wāḥidī, Abū al-Ḥasan al-Nīsābūrī. *Asbāb al-nuzūl*. Cairo: Māṭba'at Hindīya, 1315/1897.

Al-Wāḥidī, Abū al-Ḥasan al-Nīsābūrī. *Wajīz fī tafsīr al-Qur'ān*. On the margin of al-Nawāwī and Muḥammad b. 'Uthmān b. 'Arabī al-Jāwī al-Bustāmī. *Tafsīr al-Nawāwī*. Cairo: al-Bābī al-Ḥalabī, 1305/1887.

Zajjāj Abu Isḥāq Ibrāhīm ibn al-Sarī. *Ma'ānī al-Qur'ān wa i'rābuh*. 5 vols. Beirut: 'Ālam al-Kutub, 1988.

Al-Zamakhsharī, Maḥmūd b. 'Umar. *al-Kashshāf 'an ḥaqā'iq ghawāmid al-tanzīl*. 4 vols. Beirut: Dār al-Kitāb al-'Arabī, 1386/1966.

# INDEX

Romans, the 140, 141
Ruzbihā Baqlī 68 n1

*ṣa'ada* 56
Sahas, Daniel J 19, 20
Sahl al-Tustarī 65
Sa'id ibn al-Musayyib 54 n31
Salama 61
Sale, George 16, 33 n12
Saleh, Walid 91
salvation 23–4, 23 n32
Savary, M. 33 n12
Schedl, Claus 27 n2, 33 n12
Seale, Morris 18
Serjes 62
*shabḥ/shabaḥ* 147 n10
Shahrastānī 121 n16
*shakk* 124–5
*shakka* 56
al-Shaykh al-Ṣaduq 95 n59
Shaykhiyya 95 n58
*sh-b-h* 32–3, 53
Shi'ism 7, 59, 69, 87, 94, 117, 142, 147–8, 150
  Ithnā 'asharī 59, 76
  Ja'farī 59
  Twelver Shi'ism 69, 75, 87–8, 94–5, 94 n58, 97, 114, 117, 146 n8, 148
  Zaydīs 77
  *see also* Isma'ilis
*shubbiha* 34, 35 n16, 49, 102, 102 n75, 147 n10
*shubbiha lahum* x–xi, 32, 34–5, 36, 67, 102, 133, 142
  translations of 15–17
al-Suhrawardī 117
*Sitz im Leben* 140, 140 n68
*ṣ-l-b* 31
Smith, Jane 22, 45, 105, 120
Stern, S.M. 89, 90–1
Stroumsa, Guy G. 2 n1
substitution legends 3–4, 12, 17, 23–4, 33, 35, 36
  classical and medieval *tafsīr* 74–5, 88, 91, 93, 100, 101–2, 103, 105–6, 107, 108–9, 112–13
  modern era 123–4, 127, 131, 137, 140
  origins of 144–50
  pre-Ṭabarī *tafsīr* 46–7, 49–50, 56, 58–9, 60, 62, 63, 67
al-Suddī, Ismā'īl ibn 'Abd al-Raḥmān 56, 92
Sūfyān al-Thawrī 65
al-Suhrawardī 97
al-Sulamī 99
  *Ḥaqā'iq al-tafsīr* 57 n44
Sunni Islam 7, 69, 76, 87, 94
al-Suyūṭī, Jalāl al-Dīn 112–14, 112 n95, 113, 121 n16
  *al-Durr al-manthūr fi al-tafsīr bi-al-ma'thūr* 112, 112 n95
  'History of Religions' 112
  *Tafsīr al-Jalālayn* 112
Swanson, Mark N. 7 n12

al-Ṭabarī, Abū Ja'far Muḥammad b. Jarīr 11, 44, 48 n13, 49 n14, 50, 52, 53, 54, 55, 56, 61, 70–2, 70 n4, 93, 100
  *Jāmi' al-bayān 'an ta'wīl al-Qur'ān* 76
al-Ṭabaṭabā'ī, 'Allamah Sayyid Muḥammad Ḥusayn 28 n3, 139–42, 140 n68
  'Just Balance in the Explanation of the Qur'an, The' 139
al-Ṭabrisī, Abū 'Ali al-Faḍl 96–7, 121 n14
Talmud 132–3
*tashnīh* 35
*ta'wīl* 76
al-Ṭayālisī, b. Muh.ammad 29 n6
al-Tha'labī 91
  *Lives of the Prophets* 5, 91
al-Ṭūsī, Abū Ja'far 75, 87, 92–5, 97, 105, 121, 121 n14
Twelver Shi'ism 69, 75, 87–8, 94–5, 94 n58, 97, 114, 117, 146 n8, 148

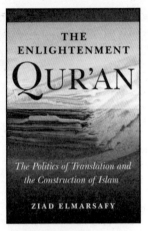

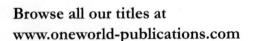